# Ethnologia Europaea

## Journal of European Ethnology



Volume 30:2 2000

MUSEUM TUSCULANUM PRESS · UNIVERSITY OF COPENHAGEN

Printed in Sweden by BTJ Tryck AB, Lund 2000
ISBN 87-7289-677-9
ISSN 0425-4597



This journal is published with the support of the Nordic board for periodicals in the humanities and social sciences.

Museum Tusculanum Press
University of Copenhagen
Njalsgade 92
DK-2300 Copenhagen S

# Editorial

## Borders and Borderlands

The current edition of Ethnologia Europaea is a thematic issue dealing with the topic of national borders from a European perspective. Cultural borders, and the spatial articulation and structure of culture are traditional objects, but at the same time hotly debated questions of European ethnology. First of all because cultural borders often have been instrumentalised politically in European history. In political and historical debates about national status of different European regions imaginary cultural borders always played a substantial role – especially in Central and Eastern Europe. The history and tradition of the ethnological study of cultural borders demonstrates not only how ethnological research can be instrumentalised, but draws our attention to probably the most important characteristic of borders, namely that they are cultural constructions and that they often represent political and historical imaginations.

This collection of papers offers a solid and sensitive survey of the current state of research in this field. The papers do not deal with cultural borders only, the common basis of the issue is that borders are complex political, cultural, and symbolical phenomena. The authors describe and analyse in their papers how borders have been created in different European regions, how traditional or historical borders have been changed, what kind of functions borders have, how people "use" borders, and what cultural and political meaning borders have for the people living there. This thematic issue gives a detailed outline of ethnological research on borders and borderlands, and at the same time contributes to further theoretical discussions in this field.

This special issue on national borders in Europe has been edited by Dieter Haller and Hastings Donnan.

# Borders and Borderlands

## An Anthropological Perspective

Edited by

*Dieter Haller*
&
*Hastings Donnan*

# Liminal no More

## The Relevance of Borderland Studies[1]

*Hastings Donnan & Dieter Haller*

Donnan, Hastings & Haller, Dieter 2000: Liminal no More. The Relevance of Borderland Studies. – Ethnologia Europaea 30, 2: 7–22.

The introductory essay suggests that for too long theories of nationalism and the state have taken a top-down approach which denies agency to local actors. One way to redress this bias is to study state borders, for here it is possible to generate insights into how people who are apparently at the periphery of the state may actively influence its policy and direction. The essay reviews existing border studies in different disciplinary fields and, to contextualise the papers that follow, argues that an anthropological approach in particular can shed much light on the cultures of the borderland, as well as on the formation and management of identities there. Special attention is paid to Europe, both to the way in which border studies as a field of intellectual inquiry were implicated in national policy in mid-twentieth century Germany, and to how our contributors suggest borderland cultures have negotiated the changes brought about by the European Union.

*Professor Hastings Donnan, School of Anthropological Studies, The Queen's University of Belfast, Belfast BT7 1NN, Northern Ireland, UK.*
*E-mail: h.donnan@qub.ac.uk*
*PD Dr.habil. Dieter Haller, Department of Comparative Cultural and Social Anthropology, European University Viadrina, Große Scharrnstr. 59, D-15230 Frankfurt / Oder, Germany. E-mail: h0920cyt@rz.hu-berlin.de*

Social scientists and historians have long understood modern nation-building, especially in the West, as a process emanating from a political core whose goal is the institutional incorporation and cultural assimilation of peripheral groups and regions through homogenising projects such as education and the media. International borders have usually been seen in context of this process, as the physical and visible markers of a nation-state's scope. The coercive and impositional nature which this approach to the national project emphasises underplays and underestimates the agency of local actors. As a result, the ways in which local developments in border regions impact on national centres of power and hegemony, helping to produce, reproduce and/or subvert a sense of national belonging, are less well understood.

By taking the border as its point of departure, this collection of essays shifts the analytical focus from centre to periphery in an attempt to generate insights into how border peoples actively influence national policies and ideologies rather than just passively absorb them. A number of the papers consider how socio-cultural processes at international frontiers – such as smuggling, environmental activism, and cross-border co-operation – can simultaneously result from and transcend political borders. Other chapters examine how cultural representations of borders – play a role in the construction and contestation of nations, ethnic groups and other social formations. At the same time, the collection offers a view of the nation-state from below: of how ordinary people ascribe or deny relevance to cultural differences, how they actively enact and modify their notions of national being, 'nation', and 'culture'. Some of the essays also show how borders can have far reaching effects on other less obvious aspects of the societies they enclose, such as body language and the performative and behavioural styles people adopt in their everyday lives.

Despite the centrality which the concept of boundary has enjoyed in anthropology, especially in relation to the symbolic boundaries between local communities and between ethnic groups, the systematic and comparative study of international borders has been relatively neglected.[2] Yet as the contributors to this collection demonstrate, these borders can offer a special insight into how subject and citizen relate to 'their' nation-state; at borders anthropologists can explore how competing loyalties and multiple identities are managed on a daily basis by those who cross borders and live alongside them, as well as by the state officials charged with their maintenance and regulation. Indeed, a focus on these liminal border zones may compel us to reconceptualise many of our most cherished assumptions about the nature of the relationships between people, place, identity and culture. Studying borders demands a translocal perspective, a view from one state to another. At the same time, many borderlanders express a striking sense of rootedness and belonging. Investigation of such apparently contradictory elements speaks to wider disciplinary preoccupations with diaspora and cultural displacement.

The study of borders is sometimes claimed as the preserve of political science, geography and international relations. Yet few studies conducted from these disciplinary perspectives have much to say about the *cultural* dimensions of international borders, or about the physical and metaphorical borderlands which radiate away from the legal borderlines between nation states. As the ethnographic accounts in this volume indicate, culture plays a decisive role in the social construction and negotiation of borders, and in the historical, ethnic and nationalist forces which generate a border's particular dynamics.

The ability and the need to draw borders have been revealed as universal anthropological constants at least since Simmel (1992: 221ff), who speaks of a psychological phenomenon: things can be brought together only by separating them from each other. Drawing borders is thus the key to human cognition: the spatial border is "only the crystallisation or spatialization of the sole true psychological boundary process" (1992: 226); the spatial border symbolises the 'dimension of power and rights' of two personality complexes, individual spheres which are distinguished by the fact "that power and rights do not extend into the other sphere" (1992: 227ff). Girtler (1992: 11ff) refers to the border as a prime symbol for being human, while Greverus (1969) similarly believes that humans are "border-drawing creature(s)" whose identity and sense of difference from others is completely dependent on the existence of borders.

## Border-Crossing Anthropology

"Whoever stands (at the village boundary) has trouble orientating themselves, fears getting lost, believes themselves exposed to all possible dangers, imagines they are threatened by evil dwarves, witches, and giants" (Müller 1987: 28).

What Müller says about the boundary of village communities also applies to other boundary situations in a broader sense. That boundaries between stable defined categories are often perceived as sources of instability, insecurity, threat, conflict, but also of new possibilities and opportunities, is particularly apparent from the ambivalent characterisation of those who move along the boundary and thus between categories. North Asian shamans transcend various cosmological levels, and come into contact with beings and demons, spirits of the dead and nature spirits of the higher world and underworld by travelling up or down the world axis. On their trips they heal the ill through trance, accompany the dead into the realm of shades, and act as intermediaries between the higher world, the human world, and the underworld. The *hagaszussa*, or witch, is capable not only of healing others, but also of destroying them. In the Winnebago myth of creation, as in that of other North American Indians, the image of the Trickster combines order and chaos. It is controlled and possessed by wild untamed desires, is egotistical, and has the mentality of a cruel child. At the same time, however, it is seen as the bringer of culture, and its travels end with a partial domestication of its compulsions. The threatening nature of the ambiguous, the fear of twilight, of the inchoate, or, as James Fernandez (1974, 1982) writes, of the darkness at the foot of the stairs, is subjected in pre-modern societies to the need to create clearly bounded categories. Such societies sometimes use *rites de passage* to restore or create such boundedness, as Arnold van Gennep (1986) long ago observed, and as Victor Turner (1967, 1969) elaborated in his concept of liminality. The use of linear borders to establish clear-cut divisions does not seem to be characteristic of pre-statal societies.[3]

If shamans, *hagaszussa*, and tricksters are characterised by the ability to move between categories in the pre-modern world, the western modern age appears to be obsessed by proscribing such movement and by maintaining strict categorical boundaries.[4] The ambiguity of transition seems to be overcome in the modern West by prohibiting ease of movement between categories. Figures constantly found between categories become a threat. The 'half-breed' subverts any assumption of pure racial categories, the homosexual becomes a monstrosity because he does not correspond to the dichotomised rendering of gender categories. Categorical clarity is maintained by revaluing the hybrid category that is perceived as threatening. Even the concept of hybridity assumes the existence of discrete cultures that can merge to form another, mixed category that can then be labelled hybrid.

Anthropologists too move along the border between the categories of self and other. "Anyone who wants to order perceptions must make distinctions. And the accuracy of the distinction made is evaluated by crossing the border." Bernhard Streck (1995: 185–195) here speaks quite correctly of border-crossing anthropology.[5] In the lives of anthropologists – as Freilich (1970), Lewis (1973), Stagl (1974), and Lindner (1987) observed for the early representatives of the discipline in general, and as Frank (1997) remarked for the Jewish founder of American cultural anthropology in particular – interfamilial, social, and geographic marginality and a feeling of exclusion, characteristics which anthropologists frequently share with their principal informants, were often the motives for dealing with 'self and the other' (Shokeid 1988: 42, Haller 1996). "Both border-crossers and anthropologists move along the border and both look beyond it. What they see, however, is not 'the other culture', but rather fellow border-crossers and (other) anthropologists" (Streck 1995: 187). In fact, the crossing of categorical and symbolic borders not only became of empirical and theoretical interest (above all in the investigation of rites of passage), it also became a key element in the methodology of the discipline with the canonisation of participant-observation.[6]

Border imagery, then, is in more than one sense part of the "family silver".[7] Moreover, much of anthropology in the past focused on peoples peripheral to the centres of power in pre-modern states, nation-states, or colonial empires.[8] All the more surprising that until recently the outer borders of these territories seldom attracted the attention of the discipline.[9] There are various sound reasons for this, as Donnan and Wilson (1994b: 7) have pointed out. State borders, especially contested borders between inimical neighbours, are highly political contexts in which regimes frequently pursue hidden agendas. If state authorities do not want to let anyone look over their shoulders, it may not only be difficult to receive permission for research in these areas, but may also be dangerous to life and limb. Furthermore, research on state borders requires a doubling of effort from the anthropologist, who may have to master at least two languages and deal with two national traditions of anthropological literature. Finance too may be a problem, since it can be difficult to find sponsors to underwrite multi-sited research. Yet in recent years this relative neglect has been reversed, following widespread predictions of the disappearance of borders in the face of globalization and transnationalism. Phenomena frequently become the object of research only when they are no longer taken for granted. With the end of the East-West confrontation in Europe, we are reminded again of Simmel's observation that state borders are neither natural nor absolute, but rather artificial and problematic.

The practice of financing mainly single-sited research is closely connected with the question of methodology. Until recently, undertaking field research largely meant focusing on one place or one region. For a long time anthropology was dominated by a sense that cultures were discrete and fixed in space (Fardon 1990; Kearney 1991; Gupta/Ferguson 1992; Haller 1994; Rosaldo 1989). Like the biologist's classifications of animal and plant species, the Trobrianders, the Dinka, and the Shoshone seemed to live in compartmentalised worlds (Hannerz 1997). Ultimately this made it possible to speak of different cultures. At the same time, other strands within the discipline took a different tack: rather than emphasising separation and isolation, diffusionism and acculturation theory, for example, focused instead on connections and commonalities. Such strands of thought are the intellectual forerunners of contemporary theories of globalization and transnationalism, and of the present interest in borders.

## The View from the Border

Where states meet the need for clear categorical boundaries and the threat of ambiguity become especially acute. Driessen (1996a) writes that it is here that societies are frequently most vulnerable, for it is here that changes and new activities arise, identities are created or rejected, and cultural categories are shifted.[10] In this special issue, we focus particularly on borders and their significance for states and nations.

Of special importance is the question of the limits of a "society" and a "community". It has often been stated that the central anthropological method of fieldwork has been limited in practice by state borders. In the case of society, this is evidently true. Societies by and large have been treated as bounded by and enclosed within state boundaries. Society, defined by most theorists as some sort of institutionalised organisation, is closely linked to state institutions. On the other hand, the other central category used to describe human forms of organisation, community, is intimately tied to the idea of small scale and face-to-face networks. The idea of cross-border networks, sometimes referred to as overlapping societies (Driessen 1996a), matches neither the institutional frame of societies nor the personal frame of community. Indeed, it is both and neither, as several of our contributors point out (Leizaola, Klomp). We suggest that a re-evaluation of these categories occurs when they are considered from the perspective of the border. Previously these categories were investigated mainly from the centre of nation-states, a perspective that regards border regions as peripheral, their inhabitants as passive and conservative in customs and morals, even as pre-modern, provincial, and backward.[11]

Too often borders are seen simply as passive, inert elements used to shape the societies and cultures which they enclose, subject to the motor of metropolitan centres.[12] This view of the border as barrier and the border region as periphery is in need of critical revision. Peter Sahlins' (1989) pioneering work on the Spanish-French border in the Pyrenees revolutionised our idea of the passivity of border regions by demonstrating that the border region of Cerdanya had a decisive influence on the development of the Spanish and French nation-states.[13] The border strip, where multiple territorial loyalties were the rule rather than the exception[14], developed into a clearly defined dividing line. In the words of Joel Kotek (1996: 23): "*L'une après l'autre, les zones-frontières floues se transforment en lignes frontières rigides.*"[15]

Sahlins conceived processes in the border area as reciprocal. On the one hand, national policies impact on local conditions; on the other hand, representative bodies and individual representatives of the national state are used by people from the border area for local and personal goals. This revolutionary perspective centred on the agent was anticipated by Georg Simmel (1992: 228). "Not the states, not the pieces of property, not the city district, and not the county district limit one another, but rather the inhabitants or owners exercise reciprocal impact." For Simmel, the border is no longer a spatial fact with sociological effects, but a sociological fact spatially expressed, a perspective which incorporates the idea that the "psychological drawing of the border is simplified and emphasised by natural territorial limits" (Simmel 1992: 227). This simplification and emphasis also applies at state borders: in concrete border situations with controls, barriers and symbols, people's behaviour and value systems are regulated by constraints which the individual perceives as largely impossible to influence.

National state borders are thus a suitable starting point for observing local, national, transterritorial and even scientific processes. The case of mid-twentieth century German anthropology offers an inspiring insight into how national policy at borders and borderland studies can be intertwined.

## State Policy and Borderland Studies. A German Example

For Simmel, the border, though a product of negotiation, implies the idea of impermeability, a conception which also finds expression in structural anthropology. The idea of division is present in the etymology of the German terms. The terms *Grenze* (border) (Slavic stem, cf. Cashubian *gran(i)ca*, (Kramer 1996) or Pomoranian *granica,* (Medick 1995: 217) actually "edge, rim") and *Grenzraum* (border area) (in the sense of *Mark* (march), Old High German *marcha* "border") imply the idea of sharp borderlines between territories and the notion of clearly definable areas on both of the borderline's sides. The emphasis on division follows in the tradition of Ratzel, who viewed the structure and territorial dimension of the state from the metropolitan centre and from the nation-state ideology of the nineteenth century.[16] At this point it is useful to introduce the concept of 'frontier', and to consider how it differs from 'boundary'.

In English, the term frontier refers to the zone which lies between civilisation and the 'interior vastness of a continent' (Anderson 1982). The anthropological usage of the term frontier in this sense originated in the dispute over the Anglo-Native American Indian frontier of North America (Alvarez 1995: 449). In contrast to the boundary, the frontier is not fixed, but is shifting. Yet it too was long considered a dividing line, albeit between rather different things: while the boundary divides states, societies, or cultures from each other, the frontier separates civilisation from the wilderness. Frontier implies the ability of people to shape what is conceived of as their "natural" surroundings. Society on the frontier is characterised by pioneers "(who) come from a civilised environment (...) (and) are set down in a natural environment, and must participate in a struggle for (their) very existence. (...) The settlers then adapt themselves to the crudity of nature, sacrificing much of the civilization they had, in favor of forms of adaptation (...) which are successful as they resemble those of the natives" (Leyburn 1933: 175ff).

In the context of the Nazi ideology of *Lebensraum* in the 1930s and 1940s, the dominant figure of post-war German anthropology, Wilhelm Emil Mühlmann advocated the idea of the frontier society. Mühlmann (1944, 1964: 276ff) theorised the border less in the sense of a boundary and more in the sense of a frontier. Since the frontier divides nature from civilisation, it is permeable, "riddled with holes, broken through." Since "interim phenomena, (which) limit structures" develop at the border between nature and civilisation, a central task for the protection of the state is assigned to the population of the border cordon, which is given the role of "peripatetic border guard" or "military elite border cordon".[17] Mühlmann thus attributed to the border a central significance for the negotiation of basic categories of national identity, a conception shared by the anthropology of Boehm (1978 [1932]).[18]

Mühlmann's work on assimilation and 're-peopling' was designed to provide a theoretical foundation for Nazi settlement policy – above all the resettlement of loyal German comrades – in the border areas of the German Reich, and to legitimate German expansionism against the wilderness inhabited by 'sub-humans'. In this project Mühlmann assigned the borderland population a major role in the protection of the 'core territory' of the *Reich*.[19] This German anthropologist considered territorial expansion and extended frontiers as a sign distinguishing "peoples (...) of political greatness" from "nature peoples" (1940: 38).[20] "Nature peoples", he suggested, are content in confined, limited spaces, while the "peoples of political greatness" are characterised by constantly expanding borders. For Mühlmann, the boundary between Germany and its eastern neighbours became a frontier, so that the Russians and Poles were practically reinvented as "nature peoples", with the

Cossack military-frontier being taken as a model for the Governor-Generals of the Third Reich, and the "finely sifted elite"[21] of the Cossacks themselves being advocated as a model for the German settlers in the East.

In Mühlmann's conception of frontier, the conquest of unsettled land, the European expansion into territories inhabited by 'nature peoples', and the German conquest of the 'wild East' are all thrown into one pot. The extremely racist and anti-Semitic element of Mühlmann's work on the border[22] should not, however, obscure the fact that some of his ideas may prove useful for the development of a contemporary anthropology of the border. In one respect at least, Mühlmann's conception of the border contrasts positively with that of the political geographers in the tradition of Ratzel: for Mühlmann the border area and border population are not merely peripheral, conservative, passive, and dependent on influences from the centre of the national states. On the contrary, he saw border areas and border populations as dynamic; while on the one hand, they are placed at the service of national-state interests, on the other hand, what they do can affect the entire state entity. With his idea of the "limiting structure" of the borderland, Mühlmann reacted against a conception of cultures and societies as clearly divided units. Moreover, he implicitly hinted at the continuity of space and the networking of culture, an idea that had already been explicitly formulated by Febvre (1922, 1962 [orig.: 1908], 1962 [orig.: 1928]).[23] For Febvre, the French co-founder of the *Annales* school, border areas act as bridges, in, for example, the creation of economic strategies specific to the border (such as smuggling), or in the development of a common medium of communication (such as hybrid languages).

## Borders, Borderlands and Border Types

As the German case already suggests, there are many different definitions of borders both within and across disciplines, and as many different approaches to studying them. In this volume we take an anthropological approach to borders, one which stresses culture and identity in border regions while recognising the ways in which these shape and are shaped by the power enacted between and within nations and their states. Informed by this approach, the contributors address a number of related themes: from how borders are being strengthened in response to forces of Europeanization and globalization, to how states may sometimes be subverted at their borders. One of the many fascinating things about borders is the way in which the people who live there can both support and subvert their state, at times being the victims of state power and at other times its source. To some extent scholars have tried to incorporate this shifting and seemingly contradictory relationship into their border typologies.

In the typology outlined by Girtler (1992: 16ff), for instance, borders are categorised according to their degree of permeability. Borders with no permeability, or "borders of fear and control", are historically the exception. Only rarely was the state border intended to be as absolutely impermeable as in the case of the border between East and West Germany or that between North and South Korea (or possibly that between Spain and Gibraltar during the period of border closure from 1969 to 1982). A second type of border, which Girtler refers to as "loose borders", divides "regions from each other (...) but yet appears permeable". This type of border, which might be labelled the transition-threshold type, is typical for western Europe after World War Two (up to the implementation of the Schengen Treaty). This type of border fulfils the classical nation-state task of controlling and channelling the flow of goods and people in and out of sovereign territory. And thirdly, the borders inside the Schengen territory are typical of borders with high permeability. These are Girtler's "disappearing borders", where "control over the constant flow of people and goods gradually" disappears.

These ideal types, of course, rarely map neatly on to reality. For borders are always historically, socially and politically marked and, consequently, the character of a border can change according to current requirements. This applies to the most varied areas. "Even the severe, strictly codified borders established by law", writes Bausinger (1997: 5), "are, upon closer examination, not completely rigid: juridical disputes (and lawyers) to some extent thrive on the fact that in many areas there are no fixed borderlines, but only relatively broad border regions." A permeable border can, in the context of the war on crime, suddenly become an impermeable border, while an impermeable border, such as the border between East and West Germany, can turn into a "loose" border virtually overnight. The idea of absolute impermeability and immovability of borders is rarely reflected in political reality.

Even at borders of the first type (those with low or no porosity), there are various degrees of permeability for certain groups of people, goods, and information. In all cases, borders allow a certain degree of permeability. Yet the idea that borders can be firmly closed and strictly regulated somehow persists as an integral component of national ideologies no matter how flexible border controls may be in practice. This idea is frequently supported by the claim that national boundaries are merely a reflection of *natural* boundaries: the Pyrenees, the English Channel, and the Rhine are perhaps the best known examples of this "naturalising" of the political.

All of this suggests that borders have an ambivalent character: they represent dividing lines as well as thresholds of passage, they have a "hinge function" (Ulbrich 1993), simultaneously bounding and excluding. To capture this dual function and to emphasise the *processual* aspect of opening and closing, we suggest the image of the zipper. Zippers, of course, are composed of two halves with interlocking rows of teeth. As the teeth engage each other, the two halves are drawn together. A zipper can be completely or partially open or closed. It is the same with state borders. Like the two halves of a zipper, bordering states may be bound together in some respects (for example, in the economy, demography, family organisation, language) but not in others (on the related concept of "differentiated integration", see Gasparini & Zago 1998). A variety of connections can be established or terminated. Links which are currently tightly meshed can quickly be loosened and vice versa. Just like a zipper, a border is never completely open or closed when seen over the long term. Even the apparently fully open zipper retains a point of contact which indicates the potential closure of the two halves. In other ways too the zipper analogy could be said to apply. Just as one row of teeth is the inverse of the other, so the two sides of the border tend to see one another in opposite and usually negative terms. The dichotomization of societies along the Iron Curtain or along the walls of 'Fortress Europe' are tangible examples of this, as is Gibraltar, where Spain, the Spanish and Spanish culture are often viewed negatively.

But we need to be careful here. The prosaicness of the image of the zipper should not obscure the fact that borderlands are often recognised as "special" places because of the part they have played in the development of states, and because of their continuing role in articulating relations between states. Their location at the edges of the state gives a particularity to the social and political lives of border peoples which distinguishes them from their countrymen in ways that researchers have found productive to explore. While in the past German-language anthropology did not devote particular attention to the border as an object of research, recent developments in its successor disciplines in European ethnology have focused on the distinctiveness of border regions, exploring the nature of their dual relationship to those within and beyond their own state lines.[24] "Beyond the border", writes Schilling (1986: 349) about the Saarland-Lorraine border area, "much is different and much is not." Apart from the division into French and German jurisdictional territories, within which the border region takes on a marginal position, Schilling (1986: 351) refers to his research area as a "new land", a "no-man's land" which emerges when "the people who live there take that which has been denied them as a resource because it here appears to be at an end: significance." To paraphrase Girtler: different 'truths' (1991: 42ff) or 'realities' (1992: 32ff) are valid on the two sides of the border. The borderland draws on both to create a third "truth", building upon the "small advantages on this side and the other side" to construct its own specific reality.

A number of scholars have identified the forces which they suggest combine to shape and define the distinctive nature of the borderlands. Anderson (1996), for example, argues that borders have a number of key functions. They act as markers of identity, are instruments of state policy, and delimit state sovereignty. As such, borders figure large in national discourse, and are often core elements in people's narratives of national and ethnic identity, as we shall see in many of the contributions which follow. Martinez (1994: 8–14) too lists a number of processes which he suggests are typical of borderlands: international conflict and accommodation; ethnic conflict and accommodation; transnationalism; otherness; and separateness. For Martinez, each of these five processes is in some way tied to borderland elaborations of cultural difference and similarity, and so to localised notions of ethnic and national identity, as borderlanders strive to differentiate themselves from or associate themselves with the majority population in their "national society", both within the state where they live and across its border.

In so far as notions of ethnic and national identity are tied to as yet unfulfilled claims to territory, they constitute a threat to the power and role of the state, as much of twentieth century history bears out even in Europe, which championed the ideal of the homogeneous nation-state. Anthropologists are sometimes less than clear about the difference between ethnic and national identity, but increasingly the distinction between the two is recognised as resting on their relationship to the state and their role within it. Banks (1996: 154) puts this very well when he says: "The expression of nationalism is ... unlike that of ethnicity in that it is harnessed to the machinery of modernity and linked to the structures of the state". Nations, then, are people tied together by common culture and whose goal is political independence. In short, nationalism "equals ethnicity plus the state" (Banks 1996: 156, glossing Eriksen 1993: 99). In this sense, ethnic groups might be regarded as "nations in waiting", as minority nations seeking political independence from states that are dominated by someone else. Whether or not they succeed depends, of course, on many factors, but few are likely to be winners, especially in Europe, the principal focus of this volume, where the idea of every ethnic group having its own state has seemed increasingly improbable since the signing of the Treaty of Versailles. Indeed, the future of the nation-state more generally in Europe has been widely debated, with popular and scholarly predictions of its imminent demise under the combined onslaught of a programme for a borderless Europe, the growing power of transnational capital and the dramatic spread of new communications technologies. While some see it wilting under global consumerism and the supranationalism of the European Union, others disagree and argue that any ground currently conceded is a constructive and imaginative response which in the long run will ensure the future of the European nation-state (Milward 1992). Certainly the growing body of ethnographic work on European identities, including that presented here, indicates that the nation continues to be a primary referent for political identity, whatever the wishes of the Eurocrats.

Nevertheless, few would deny that the nation-state is undergoing a transformation, and that this is impacting on Europe's borders in ways which scholars are now beginning to document (for a summary, see Strassoldo 1989; see also O'Dowd & Wilson 1996). This volume too is intended as a contribution to this discussion. With only one exception, all are directly concerned with processes of Europeanization and the European Union, either between member states (Leizaola, Kavanagh, Haller, Klomp), or between members and their non-EU neighbours (Berglund, Nyberg Sørensen, Svašek). Although also interested in the extent to which the state has managed to sustain its power in the face of radical change, these contributors are especially concerned with how the identities and cultures of the borderlands are weakened, strengthened and renegotiated as Europe's borders are redrawn and redefined. As anthropologists, our contributors are ideally equipped to examine this issue, for all have undertaken long-term residential field research in the communities they describe, communities which live along state borders and whose members are continuously engaged in negotiating the values, rules, and identities they live by, both among themselves and the agents of the state within whose jurisdiction they reside, as well as with their neighbours on the border's other side. Such investigations, we believe, have the potential to cast a fresh light on some of social sciences most central notions, such as nation, society and identity.

Scholars have often remarked on how life at borders transcends the borderline itself. Cross-border ties of kinship, employment, religion and leisure, for instance, frequently result in networks of contact and co-operation which generate a set of shared values and beliefs. In short, they generate a shared culture, a world-view specific to borderlanders irrespective of on which side of the border they might live, and only partially available to those from elsewhere. Such "border cultures" almost always transcend the limits of the state, and by creating transborder communities challenge any presumed fit between national culture and the sway of state sovereignty. At the same time, they also challenge the national bias which implicitly underlies much sociological and anthropological reasoning about the nature of society, how it is organised in space, and where it ends and begins (Haller 2000).

In contrast to some other disciplines, anthropology values the detailed knowledge of marginalized locations, peoples, and histories. Such knowledge allows one to formulate a critique of and resistance to metanarratives advanced from otherwise unarticulated social positions, as seminal contributions to the critique of hegemonic perspectives in other fields have shown: for example, feminist critiques of male bias, postcolonial perspectives on Eurocentrism, and queer theory challenges to heteronormative thinking. Although borders and borderlands have traditionally been described as marginal and peripheral within the national order (thereby reproducing elite metropolitan perspectives), a new approach to borders informed by anthropology can productively inform the gathering critique of dominant perspectives on centre and periphery that silence the voices of borderland populations.

We suggest, then, that anthropology, with its emphasis on listening to the voices of the borderlanders themselves, and on documenting the links between border communities and the wider social and political formations of which they are a part, offers the best way to study life in the borderlands. As our contributors show, such concerns can be explored in a number of ways. Many of the papers demonstrate how anthropologists are especially aware of the state's symbolic manifestations at borders, a dimension often missing from other borderland analyses. Not surprisingly perhaps, since they are the ports of entry and departure, borders generally are prime sites of symbolic elaboration within the state and national imaginary. Such state symbols sit side by side with the symbols used by local people to articulate their membership in local, regional, national and other communities. Anthropological sensitivity to how and why and when these varied sets of symbols conflict and contradict or overlap can shed much light on the cultures of the borderland, as well as on identity formation, management and dislocation in these border regions. At international borders people's identities too are often ambivalent, conflicting and multiple as in their daily lives they move through settings that demand different loyalties and codes of behaviour (as citizen, local resident, or someone from across the borderline). Fine tuned ethnography on this shifting contextual management and negotiation of national and ethnic identity in particular – but also of other identities such as those based on class, religion, gender and sex – helps lay bare the many ways in which the structure of state power impacts on people's lives in a setting – the border – where "state" and "people" perhaps touch more closely and more visibly than they do anywhere else. Here at the border we are able to witness with special clarity how nation and state are routinely lived and experienced in everyday life, a perspective potentially of great value to all those concerned to understand the cultural underpinnings of many of today's violent border conflicts.

In short, anthropological fieldwork is able to uncover informal connections, embodied practices and understandings of everyday routine, aspects of social reality that barely can be grasped by other methods such as surveys or textual critique. Indeed, an anthropological approach to borders and borderlands can illuminate the production, maintenance and subversion of nationality, ethnicity and identity in general. Drawing on their fieldwork, the contributors to this collection of essays, then, use the notion of border as both metaphor and place to further our understanding of multiple cultural identities amidst great world change, and as the vantage point from which to view the nation and the state from "below".

*Part 1 reflects on borders and national symbolism.*

In "From Iron-Curtain to Timber-Belt: Territory and Materiality at the Finnish-Russian Border", Eeva Berglund documents how the Finnish-Russian border changed from being a political periphery to being a focus for international ecopolitics, largely because of the way in which the landscapes on either side of the border were treated under different geopolitically informed state regimes. On the Finnish side, the landscape was transformed into uniform forests, whereas the Russian border zone was left largely unmanaged. Forests may transcend political boundaries as a natural fact but it is a natural fact, Berglund suggests, that is historically constituted as such, and imagined in ways that are specific to each side of the border. Social links which had existed historically across the border were reactivated following the end of the Cold War, and young Finnish forest activists have used these to develop new social ties on the Russian side. Their activities challenge accepted ideas of sovereign territory and, Berglund argues, beg revisions of the analytical tools for addressing processes of deterritorialisation and re-territorialisation such as those at play in ecopolitics.

Contrary to European Union rhetoric about a 'Europe without Frontiers', borders are far from disappearing in the Basque Country, as Aitzpea Leizaola demonstrates in "*Mugarik ez!* Subverting the Border in the Basque Country". Here borders not only remain symbolically significant, but control over them continues to be an issue for adjacent nation-states. At the same time, the actual porosity of the border, based on the maintenance of historical ties across it and on an increase in cross-border projects, compromises attempts at control. Claims to the Basque Country by Basque nationalist movements draw on specifically territorial notions of the Basque nation. The border has become a contested space, performatively reaffirmed or denied by a range of competing ritual events and symbolic markers. This paper suggests that these rituals have clear political aims. They advance agendas of radical political change, challenging the political border by questioning the partition of the Basque Country between two nation-states. Such overt political manoeuvrings have echoes among many ordinary borderlanders, who themselves claim that 'there is no border', even while, paradoxically, their livelihoods depend upon it.

*In Part 2, we highlight the relevance of discourses and practices that bring national identity into being.*

While it has long been recognised that borders are prime sites for the defining and redefining of nations and states, it is only comparatively recently that it has been thought worthwhile to examine closely the social reality of those actually living on international borders. In "The Past on the Line. The Use of Oral History in the Construction of Present-day Changing Identities on the Portuguese-Spanish Border", Bill Kavanagh looks at some of the oral history – the stories they tell about themselves – of the inhabitants of a part of the Portuguese-Spanish border, specifically an area of the frontier between the Portuguese region of Trás-os-Montes and the Spanish region of Galicia. Tales of bandits, of smugglers, of the Spanish Republican maquis and of the police of both sides reveal the often surprising fluidity of who is 'us' and who is 'them', as well as perhaps helping us to understand just how much the new 'Europe without frontiers' is rhetoric and how much is – or might become – reality.

In "The Smuggler and the Beauty Queen. The Border and Sovereignty as Sources of Body Style in Gibraltar", Dieter Haller explores the relatively neglected topic of how borders influence the habitus and body styles of border populations. Using data from the British Crown Colony of Gibraltar, Haller's paper examines two contexts in which the dominant body styles of men and women are shaped by the border and by questions of territorial sovereignty and integrity: smuggling and beauty contests. Smuggling is both economically lucrative and part of the Gibraltarians' struggle for political recognition and self-determination. The image of 'the smuggler' and his or her behaviour have become emblematic of this conflict. Related to the question of sovereignty and the border is the exclusion of Gibraltar from participation in many international events such as the Olympics and the Eurovision Song Contest. The only such event in which Gibraltar participates on an equal footing with other nations is the Miss World Contest, the preparatory heats for which have become major occasions in the Gibraltarian calendar, spawning a mass of local beauty contests. These examples illustrate not only how borders create and maintain national differences and distinctions, but also how such differences can come to be inscribed on the bodies of those who live at borders.

The Caribbean island of St. Martin is divided by an international border, with the north under the jurisdiction of the French Republic, and the south part of the Dutch Antilles. Yet the islanders conceive themselves as one people with a common language, a national anthem and many shared interests. In "Saint Martin. Communal Identities on a Divided Caribbean Island", Ank Klomp considers St. Martin as a special borderland case, in the sense that the centre and periphery overlap. The whole of St. Martin may be seen as a borderland. At the same time, St. Martin does not stand on its own, each part of the island is an element of a larger political formation. In this respect St. Martin is like other borderlands, which are the peripheries of larger entities. The paper identifies what unifies St. Martin as well as what divides it, focusing on the tension between the islanders' sense of shared identity and their attachment to two centres, the two European states, an attachment which threatens their perceived unity.

*Finally, in Part 3 we look across the border and follow border crossers.*

Although passage from Morocco to Spain has for centuries been a common practice in pursuit of a range of social, economic and political goals, it is usually considered in the literature from a purely economic perspective or, more recently, as a matter of strategic importance in relations between the countries concerned. In such analyses the Moroccan migrant community is reduced to an exchange commodity in international relations. In contrast, Ninna Nyberg Sørensen in "Crossing the Spanish-Moroccan Border with Migrants, New Islamists, and Riff-Raff" examines the perspective of three male border-crossers from the borderland of Tetuán: a deportee, a smuggler, and a student. Their narratives reveal a striking ambivalence towards both Morocco and Spain, which, the paper argues, can only be understood by reference to the impact which the Moroccan State has had on borderland identities. The paper explores questions of how to conceptualise notions such as 'society of origin' and 'society of settlement', as well as what it might mean to imagine one's life transnationally.

The post-1948 history of the twin Bedouin tribes of Kirad has been a series of forced mass border-crossings between Israel, Syria, Jordan and Lebanon. These migrations came concurrently with the staggered – but ultimately final – loss of their ancestral land in the Hula Valley by 1956, and their scattered diasporic existence over four states since. The Kirad's recent history of forced migration is contextualized within what Dan Rabinowitz in his paper on "Fifty Years, Five Crossings, More to Come. The Kirad Bedouins of Galilee and the Israeli-Syrian Border, 1948" refers to as 'small scale diasporic existence', a phenomenon of which the Kirad are a perfect example. The Kirad's own perception of their kinship world, fragmented and disturbed beyond recognition by impermeable political borders since 1948, is seen in terms of an analogy between the recent vivid past and ancient history, only vaguely remembered and invoked. The notions of diachronology, the subjectivity of historical perception and the place of fate and repetition therein constitute the theoretical focus of the analysis.

In "Borders and Emotions. Hope and Fear in the Bohemian-Bavarian Frontier Zone" Maruška Svašek argues that the emotional aspects of identity construction at international borders, and the ways in which different feelings and sentiments affect border people's perceptions and actions, have in the main remained an underexplored field of research. She analyses the dynamics of politics and emotions in the context of the Bohemian-Bavarian frontier zone, an area in which people's perceptions of 'those on the other side' have been influenced by memories of the atrocities of World War Two and the Sudeten German expulsion. The paper demonstrates that emotional displays and discourses of emotions have been actively used in the negation of social reality in the first post-Cold War decade. Svašek makes an analytical distinction between 'evoked', 'remembered', and 're-experienced' emotions to outline how emotionally complex memories can become a political force, weakening or strengthening national and transnational identities.

Each of these contributions is conscious of the dialectical nature of the relationship between the border and the nation-state, and while the emphasis in the collection as a whole is on the former, it is an emphasis sensitive to the wider social, cultural and political contexts of which the border is but a part. In general, then, the volume is concerned with national symbolism, national identity and agency. Its principal aim is to understand the role and place of local border communities within the wider project of nation-building. The case studies presented show how attempts to construct unitary national cultures are inevitably mediated by the specific configuration of circumstances at international borders, the cultural dynamics of which influence whether or not the national project in particular settings will be accepted, contested or subverted. And this, we suggest, is something that must be grasped to understand fully wider processes of nationalism, transnationalism, and globalization.

## Notes

1. Some sections of this introduction (namely parts of "Border-Crossing Anthropology", "The View from the Border", and "State Policy and Borderland Studies: A German Example") draw on Haller (2000).
2. For example, see the influential work of Barth (1969) on ethnic boundaries, and of Cohen (1986) on the boundaries of local communities.
3. See Barth (2000) on the Baktaman (Papua New Guinea) and the Basseri (Pakistan), and Kaufmann (1996) on Melanesia.
4. This is especially apparent in the case of transsexuality. The dichotomist rendering of the biosocial categories 'man' and 'woman' as absolute forces doctors and parents to clarify ambiguous genitalia of newborns. An in-between-category still remains unthinkable, and people born with unambiguous sexual characteristics but who feel trapped in the 'wrong' body must decide for one gender or the other, since no cultural apparatus for a third category exists. We know from comparative cultural research, however, that our Eurocentric categories are not really effective in the analysis of, for example, the 'Two-Spirits' of North America (Lang 1994), the gender categories of the Chukchee (Jacobs/Cromwell 1992), the *xaniths* of Oman (Wikan 1977), the *momak djevojka* of Montenegro and Albania (Grémaux 1996), the *mahus* of Tahiti (Levy 1971), and the *köçek* of Turkey (Tapinc 1992). See also Haller (1996).
5. See also Hauschild (1995: 13–62) on German anthropology as a border science.
6. See, for example, Spradley/McCurdy 1975; Hiebert 1976.
7. Our thanks to Michi Knecht for suggesting the term in this context.
8. See, for example, Borneman (1995) on the role of Indians in North American cultural anthropology.
9. One early exception is Cole/Wolf (1974). Since the end of the 1980s, borders have become the object of much research interest. Cf. for example Alvarez 1995; Anzaldua 1987; Borneman 1992a, 1992b, 1993a, 1993b; De Rapper 1996; Donnan/Wilson 1994a, 1999; Driessen 1992, 1996a, 1996b; Flynn 1997; Kavanagh 1994; Kearney 1991; Kockel 1991; Leizaola 1996; Nugent/Asiwaju 1996; O'Dowd/Wilson 1996; Raveneau 1996; Sahlins 1989; Thomassen 1996; Vereni 1996; Wilson/Smith 1993.
10. See also Donnan 1999.
11. Peripherality and external domination are still considered the two chief characteristics for designating borderlands by Greverus (1997: 12).
12. Even Martínez's (1994) categorization of borderlands considers border populations to be agents who merely react to national policy (e.g. the degree of openness of the border), and whose relationship to their neighbours is oriented to state limitations. Cf. Martínez's categorization of borderlands into a) alienated borderlands (border inhabitants regard their neighbours as foreign), b) co-existent borderlands (border inhabitants regard their neighbours as casual acquaintances), c) interdependent borderlands (border inhabitants regard their neighbours as friends and cooperators), and d) integrated borderlands (border inhabitants regard themselves and their neighbours as members of one social system).
13. See Medick 1991, 1995. In the Pyrenees Peace Treaty of 1659, the two powers did not divide the

Cerdenya territorially, but rather "divided a range of jurisdictions and ruling rights over the border population, over their property, exercise of religion, and payment of taxes and duties. These jurisdictions in no way matched the territories in the sense of a uniform borderline, but extended back and forth – unmeasured and a cause of frequent conflicts – beyond the border" (Medick 1995: 221). These transborder jurisdictional areas led to competing loyalties and dependencies which in turn led to conflicts between France and Spain. The local societies found themselves in a constant exchange process with their neighbours beyond the border, yet appealed for help from the wielders of state power in order to push through their own specific local interests and maintain their local cultural identity; simultaneously, however, they were pressed into the service of those wielders of power. Sahlins thereby demonstrates the border population's active role in the creation of state and national identity. In Germany, too, there were territories in a situation of transborder and competitive jurisdiction up to the seventeenth century. Ulbrich (1993: 139–146) describes a similar process for the French-German border in Lorraine.

14. In the Pyrenees, access to water and pastureland on the other side of the border is still often regulated by local custom. See Comas d'Argemir/Pujadas 1999: 255.
15. This conception is not unanimously shared. Sieber-Lehmann (1996: 80), for example, claims that borders have been considered linear dividing lines since the early Middle Ages.
16. Ratzel (1882, 1892, 1903), who himself followed in the tradition of Hegel via Ernst Kapp, and who dealt less with cultures than with states, was influenced by Carl Schmitt and Karl Haushofer in how he viewed the "nation" (Ebeling 1994). See Haller 1995: 25–33 and Medick 1995.
17. See Mühlmann 1944:8; 1962: 337; 1964: 65, 176ff, 276, 277.
18. Like Mühlmann, Boehm also developed his ideas on the border in the political context of the Third Reich and in the framework of his activities for the Institute for Border and Foreign Studies: in contrast to the border population, the 'interior German realm' was not considered to be under threat from 'border danger'. For Boehm, this danger lay in mixing with 'foreign folk elements' and, again like Mühlmann, he propounded the idea that the "'consciousness of mastery' over the border and foreign Germans (must be) raised to a race-proud 'consciousness of mission' (by National Socialism)." Cf. Weber-Kellermann 1978: 77.
19. We would like to thank Dr. Ute Michel and Prof. Carsten Klingemann for their help with these points. See also Michel 1992: 69–119.
20. Here Mühlmann is in the tradition of the German geopolitics of Carl Schmitt and Karl Haushofer, whose main theme was a revision of the borders in the Treaty of Versailles, "which, however, fostered a certain mysticism of territory, because it could not and did not want to declare openly its expansive goals reaching far beyond the borders of 1914" (Scherer 1995: 3). What they could not openly declare before 1933, however, could be openly expressed in the twelve years of the Thousand-Year-Reich – according to Mühlmann (1944), who saw precisely in the recognition of borders (in the sense of boundaries) a "sign of political weakness". Cf. Haller 1995.
21. Mühlmann 1962: 337. The terms Mühlmann uses to portray the inhabitants of the Russian-Asian border are similar to those used by Leyburn in his characterization of European settlers in North America: thus the Cossacks are portrayed as "freedom loving" (1944: 87) and as "clearly defined types of audacious, unscrupulous adventurers and individualists fully saturated with a feeling of civilized superiority and a self-righteous consciousness of mission" (1962: 36).
22. A decisive factor for Mühlmann is sedentariness: if the 're-peopled' German folk border population in the East in 1944 protected Germany against the "Jewish creature", who is characterised by "lack of roots (and is) partly nomadic" (Mühlmann 1944: 143), by 1964 the border cordon only protected the inhabitants of the German interior against "nomads", a term perhaps regarded as more politically correct (Mühlmann 1964: 251).
23. Febvre developed his thoughts on the reciprocal permeability of regions at the border in relation to cultural exchange in the Rhineland. He was more concerned with the history of the mentality of the border area and with an analysis of the world images, perspectives, and feelings of borderland inhabitants, than with issues of language, race, and origin (1970).
24. See, for example, Greverus (1969), Schilling (1986), Girtler (1991), and Jeggle/Raphaël (1997), as well as Weber-Kellermann (1978) on interethnic relations.

## References

Alvarez, Robert R., 1995: The Mexican-US border: the making of an anthropology of borderlands, *Annual Review of Anthropology*, Vol. 24, pp. 449–456.

Anderson, Malcolm, 1982: Political problems of frontier regions, *West European Politics*, Vol. 5, No. 4. Pp. 1–17.

Anderson, Malcolm, 1996: *Frontiers: Territory and State Formation in the Modern World*, Oxford: Polity.

Anzaldua, Gloria, 1987: *Borderlands / La Frontera: The New Mestiza*, San Francisco: Spinsters/Aunt Lute.

Banks, Marcus, 1996: *Ethnicity: Anthropological Con-*

*structions*. London: Routledge.

Barth, Fredrik, 1969: *Ethnic Groups and Boundaries. The Social Organization of Culture Difference*. London & Oslo: Allen & Unwin.

Barth, Fredrik, 2000: Boundaries and Connections, in: Anthony Cohen (ed.), *Signifying Identities*. London: Routledge, pp. 17–37.

Bausinger, Hermann, 1997: Kleiner Grenzverkehr, in: Jeggle, Utz/Raphaël, Freddy (eds.), *D'une rive à l'autre – Kleiner Grenzverkehr*. Paris: Ed. de la Maison des sciences de l'homme, pp. 3–15.

Boehm, Max Hildebert, 1978 [1932]: Das Volkstum des Grenz- und Auslandsdeutschtums, in: Weber-Kellermann, Ingeborg (Hg.), *Zur Interethnik*. Frankfurt/Main: Suhrkamp, pp. 78–94.

Borneman, John, 1995: American Anthropology as Foreign Policy, *American Anthropologist*, Vol. 97, No. 4, pp. 6–15.

Borneman, John, 1992a: *Belonging in the two Berlins – Kin, state, nation*. Cambridge: Cambridge University Press.

Borneman, John, 1992b: State, Territory, and Identity Formation in the Postwar Berlins, 1945–1989, *Cultural Anthropology*, Vol. 7, No. 1, pp. 45–61.

Borneman, John, 1993a: Time-Space Compression and the Continental Divide in German Subjectivity, *New Formations*, Vol. 21, pp. 102–118.

Borneman, John, 1993b: Uniting the German nation: law, narrative, and historicity, *American Anthropologist*, Vol. 20, No. 2, pp. 288–311.

Cohen, Anthony, 1986: *Symbolising boundaries – Identity and diversity in British culture*. Manchester: Manchester University Press.

Cole, John /Wolf, Eric, 1974: *The Hidden Frontier: Ecology and Ethnicity in an Alpine Valley.* New York: Academic Press.

Comas d'Argemir, Dolors/Pujadas, Joan, 1999: Living in/on the frontier: Migration, identities and citizenship in Andorra, *Social Anthropology* 1999, Vol. 7, No. 3, pp. 253–264.

de Rapper, Gilles, 1996: Frontière et transition en Albanie du sud*, Europae*, Vol. II No. 1, pp. 65–75.

Donnan, Hastings, 1999: Shopping and Sectarianism at the Irish Border, in: Rosler, Michael/Wendl, Tobias (eds.): *Frontiers and Borderlands: Anthropological Perspectives*. Frankfurt/Main: Peter Lang, pp. 101–116.

Donnan, Hastings/Wilson, Thomas M. (eds.), 1994a: *Border approaches: Anthropological Perpectives on Frontiers*. Lanham, MD: University Press of America.

Donnan, Hastings/Wilson, Thomas M. 1994b: An anthropology of frontiers, in: Donnan, Hastings/Wilson, Thomas M. (eds.): *Border Approaches. Anthropological Perspectives on Frontiers.* Lanham – New York – London: University Press of America, pp. 1–14.

Donnan, Hastings/Wilson, Thomas M., 1999: *Borders: Frontiers of Identity, Nation and State*. Oxford: Berg.

Driessen, Henk, 1992: *On the Spanish–Moroccan Frontier.* New York/Oxford: Berg.

Driessen, Henk, 1996a: At the edge of Europe: Crossing and marking the Mediterranean divide, in: L. O'Dowd/Wilson, T. M. (eds.): *Borders, Nations and States*, pp. 179–198.

Driessen, Henk, 1996b: What Am I Doing Here? The anthropologist, the mole, and border ethnography, in: Waltraud Kokot & Dorle Dracklé (eds.): *Ethnologie Europas*. Berlin: Dietrich Reimer Verlag, pp. 287–299.

Ebeling, Frank, 1994: Geopolitik 1919–1945, Karl Haushofer und seine Raumwissenschaft. Vortrag auf dem Symposion der Paul-Kleinewefers-Stiftung Krefeld und der Universität Hannover, 29.04.–30.04.94, Hannover – *Theorieentwürfe des politischen Raumes – Europäische Perspektiven*.

Eriksen, Thomas H., 1993: *Ethnicity and Nationalism: Anthropological Perspectives*. London: Pluto.

Fardon, Richard (ed.), 1990: *Localizing Strategies*. Edinburgh: Scottish Academic Press.

Febvre, Lucien, 1962 (orig.: 1928): Frontière: le mot et la notion, *Pour une histoire part entière*, Paris, SEVPEN, pp. 11–24.

Febvre, Lucien, 1962 (orig.: 1908), Frontière: limites et divisions de la France en 1789*, Pour une histoire part entière*, Paris, SEVPEN, pp. 25–29.

Febvre, Lucien, 1922: Le problème des frontières et les régions naturelles d'états, *La terre et l'évolution humaine*. Introduction géographique l'histoire, Paris, La Renaissance du Livre, pp. 359–383.

Fernandez, James, 1982: The Dark at the Bottom of the Stairs: the Inchoate in Symbolic Inquiry and Some Strategies for Coping with It, in: Maquet, Jacques (ed.), *On symbols in anthropology – essays in honor of Harry Hoijer*, Malibu: Published for the UCLA Dept. of Anthropology by Undena Publications, pp. 13–43.

Fernandez, James, 1974: The Mission of Metaphor in Expressive Culture, *Current Anthropology*, Vol. 15, No. 2, pp. 119–145.

Flynn, Donna K., 1997: "We are the border": identity, exchange, and the state along the Bénin-Nigeria border, *American Anthropologist* , Vol. 24, No. 2, pp. 311–330.

Frank, Geyla, 1997: Jews, Multiculturalism, and Boasian Anthropology, *American Anthropologist*, Vol. 99, No. 4, pp. 731–745.

Freilich, Morris (ed.), 1970: *Marginal Natives: Anthropologists at Work*. New York.

Gasparini, Alberto/Zago, Moreno: *Gorizia, Nova Gorica e le Aree di Confine Italo-Slovene: c'e un Futuro di Integrazione Differenziata*? Gorizia: Istituto di Sociologia Internazionale de Gorizia.

Girtler, Roland, 1991: *Über die Grenze – Ein Kulturwissenschaftler auf dem Fahrrad.* Frankfurt/Main, New York: Campus.

Girtler, Roland, 1992: *Schmuggler – von Grenzen und ihren Überwindern.* Linz: Veritas.

Grémaux, René, 1996: Woman becomes Man in the Balkans, in: Gilbert Herdt (ed.): *Third Sex, Third Gender*. New York, Zone Books, pp. 241–285.

Greverus, Ina Maria, 1969: Grenzen und Kontakte. Zur Territorialität des Menschen, in: *Kontakte und Grenzen*. Festschrift für Gerhard Heilfurth. Göttingen, pp. 11–26.

Greverus, Ina Maria, 1997: Island as Borderland: Experiences and Thoughts on Rügen and Usedom, *Anthropological Journal of European Culture*, Vol. 6, No. 1, pp. 7–27.

Gupta, Akhil/Ferguson, James, 1992: Beyond "Culture": Space, Identity, and the Politics of Difference, *Cultural Anthropology*, Vol. 7, No. 1, pp. 6–23.

Haller, Dieter, 1994: *Feld, Lokalität, Ort, Territorium: Implikationen der kulturanthropologischen Raumterminologie*. WZB-Diskussionspapier FS II 94–101, Berlin.

Haller, Dieter, 1995: Die Dynamik des Raumes – eine kulturanthropologische Perspektive, in: *Berliner Debatte Initial*, No. 3, pp. 25–33.

Haller, Dieter, 1996: Überlegungen zu Heteronormativität und Feldforschung, in: Kokot, Waltraud/ Dracklé, Dorle (eds.): *Ethnologie Europas*. Berlin: Dietrich Reimer Verlag, pp. 181–201.

Haller, Dieter, 2000: *Gelebte Grenze Gibraltar – Transnationalismus, Lokalität und Identität in kulturanthropologischer Perspektive*. Wiesbaden: Deutscher Universitätsverlag.

Hannerz, Ulf: Fronteras, *International Social Science Journal* 154/Dec. 1997 (Spanish version). http://firewall.unesco.org/issj/rics154/hannerzspa.html (02.08.2000).

Hauschild, Thomas, 1995: „Dem lebendigen Geist." Warum die Geschichte der Völkerkunde im „Dritten Reich" auch für Nichtanthropologen von Interesse sein kann, in: Thomas Hauschild (Hg.): *Lebenslust und Fremdenfurcht*. Frankfurt/Main, Suhrkamp, pp. 13–62.

Hiebert, Paul, 1976: *Cultural Anthropology*. Philadelphia.

Jacobs, Sue Ellen/Cromwell, Jason, 1992: Visions and Revisions of Reality: Reflections on Sex, Sexuality, Gender and Gender Variance, *Journal of Homosexuality*, Vol. 23, No. 4, pp. 42–49.

Jeggle, Utz/Raphaël, Freddy (eds.), 1997: *D'une rive à l'autre – Kleiner Grenzverkehr*. Paris: Ed. de la Maison des sciences de l'homme.

Kaufmann, Christian, 1996: Auf dem Boden der Wir-Leute – Grenzvorstellungen in Melanesien, in: Marchal, Guy P. (Hg.): *Grenzen und Raumvorstellungen (11.–20. Jh.)*. Chronos, Luzern, pp. 41–79.

Kavanagh, William, 1994: Symbolic boundaries and 'real' borders on the Portuguese-Spanish Frontier, in: Donnan, Hastings, Wilson, Thomas M. (eds.): *Border Approaches: Anthropological Perspectives on Frontiers*, Lanham – New York – London, University Press of America, pp. 75–89.

Kearney, Michael, 1991: Borders and Boundaries of State and Self at the End of Empire, *Journal of Historical Sociology*, Vol. 4, No. 1, pp. 52–74.

Kockel, Ullrich, 1991: *Regions, Borders and European Integration*. Liverpool: Institute of Irish Studies, Univ. of Liverpool.

Kotek, Joël (ed.), 1996: *L'Europe et ses villes-frontières*. Bruxelles: Éditions Complexe.

Kramer, Johannes, 1996: Bezeichnungen für "Grenze" in den europäischen Sprachen, *Tumult – Schriften zur Verkehrswissenschaft*, Vol. 22, pp. 51–61.

Lang, Sabine, 1994: "Two-Spirit-People": Gender Variance, Homosexualität und Identitätsfindung bei IndianerInnen Nordamerikas, *kea* No. 7, pp. 69–86.

Leizaola, Aitzpea, 1996: Muga: Border and Boundaries in the Basque Country, *Europaea*, Vol. II, No. 1, pp. 91–102.

Levy, Robert I. 1971: The Community Function of Tahitian Male Transvestism: a Hypothesis, *Anthropological Quarterly*, Vol. 44, pp. 13–22.

Lewis, Ioan M., 1973: *The Anthropologist's Muse – an inaugural lecture*. London: The London School of Economics and Political Science.

Leyburn, James G., 1933: Frontier Society: A Study in the Growth of Culture, *Zeitschrift für Völkerpsychologie und Soziologie*, Vol. 9, pp. 174–181.

Lindner, Rolf, 1987: Wer wird Ethnograph?, in: Ina-Maria Greverus, Konrad Köstlin, Heinz Schilling (Hgs.): *Kulturkontakt – Kulturkonflikt*, Frankfurt/ Main, pp. 99–107.

Martinez, Oscar J., 1994: The dynamics of border interaction – New approaches to border analysis, in: Schofield, Clive H. (ed.): *World Boundaries Volume 1 – Global Boundaries*. London: Routledge, pp. 1–14.

Medick, Hans, 1995: Grenzziehungen und die Herstellung des politisch-sozialen Raumes. Zur Begriffsgeschichte der Grenzen in der Frühen Neuzeit, in: Faber, Richard/Naumann, Barbara (Hgs.): *Literatur der Grenze / Theorie der Grenze*. Würzburg: Königshausen & Neumann, pp. 211–225.

Medick, Hans, 1991: Zur politischen Sozialgeschichte der Grenzen in der Neuzeit Europas, *Sozialwissenschaftliche Informationen,* Vol. 20, No. 3, pp. 157–163.

Michel, Ute, 1991: Wilhelm Emil Mühlmann (1904–1988) – ein deutscher Professor. Amnesie und Amnestie: Zum Verhältnis von Ethnologie und Politik im Nationalsozialismus, *Jahrbuch für Soziologiegeschichte* 1991, pp. 69–119.

Milward, A., 1992: *The European Rescue of the Nation-State*. London: Routledge.

Mühlmann, Wilhelm Emil, 1940: *Krieg und Frieden*. Heidelberg: Carl Winter.

Mühlmann, Wilhelm Emil, 1944: *Die Völker der Erde*. Berlin: Deutscher Verlag.

Mühlmann, Wilhelm Emil, 1962: *Homo Creator*. Wiesbaden: Otto Harrassowitz.

Mühlmann, Wilhelm Emil, 1964: *Rassen, Ethnien, Kulturen*. Neuwied, Berlin: Luchterhand.

Müller, Klaus E., 1987: *Das magische Universum der Identität: Elementarformen sozialen Verhaltens*. Frankfurt/Main & New York: Campus.

Nugent Paul/Asiwaju, A.I. (eds.), 1996: *African Boundaries – Barriers, Conduits & Opportunities*. London: Pinter.

O'Dowd, Liam/Wilson, Thomas M. (eds.), 1996: *Bor-*

*ders, Nations and States – Frontiers of Sovereignty in the New Europe*. Avebury, Aldershot.

Ratzel, Friedrich, 1882: *Anthropogeographie, oder Grundzüge der Anwendung der Erdkunde auf die Geschichte*. Stuttgart.

Ratzel, Friedrich, 1892: *Allgemeine Eigenschaften der geographischen Grenzen und die politische Grenze*. Berichte d. sächs. Ges. d. Wiss. Phil.hist. Kl. 44.

Ratzel, Friedrich, 1903: *Politische Geographie*. München.

Raveneau, Gilles, 1996: Frontière et liens à la périphérie: la Corse et la Sardaigne, in: *Europaea* Vol. II, No. 1, pp. 103–119.

Rosaldo, Renato, 1989: *Culture and Truth: The Remaking of Social Analysis*. Boston: Beacon.

Sahlins, Peter, 1989: *Boundaries – The Making of France and Spain in the Pyrenees*. Berkeley: University of California Press.

Scherer, Peter, 1995: Warum Geopolitik? Fragen zu einer umstrittenen Wissenschaft, in: *Berliner Debatte Initial*, No. 3, pp. 3–9.

Schilling, Heinz, 1986: Über die Grenze – Zur Interdependenz von Kontakten und Barrieren in der Region Saarland/Lothringen, in: *Leben an der Grenze – Recherchen in der Region Saarland / Lothringen*. Frankfurt/Main: Schriftenreihe des Instituts für Kulturanthropologie und Europäische Anthropologie an der Universität Frankfurt am Main, pp. 345–94.

Shokeid, Moshe, 1988: Anthropologists and their informants: marginality reconsidered, *Archives Européennes de Sociologie*, Vol. 29, pp. 31–47.

Sieber-Lehmann, Claudius, 1996: Regna colore rubeo circumscripta – Überlegungen zur Geschichte weltlicher Herrschaftsgrenzen im Mittelalter, in: Marchal, Guy P. (Hg.): *Grenzen und Raumvorstellungen* (11.–20. Jh.) – Frontières et conceptions de l'espace (11e–20e siècles). Zürich: Chronos Verlag, pp. 79–92.

Simmel, Georg, 1992: Soziologie des Raumes, in: *Schriften zur Soziologie*. Frankfurt/Main: Suhrkamp 1992 (4.Aufl.), pp. 221–243.

Spradley, James./M. McCurdy, 1975: *Anthropology: The Cultural Perspective*. New York: Wiley & Sons.

Stagl, Justin, 1974: *Kulturanthropologie und Gesellschaft – Wege zu einer Wissenschaft*. München: List Verlag.

Strassoldo, Raimondo, 1989: Border Studies: The State of the Art in Europe, in: A. I. Asiwaju/P. O. Adeniyi (eds.), *Borderlands in Africa*. Lagos: University of Lagos Press, pp. 383–395.

Streck, Bernhard, 1995: Grenzgang Anthropologie, in: Faber, Richard/Naumann, Barbara (Hgs.): *Literatur der Grenze / Theorie der Grenze*. Würzburg: Königshausen & Neumann, pp. 185–195.

Tapinc, Huseyin, 1992: Masculinity, Femininity, and Turkish Male Homosexuality, in: Kenneth Plummer (ed.): *Modern Homosexualities*. London: Routledge, pp. 39–49.

Thomassen, Bjørn, 1996: Border Studies in Europe: Symbolic and Political Boundaries, Anthropological Perspectives, *Europaea* Vol. II, No. 1, pp. 37–48.

Turner, Victor, 1967: Betwixt and Between: The Liminal Period in Rites de Passage, in: *The Forest of Symbols*. Ithaca, Cornell University Press, pp. 93–111.

Turner, Victor, 1969: *The Ritual Process: Structure and Anti-Structure*. Chicago: Aldine.

Ulbrich, Claudia, 1993: Grenze als Chance? Bemerkungen zur Bedeutung der Reichsgrenze im Saar-Lor-Lux-Raum am Vorabend der Französischen Revolution, in: Pilgram, Arno (Hg.): *Grenzöffnung, Migration, Kriminalität*. Baden-Baden: Nomos, pp. 139–146.

Van Gennep, Arnold, 1909: *Les rites de Passage. Étude Systématique des Rites*. Paris.

Vereni, Piero, 1996: Boundaries, Frontiers, Persons, Individuals: Questioning "Identity" at National Borders, *Europae*, Vol. II, No. 1, pp. 77–89.

Weber-Kellermann, Ingeborg (ed.), 1978: *Zur Interethnik*. Frankfurt/Main: Suhrkamp.

Wikan, Unni, 1977: Man becomes Woman: Transsexualism in Oman as a key to gender roles, *Man*, Vol. 12, pp. 304–319.

Wilson, T. M./M. Estellie Smith (eds.), 1993: *Cultural Change and the New Europe: Perspectives on the European Community*. Boulder: Westview Press.

# From Iron Curtain to Timber-Belt

## Territory and Materiality at the Finnish-Russian Border

*Eeva Berglund*

Berglund, Eeva 2000: From Iron Curtain to Timber-Belt. Territory and Materiality at the Finnish-Russian Border. Ethnologia Europaea 30, 2: 23–34.

The paper shows the Finnish-Russian border changing from a political periphery into a focus for international ecopolitics, because of how landscapes either side have been treated under different geopolitically informed regimes of government. On the Finnish side landscape was transformed into industrially managed forests, whereas the Russian border zone was left largely unmanaged. Historical social links across the border were reactivated after the end of the Cold War, and young Finnish forest activists in particular have created social links here. Their activities challenge accepted ideas of sovereign territory and beg revisions of the analytical tools for addressing processes of deterritorialisation and reterritorialisation such as those at play in ecopolitics.

*PhD Eeva Berglund, Department of Anthropology, Goldsmiths College, New Cross, London SE14 6NW UK. E-mail: e.berglund@gold.ac.uk*

In the face of environmental destruction state borders can easily seem meaningless.[1] If this is an exaggeration, border environments nevertheless throw the weakness of state sovereignty into relief. This paper sketches a picture of one region, along Russia's – formerly the Soviet Union's – 900 km border with Finland, where state sovereignty is challenged by international networks of governmental and non-governmental organisations and by ecological processes. Russian Karelia[2] has been 'open' to international traffic for over a decade though for most of the twentieth century, crossing the border was extremely difficult and access to the region from within the Soviet Union was also restricted. After all, it was part of the boundary between what US President Ronald Reagan famously called the Evil Empire and market-led democracy. Today it is an object of intense concern for Finnish and international environmentalists. It is the focus of interest because of its exceptionally unfragmented boreal[3] forests, the result of the fact that the region was so long valued as a frontier, the edge of a territory.

Here ecopolitics challenges sovereign territory, since the valued forest lies inside Russia, whilst many of those seeking its protection come from elsewhere. But Karelia is also deeply connected to the history of Finnish national identity. It has nourished ideas and practices of the good life that draw a variety of resources from forests, something that has become important economically as well as culturally in Finland. Thus this paper argues that what provokes the interest of Finnish environmentalists and fosters social links across the border is the materiality of the border's forests. Deterritorialised ecopolitical concerns articulate with Finnish historiography in which forests are both resource and symbol for the nation. Besides supporting recent critical work on territories and territorialisation (Appadurai 1996, Lugo 1997, Ó'Tuathail and Dalby 1998, Paasi 1996, Brock 1999), a broader point follows, namely that as an empirical as well as critical pursuit, anthropology needs to attend to re-territorialisation as much as to de-territorialisation.

For power remains spatialised (e.g. Brock 1999, Gupta and Ferguson 1997). The intensifying competition over access to environmental goods and avoidance of environmental evils (Harvey 1996) is but one arena where continuity and change in the spatial relations of power needs to be better understood. Flows of capital, movement of information and displacement of people do not necessarily indicate the weakening hold of territory as an organising principle of social and political life. Certainly international environmentalism challenges hegemonic notions of space (Kuehls 1996), highlighting the disjunctures between the space of ecopolitics (the politics of global risk) and the space of state control. Yet understanding the effects of such disjunctures requires further theoretical work. This paper, focussing on the border zone where the history of Cold War logic, ecological processes, and late-twentieth-century economic patterns meet, demonstrates why.

As the border opened up, the forests beckoned logging companies, especially Finnish ones, to exploit easily accessible, abundant reserves of timber. The companies were soon followed by environmental protestors who feared irreparable damage to Karelia's ancient forests. Activists thus pitted themselves against corporate power on behalf of nature and sustainable lifestyles. In so doing, they also challenged ideas about sovereign territory and about the rights to harvest natural resources for a world market. Yet on the face of it, their protest looked like a familiar romanticisation of living 'close to nature'.

A young Finn, let me call her Anna, told me she would love to move to Russian Karelia.[4] The world on the Finnish side of the border with its high-tech and consumer-oriented life contrasted unfavourably in her eyes with the almost subsistence-based village life on the Russian side. Here energy is conscientiously saved, water is carried in buckets from river or lake to the house, and waste disposal is not an issue since nothing is wasted. After a lifetime's participation in conservation, Anna had a strong desire to live out what she considered a sane lifestyle. "I'd like to move here [to Russian Karelia]," she told me. "This is where people, forests and large lakes exist side by side in a proper balance. I mean, it's selfish of me, I know, but this really is how a good life can be lived." Rather than reiterate the argument that such attitudes are typical of metropolitan coloniser (environmentalist) towards peripheral colonised (Cronon ed. 1995), I want to show that similarities in activists' and local people's ways of valuing the forests still transcend political boundaries. Environmentalists like Anna may be influenced by a media-enhanced global discourse which constructs concerned 'global' eco-citizens at the same time as it constructs differently valued others – whether backward peasants or ecologically wise savages – but they are also situated historically and geographically in ways that inflect their environmentalism.

A brief methodological note is in order here. My research was designed to examine conflicts over forest use in a country, Finland, with a powerful self-image of homogeneity and consensus. Historical records and analyses of political shifts, along with attention to various media, have provided input, as have the conversations all Finns seem to launch into when it comes to talking of forests. The current text, however, is based on ethnographic work with Finnish activists[5], which took me to both sides of the border and led to conversations with people on the Russian side. This work began to suggest alternative questions about young environmentalists' orientations to the nature and people of this region. This part of my research is limited to fewer than a dozen activists. Many more Finnish activists campaigned on Russian Karelia throughout the 1990s, publicising illegal logging, and even more young Finns and Russians have carried out biodiversity surveys of the forests in order to produce the necessary documentation for conservation measures to be implemented. News coverage and letters to editors, interviews in a range of environmental organisations, and conversations with non-environmentalists, further demonstrate that many people have supported the young men and women at the heart of the effort to prevent the introduction of Finnish-style industrial forestry in Russian Karelia. Events in its forests began to reflect Finnish values, and it is the view from Finland, which this paper presents.

## Nature, Science and Ecopolitics[6] at Borders

At first sight Karelia's belt of ancient forests seems like an obvious target for international environmentalism. As a recent publication puts it, these forests "are one of the most important boreal biodiversity centres of Europe" (Ovaskainen et al. 1999). Another refers to the area as the 'Green Belt' of Fennoscandia, noting that this "unique natural complex [...] has been preserved and offers an opportunity to sustain evolutional and distributional dynamics – the prerequisites of biological diversity – on an exceptional scale" (Kleinn 1998). However, one could ask, as many have in the Amazon and elsewhere (Kuehls 1996, Conklin 1997), what gives the wealthy and privileged the right to protect biodiversity elsewhere when they have destroyed their own at home? Why do already disempowered groups become identified with nature, a passive if highly valued object, when the rich insist on identifying with civilisation and progress even after they have destroyed their environments?

In creating copious knowledge about the ecological value of the region, sometimes together with Russian counterparts, Finnish activists throughout the 1990s acted as if their work was deterritorialised, part of the global imperative to promote economically viable and ecologically healthy resource use (Ovaskainen et al. 1999). Nature does not stop at borders and therefore by definition the environmentalist agenda is conceptualised as transnational. It is seen as scientifically based, and accordingly activists referred to the knowledge that promoted their enthusiasm as free of political or cultural biases. Finnish activists are connected to organisations like UNESCO, they work with large NGOs[7] like Greenpeace, and with the international umbrella organisation dedicated to protecting such forests in the Northern hemisphere, the *Taiga Rescue Network*, a group that brought international delegates to Karelia in 1996 to promote the political process. German organisations have fuelled the idea of the area as a World Heritage site (Kleinn 1998).

Like government officials who promote technomanagerial interventions as the only answer to ecological destruction, environmentalists here contribute to the world-wide power of ecology as a moralised scientific discourse (Takacs 1996). Many of the other actors involved in cross-border traffic speak another apparently universal language, that of economics. The *Oikos*, or household, is at the root of both these discourses: eco-nomics and eco-logy. The *Oikos* draws attention to the idea that the planet as a whole is home and its management is a shared responsibility across borders. It seems hopeful to think that problems such as global environmental degradation and global economic volatility actually carry the promise that eventually state borders will be seen for the mere human constructions that they are. But the reality so far warrants rather less optimism.

The crisis of environmental politics is inextricably bound up with a crisis over boundaries (Kuehls 1996). Ecological processes pay no heed to borders, yet states remain crucial to their government and so "ecopolitics cannot be reduced to either domestic or international policy" (Kuehls 1996: 117). But ecopolitics is also bound up with a crisis of policing (the appropriate spaces of) knowledge, science and expertise. Reliable knowledge and trustworthy expertise are necessary to the political process of environmental protest just as they are to resource management. Ecopolitics is thus a forum for generating new criteria for legitimate concern over territories, linking groups distanced in space, and reconfiguring existing networks of knowledge. It generates new collectivities held together by trust in purveyors of knowledge, as environmentalists in the border zone constantly bring different spatial scales and various scientific logics into conjunction with each other. The intensity of the traffic in these competing forms of science is an important change from an earlier condition where scientific expertise was spatialised in more fixed, often national ways, as I shall show below.

In insisting on a scientific basis for their concern, those protesting logging appear to be endorsing the official discourses that cross this border rather than challenging them. Just like employees of the Finnish Environment Ministry, Moscow-based activists, German researchers, or local conservation officials, activists connect across the border in the language of scientific ecology. Collaborative research proliferates as do publications like the report *On the Ecological and Economic impacts of wood harvesting and trade in north-east Russia* (Myllynen et al. 1996). Finnish and Russian nature enthusiasts, many of them students, spent summers in the mid-1990s mapping and surveying the region's biodiversity, and in their view, science and economics are best able to transcend cultural differences unless they are cynically manipulated. Such a Eurocentric perspective (Szerszynski et al. 1996) has allowed administrators and scientists from a range of institutions to identify common goals and carry out collective projects, for instance co-operation under the "Finnish-Russian Development Programme on Sustainable Forest Management and Conservation of Biological Diversity in Northwest Russia", administered on the Finnish side through the Ministries of the Environment, of Agriculture and Forestry and for Foreign Affairs. The process is clearly managerial and technical in character, with the umbrella project aiming to encompass "economic, environmental, social and market aspects" (NWRDP 1997:3). Forests are treated as an external resource needing to be managed for the common good – whether as industry resource or as biodiversity – through government action.

The power of modern scientific discourse in much of the world rests precisely in the conviction that it is above politics and that only the world, not society or religious dogma or even financial interest, is reflected in it. However, social studies of science have done much to demonstrate that contrary to such proclamations of transcendence, these claims are not devoid of culture or power, and that science remains a *cultural* practice (e.g. Latour 1987, Haraway 1997). Still, when wedded to the common-sense notion that we all know what nature is, it is hardly surprising that ecopolitics should make science carry so much of its argument. Technical and scientific languages remain preeminent when international agendas in the name of a healthy, global environment are articulated. And the technical language of the global economy, conceptualised as necessary or transcendent rather than historically constructed, is easily wedded to the technical languages of both resource use and nature protection, often enough with similar ends in mind (Luke 1995).

## Governing Forests

Activism thus indirectly supports the policing of resources and endorses particular forms of expert knowledge, but it also resists the Lockean conception of land as only valuable when it is productive in a way the state recognises.[8] Activists challenge older ideas about nature, territory and state power, by allowing them to be drawn in by the concreteness of the forests in ways that the state cannot dictate. As I have argued elsewhere in more detail (Berglund 2000), as they became tangible economic assets, forests were made a particular focus of social relations in Finland and until the 1980s the state's role in defining ideal attitudes towards forests, as well as policing authorised knowledge about them, was impressive and it reached practically every square kilometre of the territory (Michelsen 1995, Berglund 2000) giving substance to the ubiquitous claim that "Finland lives off the forest". This thoroughgoing government of Finland's natural landscape, as much as the isolation of the Russian border zone, is what has produced the sharp discontinuity in the biophysical characteristics of the forests on both sides of the border. The landscape that now draws activists, locals and others into collaboration is thus the direct result of policing the frontier and of constituting Finland and Russia in mutual opposition.

As Finland became increasingly connected to an international network of trade in the mid-nineteenth century, domestic life became more professionalised and increasingly governed through state apparatuses of knowledge production (Häkli 1998). The state surveyed and documented the nation's progress. Sustained interest in timber extraction as well as in the population was fostered, and Finns came to believe that their right to self-determination was as irreducibly natural as their dependency on a natural resource. They depended on the forest for timber, but also for many other goods such as berries and wild game, as well as for the many auxiliary industries that paper and pulp manufacture brought with it. Since the 1860s, Finland invested purposefully in the forest products industries, and gradually what lay within its borders became homogenous as nature and nationhood were consolidated together (Berglund 2000).

Today the border demarcates both the landscape of Finnish national pride – the homogenous landscapes of industrial forestry – and the landscape of environmentalist desire – the Green Belt of Karelia. Satellite imagery, but also the naked eye, can easily distinguish the border because of the contrast in vegetation. The Russian side of the border is the legacy of purposeful neglect, whilst on the other side, state forestry has affected practically all of Finland's surface area. Although much of Finland is forest and most of it is pleasant to wander in and to enjoy, its biological diversity has clearly suffered, from selective replanting in response to industry needs, and from management that emphasises ease of access.[9] Thus, the quality of the forests on either side of the border is one form of the "recognisable and concrete manifestations of government and politics" to which Wilson and Donnan (1998) wish to draw anthropological attention.

I believe it is of utmost importance to demonstrate or reiterate the rather obvious point, that economic and political regimes, particularly at large scales, have long-term and often irreversible consequences. Significantly, governmentality (Foucault 1991) is made manifest not only in 'correct' Finnish attitudes towards forests, influenced as they are by state-led forest science together with hegemonic aesthetic sensibilities, but also in the biophysical environment itself. With the benefit of hindsight these landscapes, which had appeared natural and unquestioned, can now be seen to be the result of sustained and transformative intervention within a sovereign space through sovereign regimes of management.

As I noted, scientific discourse gains legitimacy from appearing to be an unmediated reflection of the world. Scientific institutions seek to make it appear that the people, the institutions and the values embedded in them are an almost inconsequential background to the foregrounded facts, supposedly speaking for themselves (Latour 1987). Only facts and policy recommendations – the former unassailable, the latter prone to human fallibility – are admitted as part of the science-policy process. In Finland this process fed into the highly valued consensus characteristic of national politics, a consensus where science, well-being and government have often appeared to be synonymous. The limit of the consensus has always also been spatialised, producing the sense that it is bounded territory which guarantees order and enables life to flourish. In official post-war rhetoric, life on the Finnish side is, as the proverbial phrase puts it, "like winning the lottery", whilst life on the other side is, well, rather different.

Until the mid-1970s[10], the official rhetoric of forest-based prosperity broadly corresponded to the experiences of Finns across the country. The modern forest, intensively managed to produce a sustained yield of timber, became a focus of national as well as professional pride (Michelsen 1995) but also something that people thought about in highly personal terms. This was (and is) because most of the forests consumed by the paper and pulp industry were privately owned, not in the alienating hands of large corporations or even of the state (Berglund 2000). Orvar Löfgren (1993) argues that landscapes perceived as national become arenas of emotional resonance and, along with other material manifestations of national peculiarity, provide arenas for contesting and challenging what it means to be a nation, or part of one. It is not surprising then that in independent Finland, that is since 1917, challenging the forestry expertise has always also been seen as threatening to a national consensus.[11] Even complaints about foul-smelling paper and pulp plants were long shrugged off with the quip that money smells. Forest politics has, as a consequence, been a typical arena for socialisation into the role of social critic. Institutional continuity in forest protest is manifest for instance in an organisation called the *Nature League*, prominent when forest-industries lobbies need to name their enemy.[12] Throughout the 1990s critics of the forest sector were regularly portrayed as irresponsible, romantic and even traitors of the nation by the mainstream media and representatives of the forestry sector.[13]

Activists' efforts are probably rightly interpreted by older generations as a sign that young people's allegiances are no longer with the forest industries which used to protect fatherland and family. For earlier generations, these symbolised belonging to a land where people were free, democratic and able to fulfil themselves with the help of a market economy, to a land which, above all, saved itself from the fate of so many, developing into a liberal democracy rather than a satellite of Moscow. Consonant with these kinds of views, Russian Karelia is sometimes portrayed in the media as a site of disorder and danger, whereas for young activists, this 'wrong' side of the border is a locus of virtue.

This probably reflects economic changes, as forestry is losing out to other sectors of the economy, such as an expanding telecommunications industry. Nevertheless, for the foreseeable future the critique of forestry will remain central to alternative politics. It is also worth mentioning that forest activists are among the few in contemporary Finland who mount a sustained challenge to neo-liberal economics and foster critical debate on technology and science.

## Situated Ecopolitics

Let me now return to a more ethnographic sense of activism. In the early 1990s, after the border was opened, environmentalists accused Finnish companies of plundering Karelia's irreplaceable old-growth forests for short-term profit, and they literally followed the timber lorries crossing the border.[14] In addition to mapping biodiversity, a few activists have acted as private investigators tracking down criminals and apprehending Finnish loggers cutting down areas already set aside for conservation.[15] In the wake of political and economic upheaval, the border zone quickly became known as the Wild East, haven of unscrupulous and corrupt operators, once again drawing Finnish attention to the proximity to, even contiguity with, the Russian Other.

Unlike those who highlight the dangerousness of the border zone, Finnish activists behaved as if rather than going abroad to Russian Karelia, they were coming home and leaving the alien behind. Crossing the border is also thought of as travelling back in time, perhaps to an earlier Finland. For despite Russification policies, many inhabitants of Karelia speak a language closely related to Finnish and unrelated to Russian, and which allows locals and Finnish activists to share their experiences in an atmosphere of special intimacy. Karelia has long been romanticised by Finnish intellectuals, and there are special cultural connections to the region, not just among activists, but among state representatives and other Finns.

Significant social bonds between some activists and villagers (and, although I have little direct evidence, probably between ministry-level actors also) were created because the groups from both sides of the international frontier share ideas about the importance of forests for living the good life.[16] Knowledge about forests is constantly created in both decontextualised technoscientific discourses and in sensuous engagement. And much of the latter is utilitarian, not solely romantic. Indeed, a number of activists come from rural homes where forests are not primarily sources of aesthetic pleasure, but of financial support. Within Karelia's forests and through contacts with the inhabitants of the forest villages, historically specific forms of sociality thus articulate with world-wide, deterritorialised discourses of the biological. Even in a globalised epoch, and even among citizens of wealthier, highly modernised countries, social life remains imbricated in material processes.

What I suggest is that the tangible reality of Karelia resonated with activists so strongly because they were already familiar with making their home, albeit in a very different way, in the forest. They compared their own homeland, with its manicured forests, to what they encountered here and found it wanting. The long conversations about berry picking, saunas and building materials that these activists could carry out with locals were only possible because of a partially shared concrete understanding of the practical use of forest resources. The manipulation of the material aspect of the forest was probably the aspect talked about most when activists and locals conversed. Pragmatics and aesthetics, not biodiversity, fuelled their discussions, as did a sense of profound injustice and, often, shame for their compatriots' actions.[17]

One of the prominent young men involved often used strong language to refer to the lies, cynicism and greed promoted by the forest products industries. His long-term involvement had led to a sophisticated understanding of the politics of forest exploitation and of forest protection. A skilled negotiator and campaigner, he had closely observed how the large conservation organisations seek to co-opt smaller players and be co-opted themselves into diluted forms of intervention. Involved in these processes himself, he came to be seen for a few years as the most knowledgeable expert on the conservationist side. Yet like so many others whom I met, he insisted that an extensive old-growth forest is more than a repository of biodiversity or an object of aesthetic contemplation; it is a locus for material, but above all, spiritual regeneration.

In a taped interview one young woman, who was extremely effective in uncovering the illegal activities of timber companies, insisted that "actually, the important knowledge comes from bumping into these issues in practice. That's where you get the intuition that's so important. It's about understanding [not information]". As she continued, she shifted away from talking about the forests themselves to telling me about confrontations with drunken loggers and other Finns, about helping an injured prostitute to hospital, and about her personal motives for continuing the campaign even when criticised for romantic and utopian attitudes. "Yes", she continued without prompting, her involvement might reflect a utopian strain of thinking, but even more unrealistic was the dream of continued economic growth. What border could Finnish companies cross once these forests had been consumed? And what, activists ask, drives Finnish companies to leave such devastation in Karelia when at home at least they persistently (and cynically) argue that they take ecological fragility seriously.[18]

Activists felt that they were supporting the views of the local population in decrying the industrial use of local forests.[19] In Soviet times, as today, forests in Russia have been classified on scientific grounds and their use has been controlled by state-experts (Myllynen et al. 1996). However, state forestry reinforced customary practices according to which forests immediately surrounding villages were used for domestic purposes only. Today's clear cuts, many carried out by Finnish companies, are thus a tangible sign of how times have changed.

In Vuokkiniemi, the largest of the Karelian villages, a local teacher recounted how "we've lived from the forest all our lives," and talking of the first clear cut she ever saw, she said it had been like "entering the hallway to Hell" (see Berglund 1997). Resin collecting used to employ most men until less than two decades ago. Women still stock jams made from forest berries in their cellar along with mushroom preserves and medicinal plants. Interest is also growing in commercially viable forms of sustainable forestry, although concrete measures to promote it are in early stages.[20] Clearly, Karelia is a region where human life and ecological systems mutually constitute and frequently nurture each other. Even before Stalinist obsession with forests as security, villagers' forestry practices were sustainable, geared towards partial export from the region (as resin, formerly tar), and to hunting, fishing and domestic timber needs.

I suggest that although Finnish activists' rhetoric has often supported the international discourse about the region as a repository of the globe's biodiversity (see Kleinn 1998), much of what sustains their enthusiasm comes from their relationship with the people living there and from their sympathy with the people's attitudes to the forests. I am not, however, claiming that all those from outside Finland have the converse attitude which sees nature as an external resource only to be reified and romanticised yet still 'managed'. Indeed, the internationally run *Taiga Rescue Network* has done much to emphasise the politico-economic and cultural components of conservation itself. But my point is that Finnish activists specifically are identifying these forests as something already familiar, providing further impetus for seeking connection with people in ways that challenge the idea that specific natural resources are, and should be, under the authority of one sovereign power.

## The Cultural Significance of Karelia

The Karelian case suggests that cross-border environmentalism is complex and multi-directional and impossible to narrate into a singular argument. Part of the problem is that the connection between ecology and culture can be, and has been, used to argue that Karelia is more a part of Finland than of Russia and would thus be better off under Finnish sovereignty.[21] But even more radically, ecopolitics potentially challenges the whole concept of sovereign territory (Kuehls 1996).

In addition to the conjunction of transnational, media-infiltrated environmentalism with the truly noteworthy material characteristics of this border, cross-border traffic is also inspired by Karelia's special place in the Finnish national consciousness. Many Finns who do not join activists feel strongly about these forests simply because Karelia is thought of as the cradle of Finnish national culture. Although in the twentieth century it was associated with the unknown and frightening Soviet power, starting in the eighteenth century, peripheral Karelia in fact produced Finland's 'exotics within'. As Finnish nationalism became more confident, Karelia, which lay administratively on both sides of the border, came to symbolise a quintessentially national folklore, the locus of the cultural authenticity which nineteenth century European nationalisms needed in order to constitute the self as collective subject. Thus, when early nineteenth century Finns, after being transferred in 1809 from Swedish to Russian rule, asked the question "who are we?", the answer came from folklorists. They argued that Finland's cultural roots lie in the backwoods of Karelia, poorly connected both to Finland and to Imperial Russia, but enjoying a vibrant oral tradition, imagined to have been lost from the rest of the country along with modernisation.

The image of Karelia as some kind of proto-Finnish condition also suggested that an essential element of Finnishness was the bond between people and forest. A broadly Herderian notion of the uniqueness of all peoples informed the way that the early nineteenth century romantics imagined the relationship between people and nature. They came to celebrate the environmental circumstances of the emerging nation, drawing on Herder's ideas about the significance of varying physical environments for the evolution of national character (Wilson 1976).

Karelia came to symbolise true Finnish character, as the folklore collected by the young intellectuals of the early nineteenth century inspired an emergent vernacular, non-Indo-European literature. The documentation of Karelian oral tradition inspired high art which came to be seen as belonging to Finns as a fully recognised collectivity, not just an uncultured adjunct to either Sweden or Russia. Today, with the opening of the border, Karelia is increasingly represented for public consumption as an ideal tourist destination, a place where time has stood still and where even Soviet power has failed to crush the vitality of the Karelian spirit, one connected far more closely with Finnish than with Russian or Soviet identity.

And even this overtly cultural significance of Karelia does not exhaust the reasons Finns today are keen on cross-border connections. After the Second World War a large area of Finland, over 10 per cent of the territory, known as the Karelian Isthmus, was ceded to the Soviet Union. This experience solidified a sense of shared Finnish identity across language and class boundaries (though arguably Sami and Gypsy minorities have a different view) such that the name Karelia rings louder than others in contemporary consciousness[22], and that is in many senses an unstable, liminal space, one that inspires both desire and fear.

Through most of its independence the Finnish collective imagination has easily accepted a self-image of a homogeneous, consensual people, and when the border was shown to be permeable, those inside Finland overcame internal squabbles in order to keep the enemy out. Importantly, the strengthening consensus was accompanied by an enhanced self-consciousness of being at home in forested landscapes. Some of the mechanisms of this homogenisation were top-down like the spread of forest professionals across the territory, or the fashion for painting forested landscapes, but many were bottom-up, like collective resistance by smallholders to company ownership of land. Because of the way they have been constituted through the nation-state apparatus as citizens with both rights and responsibilities towards that state, Finns value forests in both utilitarian and in aesthetic terms (Berglund 2000).

Because of this history, it is no surprise that Finns are quick to respond to forests beyond the border. After all, for some Finns Karelia ought to come under Finnish rule. Arguments for organic as well as exclusive human-nature relations that have hovered in political debate for over 100 years (Paasi 1996) continue to flourish, for instance that people there speak a related language and should be part of the economic, political and cultural system of the West. And yet my ethnographic work, combined with efforts to question the applicability of territorial logic in the contemporary political conjuncture suggests, perhaps provocatively, that for the activists I have talked about here, such politics of authenticity are marginal to, if not outright contrary to their goals.

Thus activism does generate deterritorialised collectivities that cut across such politics, as Appadurai highlights. And although state-based practices of nature inform Finnish activists, their encounters with nature and people go beyond what the state can govern. The significance of forests for young activists increasingly diverges from the experiences of older generations, who were perhaps more empowered by the earlier national imaginary. One last example may make the point. On one of my trips to Russian Karelia, an elderly Finnish woman visiting as a tourist bemoaned the state of the forests there, aghast at the lack of management. Yet it is precisely this feature which has attracted the positive attention of the activists. The ecopolitical challenge to territorial thought is only provoked by the fact that these forests, in this place, have been here a certain time. They are irreducible both to state-protected market values and to arguments about the exclusive property of any ethnic group or state.

The critics' joint agendas thus draw attention to what Kuehls calls the "nonsovereign territorial nature of ecopolitics" (1996: 118), that logging is in any case not confined to any bounded territory, but both fuels and is fuelled by world-wide consumer desire for its products. What is going on in Karelia cannot therefore be analysed simply as a conflict over who is master in the region. Such an analysis would remain as impotent as the appeals to nature and to territory it sought to explain. This is because ecopolitics already crosses borders with little heed to national sovereignty.[23] Even modern states are not capable of imposing exhaustive injunctions on how their populations should connect with the environment. In Finland, despite a century of state rhetoric in which the perfect forest is the productive forest, commercial utility – whether for industry or tourism – hardly exhausts the ways nature is actually practised let alone dreamed of. And for those who currently make their home in Russian Karelia, state fantasies of control and progress have long been at odds with place-bound realities.

## Conclusion

Borders thus remain salient spaces for comparing and contrasting similarity and difference, in biophysical or infrastructural terms, and in terms of authoritative knowledge. As Russian Karelia demonstrates, this recently opened border zone produces trajectories of trustworthy knowledge and of images of the good life that travel as much through contiguous, if partially bounded space, as they do along the hierarchies of state institutions. That is, activist encounters with local villagers, though they may be few in the grand scheme of Finnish life, nevertheless open up conceptual spaces, mediated by the materiality of the region, where territoriality and the idea of home are important, but are not defined in the terms of state institutions. And although the language of international science remains important, I have argued that it hardly promises to create truly global collectives with identical commitments leading to a sense of global identity. Such an identity, I suspect, is not going to emerge out of grassroots environmentalism.

Ecopolitics is then neither national, confined within borders, nor truly global. But it remains played out both within and against territorial logics. There is still a huge market for wood products, and everywhere that forests (or other renewable resources) and people share a territory, these forests and the people become entangled. This applies not just to Russian Karelia but to many areas, especially in the tropical world (particularly South East Asia) where northern forest-products companies are transforming more and more places into profit machines (Carrere and Lohmann 1996). At an empirical level, neither the exploitation of timber nor environmentalism can be said to have become de-territorialised. Instead, they are being re-territorialised.

As more and more space is consumed by productive machinery and waste disposal, the fight over some territory promises to intensify. What needs to be pursued is not the question, to whom does a certain territory belong, but rather: is the hype of deterritorialisation prematurely displacing questions about what new boundaries and barriers are emerging in the world today? And at what level of analysis does the drive to de-territorialise prove analytically productive? Since political practice and social theory have unfolded for 300 years in matrices of space and time that operate territorially, such questions are difficult to articulate let alone answer conclusively. But oddly enough, it seems to be at the edges of territories, at borders, that one might best turn to examine them.

## Notes

1. Thanks to Hastings Donnan and Dieter Haller for organising the panel and for comments.
2. I use this formulation because the contiguous region inside Finland is also known as Karelia.
3. A type of forest with much spruce and pine, interspersed with rivers, lakes and mires. The fact that these forests are continuous across a large expanse is significant ecologically, as is their age.
4. I have since learned that she did purchase a home there.
5. Nine months in 1996 including three trips to Russia of a few days each, interviews in Finland since then, and two trips to Russia in 1999.
6. To foreground the fact that environmentalism is not a straightforward practice let alone a self-evidently virtuous one, borrowing from the geographer Thom Kuehls (1996) I shall refer to the struggles over Karelia's forests as ecopolitics.
7. Non-governmental organisations.
8. Kuehls (1996) elaborates on the connection between ecopolitics and Lockean conceptions of sovereignty over productive land.
9. See Lowood (1990) on scientific forestry and its impact.
10. Increased mechanisation and transformations in the political economy of forest products has meant relative decline since the mid-1970s. Marchak (1995) and Donner-Amnell (1991).
11. Twentieth century domestic politics was always accompanied by forest debate (Lehtinen 1991, Berglund 2000).
12. More ethnographic detail can be found in Berglund (forthcoming).
13. This is borne out in professional publications and was abundantly clear in encounters, including nine interviews with high-ranking representatives from corporate and state proponents of industrial forestry.
14. Information is available from environmental organisations in electronic form, and Finnish research continues to expand (http://www.luontoliitto.fi/forest/russia/index.html, and Haapala 1999.)
15. Kleinn (1998) provides detail.
16. Bonds between the activists from Finland and those from Russia, especially Moscow were also clearly close, but I had little opportunity to become familiar enough with them to make a stronger argument.
17. Motives for interaction are, of course, heterogeneous on both sides, and understandings of ecopolitics are also highly varied. Complicating the picture is also the fact that a partial moratorium on logging Karelian old-growth was instituted by the largest Finnish companies in 1997.
18. In Finland where plots are often small by international comparison, extensive clear cutting is illegal. In Karelia, however, many companies claim that they are following local custom, in other words regulations inherited from the Soviet era, where they denude hectare upon hectare of forest paying little if any heed to replanting. See Marchak (1995).
19. Attitudes are varied. Also, revenues from local timber have, despite administrative and politi-

cal set-backs, been used to pay for instance for the Vuokkiniemi School (See map).

20. Based on personal communications on both sides of the border and newspaper articles. E.g. 'Runokylä ei elä yksin suojelusta', *Karjalainen*, 27/10/97.
21. Debate still surrounds the injustice of the loss of 'southern' Karelia to the Soviet Union in the Second World War. For the context see Paasi (1996) and below.
22. But see the argument in Paasi (1996) that it was only the war that really secured homogeneous identity and unquestioned allegiance to the Finnish nation-state.
23. Ecopolitics is equally inconsonant with pan-European or global claims to sovereignty such as demands that Karelia or the Amazon be 'saved' from their inhabitants in the name of biodiversity.

## References


Appadurai, Arjun 1996: *Modernity at Large: Cultural dimensions of globalization*. Minneapolis: University of Minnesota Press: University of Minnesota Press.

Berglund, Eeva 1997: 'Clear Cut Madness in Russian Karelia'. *The Ecologist*, Vol. 276.

Berglund Eeva 2000: 'Forestry expertise and national narratives', *Worldviews* Vol. 4 (1).

Berglund, Eeva (forthcoming): 'Ecopolitics through ethnography: the cultures of Finland's forest-nature'. In: Biersack, A. and Greenberg, J. B. (eds.): *Culture / Power / History / Nature: Ecologies for a new Millennium*, London and New York: Routledge.

Brock, Lothar 1999: 'Observing Change, 'Rewriting History': A Critical Overview'. In: *Millennium: Journal of International Studies*, Vol. 28(3): 483–497.

Carrere, Ricardo and Lohmann, Larry 1996: *Pulping the South: Industrial tree plantations and the world paper economy*. London: Zed Books.

Conklin, Beth 1997: 'Body Paint, feathers, and VCRs: aesthetics and authenticity in Amazonian activism', *American Ethnologist*, Vol. 24(4).

Cronon, William (ed.) 1995: *Uncommon Ground: Rethinking the Human Place in Nature*. New York and London: Norton.

Donner-Amnell, Jakob 1991: Metsäteollisuus yhteiskunnallisena kysymyksenä. In: Massa, Ilmo & Sairinen, Rauno (toim.): *Ympäristökysymys: Ympäristöuhkien haaste yhteiskunnalle*. Helsinki: Gaudeamus: 265–306.

Foucault, Michel 1981: *The History of Sexuality, Volume I: An Introduction*. London: Penguin.

Foucault, Michel 1991: Governmentality. In: G. Burchell, C. Gordon, P. Miller (eds.): *The Foucault Effect: Studies in governmentality*. Chicago: University of Chicago Press.

Gupta, Akhil and Ferguson, James (eds.): *Culture, Power, Place: Explorations in Critical Anthropology*. Durham and London: Duke University Press.

Haapala, Henna 1999: *Karjalan tasavallan metsiensuojelukeskukstelun retoriikka-analyysi*. Helsinki: Suomen Ympäristökeskus.

Häkli, Jouni 1998: Manufacturing Provinces: Theorizing the Encounters Between Governmental and Popular 'Geographs' in Finland. In: G. Ó'Tuathail & S. Dalby (eds.): *Rethinking Geopolitics*. London & New York.

Haraway, Donna 1997: *Modest Witness Second Millenium: FemaleMan Meets Onco Mouse Feminism and Technoscience*. London & New York: Routledge.

Harvey, David 1996: *Justice, Nature and the Geography of Difference*. Oxford: Blackwell Publishing.

Kleinn, Eva 1998: Planning and Geoecological Assessment for a World Heritage Site Nomination in the "Green Belt of Fennoscandia". Diplomarbeit, Universität Karlsruhe (TH), Institut für Geographie und Geoökologie.

Kuehls, Thom 1996: *Beyond Sovereign Territory*. Minneapolis: University of Minnesota Press.

Lash, Scott et al. (eds.) 1996: *Risk, Environment and Modernity: Towards a New Ecology*. London and New York: Sage

Latour, Bruno 1987: *Science in Action*, Cambridge, Massachusetts: Harvard University Press.

Lehtinen, Ari A. 1991: 'Northern Natures: A study of the forest question emerging within the timber-line conflict in Finland', *Fennia*, 1691: 57–169.

Löfgren, Orvar 1993: Materializing the Nation in Sweden and America. In: *Ethnos* 58(3–4): 161–196.

Lowood, Henry 1990: 'The calculating forester: Quantification, Cameral Science, and the Emergence of Scientific Forest Management in Germany'. In T. Frängsmyr et al. (eds.) *The Quantifying Spirit in the 18th Century*. Berkeley, Los Angeles, Oxford: University of California Press.

Lugo, Alejandro 1997: Reflections on Border Theory, Culture and the Nation. In: S. Michelsen & D. E. Johnson (eds.): *Border Theory: The limits of cultural politics*. Minneapolis: University of Minnesota Press: 43–67.

Luke, Timothy 1995: On Environmentality: Geo-Power and Eco-Knowledge in the Discourses of Contemporary Environmentalism. In: *Cultural Critique* 31: 57–81.

Marchak, Patricia M. 1995: *Logging the Globe*. Montreal & Kingston: McGill-Queen's University Press.

Michelsen, Karl-Erik 1995: *History of Forest Research in Finland. Part 1: The Unknown Forest*. Helsinki: The Finnish Forest Research Institute.

Myllynen, Anna-Liisa et al. 1996: *On the ecological and economic impacts of wood harvesting and trade in North-West Russia*. OY FEG – Forest and Environment Group Ltd. Joensuu, Finland.

NWRDP (Finnish-Russian Development Programme on Sustainable Forest Management and Conservation of Biological Diversity in Northwest Russia) 1997: Forest & Nature in *Northwest Russia*. Helsinki: Indufor Oy.

Ó'Tuathail, Gearóid and Dalby, Simon 1998: Introduction: Rethinking geopolitics: Towards a critical geopolitics. In: G. Ó'Tuathail & S. Dalby (eds.): *Rethinking Geopolitics*. London & New York: Routledge: 1–15.

Ovaskainen, Otso; Pappila, Minna; Pötry, Jyri 1999: *The Finnish Forest Industry in Russia: On the path towards ecological and social responsibility.* Helsinki: The Finnish Nature League Publications.

Paasi, Anssi 1996. *Territories, boundaries and consciousness*. London: John Wiley and Sons.

Szerszynski, Bronislaw, Lash, Scott, Wynne, Brian 1996: Introduction: Ecology, Realism and the Social Sciences. In: S. Lash et al. (eds.): *Risk, Environment and Modernity: Towards a New Ecology*. London and New York: Sage: 1–26.

Takacs, David 1996: *The Idea of Biodiversity: Philosophies of Paradise*. Baltimore & London: Johns Hopkins University Press.

Wilson, William 1976: *Folklore and Nationalism in Modern Finland.* Bloomington: Indiana University Press.

Wilson, Thomas M. & Donnan, Hastings 1998: Nation, state and identity at international borders. In: T. Wilson & H. Donnan (eds.): *Border Identities: Nation and state at international frontiers*. London & New York: Cambridge University Press: 1–30.

# Mugarik ez! Subverting the Border in the Basque Country

*Aitzpea Leizaola*

Leizaola, Aitzpea 2000: Mugarik ez! Subverting the Border in the Basque Country. – Ethnologia Europaea 30, 2: 35–46.

In what could be considered a paradox in the present globalisation era, political borders, frontiers and boundaries in general, have become more than ever a point of interest and research focus of an increasing number of scholars, as the extensive and burgeoning literature on the topic highlights (Alvarez 1995, Donnan and Wilson 1999, Pujadas 1999). Now that national structures seem to be overwhelmed by the enforcement and consolidation of all kind of supranational structures and organisations, economic and political among others, talking about borders as sovereignty limits would not seem to make much sense. However, states are not as eager to relinquish their grip on territory and control on its borders as could be expected. This article aims to point out how borders can be considered significant places in the political arena, stages at which divergent representations of sovereignty and territoriality are performed.

*Dr Aitzpea Leizaola, European Studies Centre, St. Antony's College, Oxford University, Oxford OX2 6JF, UK. E-mail: aitzpea_leizaola@hotmail.com*

The Basque Country is a good example of how state policies can contradict EU policies, particularly in a Europe now nominally 'without frontiers', as in the case of the maintenance of borders despite their official shut down. This territory of 20. 864km$^2$, approximately the size of Slovenia, is divided since the 17$^{th}$ century by the state boundary setting apart France from Spain.[1] As will be discussed below, borders are far from disappearing in the Basque Country. Not only do they continue to have major symbolic significance, but also control over the border area remains an important issue for adjacent states, which still continue to close border posts at particular dates. At the same time, the actual porosity of the border, based on the maintenance of historical ties across it and the important increase of cross-border local or EU promoted projects and initiatives, compromises any attempt at control. In this paper I argue that borders still are contested places, frontiers in the original sense of the word, front-lines where nation-states battle for their maintenance despite European integration, and where nations divided by such frontiers, as in the Basque case, struggle for their abolition, not only in discursive ways, but also through symbolic actions.

## Mugarik ez!

Coinciding with the 1986 widely diffused slogan "a Europe without frontiers" nationalist movements have incorporated similar slogans in various campaigns aimed to strengthen the notion of national unity despite and above the border. Slogans like "*mugarik ez*" (no to the border), "*ez da mugarik*" (there is no border), or "*mugak apurtu*" (dismantle the borders) have become common and recurrent in the Basque nationalist political agenda. Referring to the border as *muga*, these slogans point out the complexity of this concept and its meanings (Leizaola 1996). *Muga* is the usual Basque term designating any kind of boundary or limit, encompassing among others both spatial and/or temporal meanings, although the former is much more usual than the latter. In the traditional society, this concept is particularly relevant. *Muga* designates both the location where some-

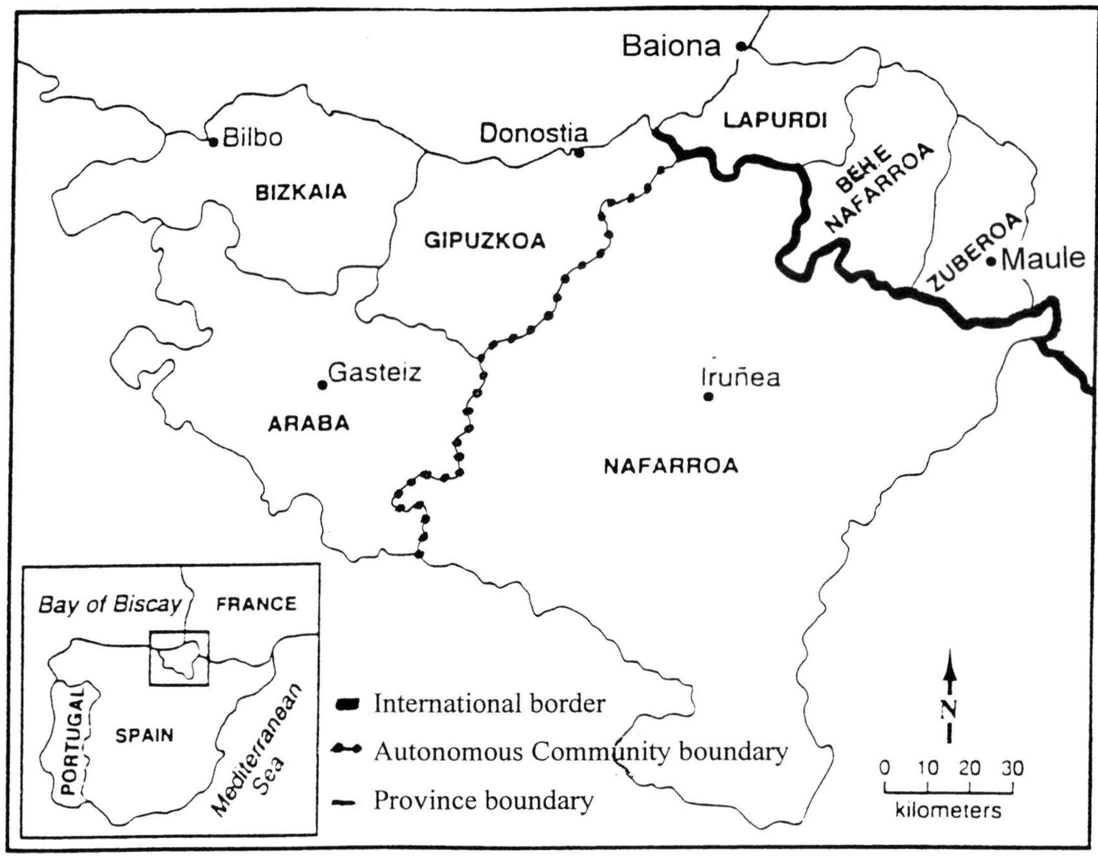


Borders and boundaries in the Basque Country.

thing ends and its limits. It refers to the linear division separating two territories as well as to the physical elements marking those limits. As many scholars have noted (Del Valle 1988, Descheemaeker 1946, Barandiaran 1972), the *muga* was rarely imposed, but resulted from negotiation. In contemporary Basque, *muga* includes the notion of "political border" among its meanings. Furthermore, nowadays, when no other precision is given it refers explicitly to *the* interstate border in the Basque Country. *Muga* is one of the few words Spanish has borrowed from Basque.

In the past, the location of the *muga* and of the *mugarri*, boundary stone, had to be approved by all the parties involved. According to historians, the councils of limiting villages decided the setting of the *muga* and this had to be respected by the communities involved. The location of limits and the setting of landmarks marking the boundaries between villages had thus to be approved by each of the limiting units. Removing *muga* boundary stones was a serious offence, formally defined as such by customary laws, and even punished with death[2] at certain periods. Many myths too, refer to this conventional aspect of the *muga* and to the fatal consequences of removing them without permission, such as the wandering of the soul of the remover until the *mugarri* was returned to its original location (Barandiaran,1972:173–175). Boundaries were thus to be highly respected.

As many scholars have pointed out (Del Valle 1988, Descheemaeker 1946, Gómez-Ibáñez 1975), the present political border resulting from the Pyrenees Peace of 1659 and the demarcation of the mid-19th century overlaps *muga* limits previous to the border. In contrast with other Pyrenean regions such as Catalunya, the state boundary in the Basque area was drawn along the old inter-communal lines (Gómez-Ibáñez, 1975:49). Although some exceptions are to be noted in parts of the borderland disputed in the past, such as the Kintoa, this could be considered as a rule in this part of the Pyrenees. Hence, some boundaries happen to be at the same time limits between villages, region or province boundaries, and even autonomous region boundaries and, in the bordering area, inter state boundaries. It is common to have various territorial markers at the same spot. This overlapping is reflected in language too, as it has been referred previously. Referring to the border the term *muga* may be ambiguous because of the multiple meanings this words conveys. Playing with that multiplicity of meanings, explicit reference to the border can be somehow blurred when using the term[3]. The interstate frontier concept, with its administrative and political dimension shades off and the idea of boundary comes out. This is particularly noticeable when using the Basque word in a Spanish speaking context: in appearance, the border becomes a boundary like any other.

## Drawing the Line. Landmarks and Territoriality

The present political border between France and Spain, said to be one of the most stable borders in the political map of Europe, was defined as a result of the Treaty of the Pyrenees (1659) putting an end to the long-lasting confrontation for the control of the oriental area of the Pyrenees (Sahlins 1989). The boundary line was not demarcated until the middle of the 19th century, though. In 1856, the signing of the Treaty of Bayonne set down the border's definite delimitation, drawing an imaginary line between France and Spain at which the sovereignty of each of the states ends. This boundary line is since marked out with tall granite stone landmarks. Starting from the most occidental point of the border at the very mouth of the Bidasoa river, to the most oriental one on the Mediterranean coast, 602 numbered landmarks, deeply buried on earth stand up at a certain distance one from another drawing an imaginary line.

Situated strategically on one of the two main entrances from the North of Europe to the Iberian peninsula, on the way to Portugal and the North of Africa, the Basque Country has a long tradition of being a passage region. As such, this land has known all throughout history non-stop flows of people and cultures crossing it in both directions. Following the course of European history, the imposition of a state boundary with all the structures and control paraphernalia it entails affected not only local people, specially borderlanders' life, but also population movements in a broader sense, mainly economic migration flows, as well as other population transfers. Particularly during the 20th century, the border area became one of the gateways of a European version of Eldorado for thousands of migrants willing to enter France and Northern Europe – Portuguese workers in the 60s, and later, labour from Maghreb and other areas of Africa – as well as the shelter for political refugees and Resistance fighters at different historical moments.[4]

All through this last century, and particularly due to the recent history of Spain, the border became, as in other areas of Europe, a highly controlled and militarised area. From the first years of Franco's dictatorship and for more than three decades, the border was formally closed, preventing the exit as well as the entrance of many Spanish nationals, namely all those considered to have lost the 1936 war, republicans, partisans of nationalist movements in Spain (Basques, Catalans and Galicians among others), anarchists etc. This highly militarised control of the border was temporarily intensified by the German border patrols during the occupation of France in the Second World War. Crossing the border was not free and it entailed a long bureaucratic process to obtain the papers to leave the country, which were denied in many cases. Limited in time, one-day permits were nevertheless frequent in the borderland area. Even if the opening of Spain to tourism in the 1960s signified a certain loosening in border control, the revitalisation of nationalist movements and independence claims together with the emergence of ETA were accompanied by the strengthening of control on the border area.

## The Front Line. The Border as a Space of Contest

The dismantling of borders has frequently been analysed as part of the weakening of state sovereignty resulting from the consolidation of supranational structures all over the world. Over the last decades, scholars had somehow predicted such an evolution together with the fall of nationalism as a consequence of globalisation. Paradoxically, at least in the case of Europe, together with a significant rise of nationalisms, not only the reinforcement of supranational structures, such as the European Union, has not signified the end of internal borders as anticipated. It has also led to the creation of real"border states", states that practice borders' main functions all over their territory, as Spain in the EU or Mexico in the North American context. This is particularly relevant concerning immigration control. Spain has become one of the main gateways to the EU, mainly for African migrants willing to reach Europe but also for South American migrants that choose Spain, "la *Madre Patria*" as their first and often final destination in the Old World. Trying to prevent this non-stop and increasing affluence of illegal migrants, border controls have been stepped up, particularly all over the Mediterranean coast. Here too, following Anzaldúa's words (1987:2–3), the border is an "open wound", a wound that bleeds taking away every year the life of hundreds of people.

Applied to the Basque context, the metaphor of the wound takes another nuance and strongly renders a conception of the border shared in nationalist spheres and not unknown to borderlanders. Although in many cases it has contributed actively to the strengthening and maintenance of various links astride the border, the frontier is conceived as a dividing line, a line splitting up a unity, putting it apart. The slash is then a source of pain, one of the recurrent representations of the border in Basque contemporary imaginary. As the *bertsolari* Otaño, a well-known oral poet of the turn of the $19^{th}$ century, put it in improvised verses, the Basque Country is "the cloth of seven sisters, cut in the middle"[5], the border being the scissors setting apart the seven provinces or "sisters". Considered one of the most beautiful and meaningful metaphors of the Basque Country, it represents an idea of the Basque Country based on shared cultural and linguistic grounds.

Claims to the Basque Country by Basque nationalist movements draw on specifically territorial notions of the Basque nation. Although since the 1960s Basque nationalism can not any longer be considered as a homogeneous movement, territoriality as a concept is largely agreed upon. Nevertheless, the various nationalist projects have specific political goals as well as differing ways of implementing political action. Despite a shared representation of the extension of the Basque Country, concrete proposals and policies are not applicable to the whole territory. For some, the present administrative and political frame is the basis and the setting for political action, while for others territoriality constitutes one of the major goals of political action. Thus, for those whose project is the independence of the whole Basque Country, the present political frame has to be substantially changed. This later representation calls into question Spanish and French states' territoriality, and as such, it is considered as a direct attack on their sovereignty. The state boundary is one of the most representative places where these differing and opposed conceptions of territory are to be materialised.

In this context, the border becomes a contested place where symbolic events and political actions are performed to deny the political border. Considering borders as "meaning-making and meaning-carrying places" (Donnan and Wilson, 1999:4), special attention will be paid to rituals highlighting the border as a place of contest. Many of these rituals challenging the partition of the Basque Country, attempt to subvert the state border, mainly denying its legitimacy. Such rituals have identifiable political aims, and advance agendas of radical political change. I argue that the importance of the border is not merely a concern of nationalist or pro-independence movements or other political organisations challenging state sovereignty and legitimacy and leading such subverting rituals. It also concerns the states, which in response, by different means, emphasise the role of the border as a marker of territorial sovereignty.

Now that the European Union has encouraged the dissolution of internal borders, particularly since the Single European Act and the Maastricht Treaty, and more recently with the signing of the Schengen Treaty, such symbolic, and too often real battles do not seem to make much sense. However, the fact is that since the border was officially shut down, it has become a major space of contest. Besides the frequent protests of truck drivers who in the last years have chosen border areas as one of the main scenes for their road blocking, the border has become a particularly meaningful arena for demonstrations and protest actions. Since Spain's inclusion first in the European Market and later in the European Union, the Spanish-French frontier has known an increasing number of demonstrations held in the border. Location and symbolic value of space have to be considered when dealing with demonstrations (Raento 1997:199), especially when the place is as symbolically meaningful as the border. However, far from being a simple scene of protest, the border is explicitly called into question through these examples of political activism. Hence, the frontier is a terrain of resistance and in most of the cases it is at the very core of the political mobilisation's *raison d'être*.

This is the case of demonstrations or marches willing to cross the border and thus unify symbolically both parts of the Basque Country. As will be discussed further on, most of the times and until very recently, they were not officially permitted to do so. Either one or both states have closed the border at different times in order to prevent such demonstrations from crossing the border. Border checkpoints at which until recently states materialised in the form of customs and police posts constitute the favourite frame for these political rituals. Nevertheless, as Douglass (1998) pointed out, the borderland is far from being a homogeneous area all along its layout and whilst some spots in the border are the scene of major contest actions, other areas are rarely concerned. Most of the protest actions and rituals aimed at subverting the political boundary are performed at three checkpoints, the busiest of the whole French-Spanish border[6]. The traffic is extremely heavy and chaotic at Behobia and specially at Biriatu, on the highway, as the main bulk of truck traffic transporting goods not only to and from Spain, but also to Portugal and Morocco crosses the border at one of these points. Seasonal traffic is important too, as this is the route thousands of Portuguese and Moroccan migrants choose to cross the peninsula every year to spend the summer holidays in their countries. All this explains the fact that Biriatu is considered one of the places in Europe to have the heaviest road traffic. Hendaia, remains a crossing point frequented by more local and occasional traffic.

Border landmarks and other markers, such as customs houses, frontier posts or even traffic signs, convey a particular meaning, they represent the state at its limits. As such, they are comparable to monuments, "the most conspicuous concrete manifestations of political power" (Hershkovitz 1993:397). However, in the case of border markers, their meaning is directly linked to space, to the location where they are placed. Because of the symbolic weight of the border as evidence of state imposition, the frontier and its markers have deliberately been attacked several times. Among other various actions, attacks on state sovereignty through its territorial limit markers constitute the most visible example of subverting the border. Attempts to eliminate the border have been quite common and popular before border controls were officially dismantled after the Single European Act and the Schengen Treaty came into effect. Attacks have been quite frequent in the last two decades. They recall similar destructive actions against monuments and the symbols they represent, as in the case of the Nelson pillar in Dublin dynamited by the republicans in the 1960s (Johnson 1995:62). Mostly they have consisted of symbolic sabotage, such as countless erasing of road signs displaying "France" or "Spain" and spraying of "E.H", standing for Euskal Herria, the Basque name of the Basque Country, or the corresponding province name. These actions have to be considered as part of a broader movement including campaigns led by different organisations at various levels demanding the displaying of Basque place names correctly spelled instead of the Spanish/French versions.

In other cases, state territorial landmarks have been totally destroyed. The case of the border-stone sculpture by the well-known sculptor Oteiza in the middle of the Santiago-Saint Jacques international bridge over the River Bidasoa which has been pulled down several times is particularly meaningful. For a long time, it was reduced to nothing more than a pile of rubble until it was roughly repaired. After it was returned to its original landmark, tied with wire, the engraved mention of France and Spain was painted out. Instead, the name of each of the bordering provinces, Gipuzkoa and Lapurdi were spray-painted in red on it. Today, the boundary stone is non-existent and there is nothing left on this site other than some scarcely visible marks of its previous emplacement. Similarly, border checkpoints and customs have been a main target for armed groups in the North Basque Country.

Protest is not always violent though. Following these last years ever increasing trend to think up innovative ways of protest and denunciation, a spectacular action was recently carried out against the border. Calling to rebellion against French and Spanish states, two people tied themselves with a rope hanging from the Santiago-Saint Jacques international bridge.[7] It took some time until the police were able to free both of them without letting them fall into the river. Such actions intend to redefine the territory, denying the border, giving place to a reformulation and reshaping of Basque land according to nationalist conception.

Other dimensions apart from the ones presented above have to be taken into account, too. The destruction of some twenty boundary stones in 1997 aroused the border issue in the context of European integration. At the time, the MLNV[8] had launched a broad campaign to raise public awareness about territory and one of its major repercussions was the questioning of the legitimacy of the border and the role of the *muga* in the Basque territory definition. Related to this, a group of youths from both sides of the border decided to undertake the systematic destruction of state boundary stones to protest against an "imposed and artificial border".[9] Many of those landmarks are situated in not easily accessible spots, on the top of mountains, as the boundary line follows the crest line. Local people from a village north of the border reported the sabotage and the French gendarmerie took charge of the issue, patrolling the border area, specially the boundary stone emplacements. Some days after the first actions were reported, four young people from the North were caught red handed, hammer in hand as they tried to smash into pieces one of the 276 boundary stones in the Basque area. As one of the activists explained some months later during the trial, the sabotage was conceived as "a symbolic action against the border dividing our country in two." This event did not provoke any substantial reaction from local authorities who did not even present a complaint to superior authorities. Surprisingly enough, France was the only country to feel involved by the attack and to present charges against the activists who were taken to court and lightly charged, while Spanish authorities did not mention a word about it – even if the landmarks are under their jurisdiction too. The incident came quickly to public notice though: a picture of one of the smashed boundary stones was later used as a poster displaying a slogan explicitly referring to the dismantling[10] of the border and claiming the unity and sovereignty of the Basque Country.

## Making Up One from Two: Unifying the Basque Country Symbolically

In 1992, *Bai Independentziari* "Yes to independence", a large platform gathering most of the Basque nationalist parties[11] from both North and South called what was considered the first united National Day since the 1936 War. This *Aberri Eguna*, literally "the day of the Basque Fatherland" was to be held that year on both sides of the border. Two villages on the banks of the Bidasoa River, Hondarribia and Hendaia, were the setting of the commemoration. Organisers had been careful to acknowledge prominence to both sides of the border, and the main events of the day were a demonstration in Hondarribia in the morning and a political meeting in Hendaia in the afternoon. The scheduled programme went ahead despite the fact that the border had been closed since very early that morning preventing any circulation across the frontier. The border closure generated a spontaneous reaction amongst the crowd gathered on both banks of the Bidasoa and resulted in a dialogue-like shouting of slogans from each side of the river. Songs, *irrintziak* – loud, long and joyous yells – and slogans were shouted from one side to the other, establishing communication over the closed border. As two traditional rowing boats crossed the river and met at its centre, where the border line streams into the sea and pulled up their oars in a symbol of victory, the climax was reached. Slogans for independence, against the border and the French and Spanish states were vigorously shouted from both banks.

Four years later, in 1996, in the same year when Spain signed the Schengen Treaty, the *Aberri Eguna* was once again to be held in the borderland. This time, it was a common call by the South left pro-independence party *HB* and the North nationalist coalition *Abertzaleen Batasuna*. This was the first visible result of advanced concrete cooperation efforts for the implementation of a common policy for the whole Basque Country. The scene chosen for the celebration of the *Aberri Eguna* was to be again the Bidasoa area. This time though, the main event was not to be held on both sides of the border, but consisted in the actual crossing of the border itself. A huge demonstration of several thousand people from North and South crossed the border from Hendaia to Irun. It was the biggest march in the borderland, comparable to the so-called "national demonstrations"[12] usually taking place in the main cities.

From the last decade of Francoism to the present, popular mobilisations occupy a prominent place in politics, as the demonstration culture that has flourished in the Basque Country highlights. Apart from some exceptions (Chaffee 1988, Raento 1997), scholars have paid little attention to street campaignings. However, mass protests have become common in the political arena and street mobilisations play an important part when considering political stakes. Demonstrations and counter-demonstrations are thus considered a way both to measure forces and to challenge the status quo. As part of this protest tradition and following a practice that has become usual in the last twenty years, many people arrived to the borderland by bus. Coming from towns and cities as far as almost three hours drive, the buses, organised for the occasion, stopped before the border as a precaution, fearing that they would not be allowed to cross the international bridge. Some hours before the demonstration, the Spanish police in riot gear had taken up position at the abandoned customs checking point on the demonstration route. The French police, more discreet, guarded the other side of the bridge. People from the South thus crossed the border on foot choosing an adjacent bridge to avoid the main border post under extraordinary police surveillance.

From the Town Hall of Hendaia, the demonstration made its way towards Irun, the first town on the other side of the border. The increasingly elaborate icons carried in mass protests and presenting a carefully prepared setting, the demonstration was spectacular. An impressively huge *ikurrina*, the Basque flag, carried by dancers in traditional dress followed close behind by big size emblems of the six historical Basque lands or provinces (Behe Nafarroa being represented by the coat of arms of the kingdom of Nafarroa) marched at the head of the demonstration. Immediately behind, the main banner, with the slogan Euskal Herriak, Askatasuna (Basque Country, Freedom) was carried by politicians of the organising parties and coalitions. As the demonstration was getting closer to the international bridge, tension grew. Since very early in the morning, because of previous unsuccessful experiences and above all because of the police in assault uniforms, there had been a lot of expectation about crossing the border. Anticipation of crossing the border was the main topic of conversation among the demonstrators. Suspicion and fear about whether the border crossing would be peaceful was evident among the crowd. As the demonstration passed the border controls, tension dissipated. Enthusiastic comments like "this is a historical moment", "we got it", could be heard at the very moment of the crossing. The political leaders who spoke at the meeting giving an end to the march in Irun described the demonstration as a success and defined it as a "historical event". In fact, never before had such a demonstration succeeded in crossing the border.

There had been several precedents prior to the 1996 *Aberri Eguna*, though. Both states in turn or together had prevented any demonstration from crossing the frontier either by closing the border, or by firing plastic bullets against the demonstrators. As Del Valle (1988:122) points out in her study on the Korrika, a popular footrace for Basque language speakers all through the Basque Country, the border crossing is particularly meaningful. Through the ritualisation of crossing, the border is transcended materialising symbolically the metaphor of Basque unity. For years, various protest actions, including that of Korrika had systematically been denied crossing the border. Even the funeral procession marches accompanying the transfer of the corpses of *political refugees*, ETA militants living in the North were blocked. As Aretxaga reports in her study of funeral rituals in Basque radical nationalism, border crossing is particularly meaningful. The territorial unity symbol for which the militant has struggled and died becomes significant as the mortal remains are returned to the family on the other side of the border (Aretxaga 1988:47). At this very moment is enhanced another strong and recurrent metaphor of the border, that of the divided family – present in Otaño's verses. Although the funeral cortege, wife and children, friends and militants are not permitted to cross the state boundary, the border does not stop the funeral procession. Frequently, as in the Korrika case, a relay system is organised, the border being the end and starting point of a divided demonstration. Slogans and songs would unite people – and family – astride the borderline, symbolically transcending it.

The following year, and as a continuation of the 1996 experience of bringing together North and South on such a special day, there was again a call for a united National Day. The celebration of the *Aberri Eguna* was part of a large campaign of co-operation between nationalist parties and social movements astride the border. The celebration had two different settings, Baiona, provincial capital of Lapurdi and the main urban centre in the North, and Iruñea, an emblematic city of high symbolic value, capital city of the former Kingdom of Nafarroa in the South. Although the idea was not new – the PNV for instance had organised double events of this kind before – the aim was to bring together people from both sides. Because of the distance between the two cities, about 140 kilometres, organisers had foreseen that people would mainly join one of the two events. Nevertheless, responding to the unity idea of the call the celebration was organised to make it possible to attend both. That way, demonstration traditions of North and South were respected too: as in previous years, the demonstration in Iruñea was scheduled in the morning and that in Baiona in the afternoon. Hence, a bus link was to operate between the two cities. However, the unexpected finding of the corpse of an ETA activist found dead in strange circumstances the day before the *Aberri Eguna* disrupted the scheduled programme.[13]

## The Reification of the Border. Opening and Closing Policies in a "Europe without Frontiers"

Until the present, borders have been highly significant all through the process of state formation. Examples taken not only from the European context, but also in other settings show the importance of the frontier concept worldwide in the definition and consolidation of states at different periods. Now that the European Union has stressed the need to open economic and political borders in order to achieve European integration, the meaning and role of borders and territorial boundaries in general, seem to have altered radically. I will argue, though, that states still manifest their willingness to maintain and even emphasise their territorial jurisdiction as a means of sovereignty. To do so, rituals and specific actions are again activated. The most visible one is without any doubt the presence of police corps at former checkpoints despite the closing down of frontier posts.

Other visible examples of border maintenance are related to space and to the inscription of memory through monuments. As in other cases that have deserved special attention, particularly the war monuments to the dead as a way to embody national identity through the highest sacrifice to the Nation, the location of the monuments remains an outstanding matter. Johnson points out the relation of space and more particularly territory, defining it as "as intrinsic to memory as historical consciousness in the definition of a national identity" (1995:55). The location of monuments is rarely left to the whims of fate. Rather, it responds to an often previously well planned conception of space and its meanings. However, it can be seen in the case of border markers sabotage, monumental space becomes social property and can thus be "used in ways that are different from and even contrary to the uses to which their builders or "owners" intended they be put" (Hershkovitz, 1993:397). This raises again the issue of place and monument location. Some months before the formal abolition of customs and traveller controls, twelve huge pillars where erected at the Biriatu no man's land, between the border post and the highway toll barrier. Apparently, the pillars had no special function or purpose. They had no name either. Their emplacement was significant though: if borders were to disappear together with the paraphernalia signalling them, the pillars would be a visible outstanding mark at the very location of the former border.

Apart from maintaining the border icons, states still actively emphasise their role at the borderline. One of the less known rites reasserting the border is the reconnaissance every two years of all the boundary stones on the Pyrenean borderline. Through a ritual recalling very much the *muga* reviewing, quite frequent nowadays in many Basque villages and towns, authorities from both states meet at a pre-fixed date in order to check together the condition and correct situation of the landmarks. As can be noticed from the analysis of reports at the municipal archives of bordering villages where fieldwork was conducted, this ritual has evolved. Since the 80s, state representation is not any longer ensured by state agents and officials, such as the *préfet* for the French side, or the *gobernador* for the Spanish one. Even the police, which in the past witnessed the operation, are no longer present. In a movement that could be very much considered as part of the actual European trend towards regionalising politics, states have delegated their representation to village mayors.

Too often, though, states continue to hold control of the frontier in what could be easily understood as a way of publicly displaying that they still master border matters. As it happens in the case of subverting rituals, states are aware that "political understandings are mediated through symbols" (Kertzer 1988:79). The border becomes thus one of the most visible and concrete symbols of power legitimacy and control. As has been described in the case of the National Day celebrations and other protest events, the presence of the state at the border becomes more than evident on particular dates. On dates significant to the Basque nationalist agenda, control measures are reinforced and police return to the abandoned border posts and to checkpoints that no longer exist. On such occasions, and without giving any consistent explanation, main-crossing roads – even the highway – can be closed for some hours or for a whole day. Other minor routes are also affected by these measures. When the border is not totally closed, despite the free circulation agreements, people are stopped at the border. Police start what is known as "filter operation": crossing is controlled and can be refused. The consequences of border closing affect anyone wishing to cross the border on these dates. That means that on such occasions commercial and private traffic is stopped at the border and compelled to wait for the opening and regularisation of the situation. This situation provokes above all important traffic jams. No mention is ever made of the fact that these actions go against one of the main bases of the Single European Act. As a matter of fact, most of the time the media consider it only as locally relevant news.[14]

However, border closing does not affect only events specifically linked to Basque nationalism. Cultural events and other kinds of celebrations are also touched. For the last 25 years one of the most significant dates for border closing is the *Herri Urrats*, a festival to raise funds for *ikastolak*, Basque schools in the North. Because of the frequency of controls and the difficulty of crossing the border, border crossing has become part of the day's program for thousands of people from the southern provinces willing to join the festival. Due to this, drivers plan the trip thinking of alternative routes and taking extra time as a precaution against possible disturbances and objections.

When “national demonstrations” are called in the North, the border is very likely to be closed by either one or both states. It may occur too, when protest actions are scheduled in France as happened on 10 November 1995. That day France closed the border to prevent 22 buses from crossing the border on their way to Paris. Almost 1,500 people from the South were in the buses to take part in a demonstration the next day in Paris to protest against a case involving 80 people, Basques and Bretons, charged with collaboration with, or membership in the armed group ETA. The border in Behobia remained closed from late afternoon until the next day, under the surveillance of the French army. This year, on the 11 March 2000, the day before the general election in Spain, a huge demonstration was called in Baiona “to claim the right of political prisoners to take part in the political process”. The border was again the object of intense control by both Spanish and French police. Buses were diverted and cars stopped. Carrying out orders from the French Ministry of Interior and appealing to the second article of Schengen, the French police corps closed the border some hours before the beginning of the demonstration. More than 200 French police in riot gear, shields in hand, had taken up the Biriatu crossing point, forming a real front line, a human frontier.

## Blurred Borders?

More than ever, as the Basque case shows, borders are being continuously transcended particularly in recent decades. The variety of examples stresses however, that this transcending is not exclusively related to the Basque nationalistic cause. While local co-operation astride the border has increased, to the extent of establishing formal agreements between several political institutions, states too have felt the need for co-operation more than ever. This has resulted mainly in ensuring an active co-operation policy between French and Spanish authorities concerning terrorism matters. To achieve this, both states have evoked at different times the European integration, stressing the need of implementing the necessary means to bring an end to the “Basque problem”. However, both states have too quickly silenced their responsibility in border transgression issues such as the GAL[15] affair. During the 1980s paramilitary forces co-ordinated by the Spanish state carried out on French soil countless bombings, killing about 30 people, most of them Basque refugees. As it has been recently proved during the criminal proceedings against former Spanish government ministers and high ranking military and police officials, Spanish police members and mercenaries had crossed the border several times during that period to operate with total impunity on French soil. Significantly, France never reported any formal complaint nor undertook any measure to prevent those attacks, although some of the victims were French citizens.

Paradoxically, in the present times, France seems very much concerned by events on the other side of the border. When dealing with the Basque department claim, a demand supported by the vast majority of the population in the North Basque Country, nationalists and non-nationalists alike, the French government appealed to unexpected arguments, more concerned by the neighbouring state than by the demands of its own citizens. As Mr. Chevenement, the French Interior Minister announced in the meeting with the local councillors, representatives of the movement for the department, “the Basque department could weaken the unity of Spain” (*Euskaldunon Egunkaria*, 2000-03-10). The issue, once again, raises the question of the legitimacy of borders and the way they are conceived, used or subverted depending on the interests at stake. Thus, the Basque example, a case of contest on an EU internal border, is particularly interesting as it points out not only the difficulty which states have in relinquishing their grip on borders but also the strategies used by Basque nationalists to subvert a border non recognised as such. It also highlights their contradictions and ambiguities, particularly concerning EU related conceptions and their application, a subject that needs to be deepened and deserves further analysis.

## Notes

1. Further administrative divisions complicate the map: south of the border, two Autonomous Communities, the Basque Autonomous Community (Araba, Gipuzkoa and Bizkaia) and the Foral Community of Nafarroa. North of the border, the Basque provinces (Lapurdi, Behe Nafarroa and Zuberoa) lack any decision taking institution and are included in the Atlantic Pyrenees Department. For simplicity, Basque toponyms will be used throughout the text. Similarly, to ease the reading, the terms South and North will be used instead of the Basque terms *Hegoaldea* and *Iparraldea*, when referring respectively to the Spanish and to the French side of the border.
2. The *fueros*, or charters specific to each of the Basque territories, give clear indications of the offensive nature of such actions and the punishment that they incurred. For more details, see Leizaola 1996:95.
3. There are other cases of avoiding explicit reference to the border. One of the most interesting to analyse is the use of the phrase "the other side", either in Basque, Spanish or French when talking of the border, where the state boundary is euphemistically mentioned.
4. Even though most of the references emphasise the role of the borderland as a "sanctuary" for ETA militants (Douglass 1994:48), it must not be forgotten that during 1936 and later during the Second World War, the borderland was a relatively secure shelter.
5. The whole poem highlights the central role of the border as a dividing line (the original is in Basque, the translation is mine): "Cloth of seven sisters cut in the middle, three dresses in one side, four others left on the other. Even if cut with scissors, each of them apart, it is known that all seven are dressed with one same cloth. Consider Basque language the cloth, the Bidasoa river the scissors, it is a mere stream compared to the sea. All seven are close from each other, the border is called Pausua – the passage. Why can not we be a single family?".
6. It is significant too that the N1, the main Spanish national road heading to Madrid, starts precisely at the very border, in Behobia. Straddling the Bidasoa river marking the international boundary, Béhobie-Behobia is a clear example of border influenced development.
7. *Euskaldunon Egunkaria* 04-03-2000.
8. The MNLV, the Basque National Liberation Movement, through some of the organisations under its patronage, mainly the political party Herri Batasuna, launched in the mid-90s the campaign "This is not France nor Spain" to condemn the present political frame – the non recognition of the Basque Country as a nation – as well as to increase public awareness on territoriality.
9. Interview, June 1997.
10. Even through the poster was not signed by any particular organisation, the message, "*Above all borders, the Basque Country. No to the border. This is not France, nor Spain. It is the Basque Country*", recalls the motto of the mentioned HB. Following an ever spreading trend since the 90s in this kind of alternative mass communication and willing to target not only local population, but tourists too, the last two sentences were written in five languages: Basque, French, Spanish, English and German.
11. There were significant exceptions, though: the PNV, the main nationalist party in the South did not join in.
12. The so-called "national demonstrations" are major protest actions taking place in the main cities gathering many thousands of people from all over the Basque Country called by political parties or organizations, defined as left-independens.
13. Following one of the main traditions of the radical or left nationalist movement (for more details, see Aretxaga 1988), a political homage organised in the activist's home village that afternoon attracted most of the demonstrators concentrated in Iruñea.
14. This is not the case, for instance, when the border is blocked by truck drivers. The way the media deal with these two new events is completely different. The road-blocking is treated as national or international news, while on the rare occasions when the border closing has been mentioned on the TV daily news, it is considered as local information.
15. GAL stands for Antiterrorists Groups of Liberation. It is the most known of the many paramilitary groups (AAA, BVE...) that emerged after the end of Franco's dictatorship and carried out terrorist attacks against Basque activists.

## References


Abeles, M. 1997: "La mise en représentation du politique", in M. Abélès and H. P. Jeudy (eds.), *Anthropologie du politique*, Paris: Armand Colin, pp. 247–271.

Alvarez, R. R. 1995: "The Mexican-US border: The Making of an Anthropology of Borderlands", *Annual Review of Anthropology*, Vol. 24, pp. 447–470.

Anzaldua, G. 1987: *Borderlands. La frontera. The new mestiza*, San Francisco: Aunt Lute Books.

Aretxaga, B. 1988: *Los funerales en el nacionalismo radical vasco*, Donostia: Baroja.

Barandiaran, J. M. de 1972: *Obras completas*, Bilbao: La Gran Enciclopedia Vasca.

Chaffee, L 1988: "Social conflict and alternative mass communications: public art and politics in the service of Spanish-Basque nationalism", *European Journal of Political Research*, Vol. 16, No. 5, pp. 542–572.

Descheemaeker, J., 1946: *La frontière pyrénéenne de l'Océan à l'Aragon*, Paris.

Donnan, H., Wilson, T. M., 1999: *Borders: Frontiers of Identity, Nation and State*, Oxford: Berg.

Douglass, W., 1994: "Las fronteras: ¿Muros o puentes?", *Historia y Fuente Oral*, Vol. 2, pp. 43–50.

Douglas, W., 1998: "A western perspective on an eastern interpretation of where north meets south: Pyrenean borderland cultures", in T. M. Wilson and H. Donnan (eds.): *Border identities. Nation and state at international frontiers*, Cambridge: Cambridge University Press, pp. 62–95.

Gomez-Ibanez, D. A., 1975: *The Western Pyrenees. Differential Evolution of the French and Spanish Borderland*, Oxford: Clarendon Press.

Johnson, N., 1995: "Cast in stone: monuments, geography, and nationalism", *Environment and Planning D: Society and Space*, Vol. 13, pp. 51–65.

Hershkovitz, L., 1993: "Tiananmen Square and the Politics of Place", *Political Geography*, Vol. 12, No. 5, pp. 395–420.

Kertzer, D. I., 1988: *Ritual, Politics, and Power*, New Haven & London: Yale University Press.

Leizaola, A., 1996: "Muga: Border and boundaries in the Basque Country", *Europaea. Journal of the Europeanists*, Vol. II. No. 1, pp. 91–102.

Pujadas, J. J., Martin Diaz E., Pais De Brito J. (coord.), 1999: *Globalización, fronteras culturales y políticas y ciudadanía,* VIII Congreso de Antropología de la FAAEE, Santiago de Compostela, Asociación Galega de Antropoloxía.

Raento, P., 1997: "Political Mobilisation and Place-specificity: Radical Nationalist Street Campaigning in the Spanish Basque Country", *Space and Polity*, Vol. 1, No. 2, pp. 191–204.

Sahlins, P., 1989: *Boundaries: the Making of France and Spain in the Pyrenees*, Berkeley: University of California Press.

Valle, T. del, 1988: *Korrika. Rituales de la lengua en el espacio*, Barcelona: Anthropos.

Wilson, T., Donnan, H. (eds.), 1998: *Border identities. Nation and state at international frontiers*, Cambridge: Cambridge University Press.

# The Past on the Line

## The Use of Oral History in the Construction of Present-day Changing Identities on the Portuguese-Spanish Border

*William Kavanagh*

Kavanagh, William 2000: The Past on the Line. The Use of Oral History in the Construction of Present-day Changing Identities on the Portuguese-Spanish Border. – Ethnologia Europaea 30, 2: 47–56.

While it has long been recognised that borders are prime sites for the defining and redefining of nations and states, it is only comparatively recently that it has been thought worthwhile to examine closely the social reality of those actually living on international borders. This paper looks at some of the oral history – 'the stories they tell about themselves' – of the inhabitants of a part of the Portuguese–Spanish border; specifically an area of the frontier between the Portuguese region of Trás-os-Montes and the Spanish region of Galicia. Tales of bandits, of smugglers, of the Spanish Republican maquis and of the police of both sides reveal the often surprising fluidity of who is 'us' and who is 'them', as well as perhaps helping us to understand just how much the new 'Europe without Frontiers' is rhetoric and how much is – or might become – reality.

*Professor William Kavanagh, Universidad Pontificia Comillas, Madrid; Universidad San Pablo-CEU, Madrid; Velázquez, 7, ES-28006 Madrid, Spain.*
*E-mail: su.kavanaghw@profesor.sumadrid.es*

Talking not long ago with one of my friends – there was a time when we used to call them our 'informants' – of the changes brought about at his village on the Portuguese-Spanish border by the so-called 'Europe Without Frontiers' (or at least without internal frontiers), he thought for a moment and then he replied, carefully and repeating his words: 'You may remove the door, but the doorframe remains . . . you may remove the door, but the doorframe remains.'

We are told that borders are important places for understanding such things as states and nations – ideas, abstractions, 'imagined communities', to be sure – but with administrative powers which have very real practical consequences for those who live in them and, in a special way, for those who live on their borders. I suggest it may be interesting to listen to those living on the border, to listen to their oral history – 'the stories they tell about themselves' – to perhaps help us understand just how much a 'Europe Without Frontiers' is rhetoric and how much is – or might become – reality.

The research I have been carrying out on a section of the Portuguese-Spanish border is long-term and on going. The object is to observe at close hand, at one specific location, the much-heralded transformation of Europe's 'internal' international borders from 'barriers' to 'bridges'. Although these frontiers always have been – and according to my friend in his border village, always will be – a bit of both. The area of the Portuguese-Spanish border – or Spanish-Portuguese border, if you prefer – I have been looking at is the land border known as the *raia / raya seca* ('the dry borderline') between the Portuguese region of Trás-os-Montes and the Spanish region of Galicia, specifically between three villages – a Galician village whose territory juts like a spur or wedge into Portugal and the two Portuguese villages on either side of it. One of the Portuguese villages is only two kilometres to the south of the Spanish village, while the other Portuguese village is somewhat further away to the west. All three villages are at approximately the same altitude and their soils

In a field divided by the border, a man from one of the Portuguese villages who is married to a woman from the Galician village.

and climates are similar. As may be seen in photograph 1, the landscape does not appear to change in any significant way at the border. The same may be said for the languages spoken on either side of the border – the Galego of the Spanish village is not that different from the Portuguese spoken in the Portuguese villages. The older village houses appear to be the same on both sides of the boundary – and most still have hollowed out spaces in their walls (known as *secretas*) where the smuggled contraband could be hidden when the border guards came to inspect. Yet these villages have had very different national histories, different political systems and different state administrations for hundreds of years. It comes as no surprise then that many things change radically when one crosses the border. Take the religious celebrations, for example, which people from both sides will attend. While at the romerias/romerías, which are gatherings at a local shrine, the priests from both sides will be present and there will be two masses said, one in Galician and one in Portuguese, and the priests will also be present at the religious processions held in the neighbouring villages of the other country, the look and feel of these ceremonies are very different on one side or other of the international border, as may be clearly seen in photographs 2 and 3. The decorations of the images of Christ, the Virgin and the saints in the Galician religious procession are very simple, while those of the Portuguese religious procession are extremely ornate. The music played on either side of the frontier is very different as well. The Galicians play the bagpipes, the Portuguese do not; the Portuguese play the accordion, and the Galicians do not. And the fact that Portuguese emigrants went preferentially to France or to the United States, while the Galicians went to Germany or to Switzerland means that the new houses they built on their return give a very different look to the villages today. Yet some of the most important differences are 'invisible' at first glance – all those aspects where the modern nation-state has control over the lives of its

A religious procession at the Galician village.

citizens, such as health, welfare, education, justice, taxes, etc. Even the time changes at the borderline, with the clocks in Portugal set an hour behind those in Spain.

It has been said that, as reminders of the past, borders are 'time written in space'. This is certainly true in the case of the border between Portugal and Spain, which as one of the oldest in Europe – dating from the founding of Portugal as an independent nation in the 12th century – has been altered very little since then. It has not always been a peaceful border, as the many fortifications on both sides of the border show only too well. Portugal is only one-fifth the size of Spain and has only a quarter of the population of its larger neighbour. Not surprisingly the Portuguese have always looked with certain apprehension at the Spanish, especially since the period of some sixty years (1580 to 1640) when Portugal was incorporated in the Spanish crown. However, things have been changing since both Spain and Portugal joined the European Union (then known as the 'European Community') in January 1986. Communications have improved. New roads and new bridges have been built between the two countries that occupy the Iberian Peninsula. Two countries that lived for many years back to back, ignoring each other. At least that was what Lisbon and Madrid did. What happened at the border was another matter.

Border regions are often peripheral areas of peripheral regions. The very name for the Portuguese border region, Trás-os-Montes (which means 'beyond the mountains') reveals the isolation and the marginality of the area, whereas Galicia, on the map the bit of Spain that sits on top of Portugal, has been characterised as 'poor, damp and difficult to reach'. Both are agricultural regions with little industry and poor communications. The only alteration since the 12th century to that section of the border under study, was made in 1864 when Portugal and Spain signed a treaty which gave the village which had been divided by the boundary line – the line passed through the centre of the village

A religious procession at one of the Portuguese villages.

– in its entirety to Portugal and the borderline was moved a hundred metres to the north. This was expressly done to control the smuggling, which, with many houses having a door giving onto Spain and another door giving onto Portugal, was inevitable, and the order of the day. The village was known as a *povo / pueblo promíscuo* and is recorded as having been so since at least the beginning of the 16th century.

A common characteristic of borders is that they are liminal areas where one may more easily elude control by the authorities. In troubled times the border provides the perfect escape for those in difficulties. During the Spanish Civil War (1936–39) there were quite a few who saved their lives by crossing the border in time. And Portuguese who wished to avoid military service have often made their way to Spain. Even after the end of the Spanish Civil War, there were a number of Spaniards living in Portuguese villages along the border. Some, if they had been identified as politically suspect by the Franco regime, were there merely for their safety, while others were operating as anti-Francoist maquis, crossing the border to murder members of the Spanish Guardia Civil and the local heads of the Francoist regime's single party, the Falange, and then returning to their bases in Portugal.

In some circumstances, the fact that the Church is the same on both sides of the border may also be utilised by the inhabitants of the borderland. A woman of the Galician village whose husband was killed in the Civil War has been receiving a war widow's pension ever since. She has been living with another villager for many years, but has not lost the pension through remarriage. The couple simply married in the next village – in Portugal. Thus, as far as the Spanish State is concerned, the woman remains an unmarried widow, while in the eyes of the Roman Catholic Church and of their neighbours, the couple are not 'living in sin'. On the other hand, not long ago a young Portuguese couple were married in the Galician village and immediately left for the United States – separately. The woman had no trouble in getting an entry visa as her parents are already living and working there and she applied as a single woman. The man did the same. Had they asked for a visa as a married couple, it would apparently have been much more difficult to obtain. So a Spanish marriage meant that neither the Portuguese State nor the American immigration authorities knew the real situation of the couple.

However, it is smuggling, more than any other activity, which exhibits the tendency of those who live on a border to live outside national laws. Smuggling is culturally acceptable behaviour on the border. 'It was lovely', one Portuguese woman told me of her years as a smuggler from the age of fourteen until she went to Paris to work when she was eighteen; of having made various journeys each night with rucksacks of whiskey and tobacco weighing some twenty-five to thirty kilos; and (the part she says she never told her mother about) of having being shot at by the guards. Border people structure much of their lives around their relations with 'foreigners'. In this sense, the border is a bridge and not a barrier. The laws against contraband, made by distant politicians insensitive to the local realities of the border, are felt by those who live on the border to be unjust and unreasonable. The borderland villagers are a 'we' group to whom the authorities are 'they'. Especially when they know that the state officials themselves have cashed in on the illegal border trade. Many villagers on both sides of the frontier tell stories of having a pair of shoes for their child confiscated as they got to the border, only to see the same pair of shoes a few days later on the feet of the son of the border guard who confiscated them. Apparently, the border police kept most of what was confiscated. It may have been only a few kilos of rice or pasta or sometimes a much larger shipment. One man told me that he had once had five thousand kilos of bananas taken by the border guards. What most annoyed him, he explained, was that he was caught even after he had taken the precaution of first bribing the corporal then in charge of the border post. He admits, however, that it was probably thanks to the bribe that in the end he was allowed to keep half the load of bananas. Portuguese villagers tell other stories of having to sell their fields on the Spanish side of the border because of the difficulties given them by their own border police. Not only were they required to get a special permit to farm their land and could only cross the border during the hours of daylight, but the guards would often, with the slightest pretext, confiscate the crops the farmers were bringing home. Some villagers claim that the only people who would ever risk going past the border post were the smugglers – in order to pay bribes to the border guards.

Many stories are told of the frequent abuse of their position of power on the part of the border guards – of both sides – and of their not infrequent brutality. A Galician woman married to a Portuguese man said that, the day after her wedding in the Galician village, she accompanied her new husband to visit his relatives in the nearby Portuguese village only to be stopped at the border by a Portuguese border guard, who sent her back to her village, while he let her husband cross into Portugal. She explained that it was only when she mentioned the incident to the priest of her village, that she learnt she had a right to enter Portugal as the wife of a Portuguese man. Others say that when there was a feast-day celebration at either village, the border guards would sometimes turn people back at the border. At other times they might even fine someone for 'crossing the border clandestinely'; one Galician villager told me that he had been fined various times for crossing the border because the guards 'felt like it'. Villagers say that while Spanish and Portuguese border guards were both bad and that both would confiscate whatever you were carrying, the Portuguese *guardinhas* were more likely to beat you up as well. When asked why this was so, one Portuguese man replied: 'Because they were poorer, more backward'. Another Portuguese man told me that when he was fifteen he was stopped on the borderline by the Guarda Fiscal and accused of smuggling. He says that, although he was carrying nothing, he was hit on the head so hard by one of the *guardinhas* that he was knocked unconscious. When the boy's family went to complain, the head of the border post asked the guard involved why he had hit the boy so savagely. 'Because I thought he was a Spaniard', replied the guard. He was expelled from the corps. Other stories tell of smugglers shot dead on the *raia* / *raya* by the border guards. One Galician man was a bit luckier: he told me how his contraband group had been challenged by a patrol of *guardinhas* at the border. But while his companions bolted off in different directions and escaped arrest, he had tried to push his way past the guards and one of them had shot him in the testicles, though luckily he suffered no permanent injury. What most angered him, he told me, was that he was 'already some two hundred metres into Spain, where the *guardinhas* have no jurisdiction whatsoever'. Many people say that the border police 'were hated by everyone'. One could, of course, sometimes hope to rely on divine intervention to save oneself from the wrath of the border police. There is a splendid mural painted on an inner wall of the church of the Portuguese village closest to the borderline, which depicts three Portuguese border guards on horseback in full gallop. The object of their chase is not shown, but the mural speaks of the *milagre* ('miracle') of a smuggler's escape from the guards thanks to the intervention of 'Santo Antonio' (St Anthony). However, quite a few villagers on both sides of the border have spent time in prison (usually just a month or so) on account of their contraband activities.

It could be claimed as an 'anthropological constant' of the Iberian Peninsula that the people of the nearest neighbouring village are always your 'enemies' and are your rivals because in some sense they are your equals. It follows from this that the village on the far side of your traditional 'enemies' are regarded as 'friends' following the simple logic that 'the enemy of my enemy is my friend'. And this holds true in these border villages. For this reason, it is not as straightforward as might first appear to discover what each side thinks of the 'Other'. It appears that often people speak of those on the other side of the frontier with ambiguity, sometimes with admiration and at other times with disdain. In many ways they appear to treat each other as simply neighbouring villages and without taking into account the political boundary. Thus, while those of the Galician village often speak badly of their neighbours in the nearest Portuguese village, they say the same about their Galician neighbours just down the road and, what is even more revealing, they speak of those of the Portuguese village on the other side of them (naturally, the arch-enemies of the Portuguese village nearest themselves) as being full of excellent people who make the best of friends.

Yet when one asks people what they feel about those of the other country without specifying the inhabitants of any particular village it is often mutual dislike which is the first thing to surface. The Galicians claim that, on first meeting, the Portuguese 'appear to be *muy formales*' (very serious, responsible), but when one gets to know them, they are *falsos* (deceiving). The Galicians claim that the Portuguese are 'backward, small and have big ears', while the Portuguese say that the Galicians are 'loud and stuck up'. The stereotypes come thick and fast. 'The Portuguese are poor', say the Galicians. 'The Galicians don't work', say the Portuguese, 'they sit back and live off their pensions and the dole'. 'You can never trust a Galician', say the Portuguese. 'You can't trust the Portuguese', say the Galicians, 'they are just like the Gypsies'. 'The Galicians beat their wives', say the Portuguese. 'The Portuguese beat their wives', say the Galicians. And so on and so forth, though some people do make the correct observation that 'they probably say the same thing about us.' When one asks people whether they would like to see a child of theirs marry someone from the other country, the most frequent reply is: 'No, they are very different from us'.

And while people from both sides attend the feast-day celebration in the neighbouring village, the Galicians claim that the Portuguese regard the festa as not having been a really good one if no one is killed during the day and, in support of their argument, will cite the case of the man from the Galician village who 'many years ago' was murdered by his Portuguese neighbours while attending the festa at the village next door. The Portuguese, on their side, state that the real violence happens at the Galician celebration. When speaking of their nearest Portuguese neighbours the Galicians say 'The best person at X is Jesus and even he is behind bars', referring to the image of Christ behind the grilles on the windows of the chapel at the entrance to the village. The Galicians explain that the Portuguese do not celebrate the feast day of Santiago (St James) – an important feast day in Spain – because St James was a Portuguese who 'escaped' from (a supposedly inferior) Portugal to (a supposedly superior) Spain.

The Portuguese claim that a Galician would never be generous, as a Portuguese would. On their side, the Galicians tell the story of the Portuguese who invites some Galicians to dinner and then gives his guests very little to eat. However, they were cheered up when they heard the man tell his wife to 'Bring out the chicken', until they realised that it is a live animal brought in to take advantage of the few crumbs dropped on the floor. This legendary tale is told in many places and the main character is generally 'a poor man', but at the border he becomes the 'Other'. Something of the same sort happens in the story about a woman – again, a Portuguese, as the tale was told by a Galician – who is in church talking with an image of St Anthony. The woman is annoyed with the saint since she has prayed long and hard to be sent a husband, all to no avail. In her anger and frustration, she throws a stone at the statue, which gives off a small cloud of smoke when hit. 'There you are', says the woman, 'smoking without burning and here I am, burning without smoking'. The same story is told by the Portuguese, who naturally make the protagonist of the tale a Galician woman.

Even the apparently true stories they tell about each other frequently underline their mutual disdain. This one, for example: A Galician was working in his field on the border, when his Portuguese neighbour in the adjoining field began shouting insults at him. The Galician told his neighbour to watch it or he would let him have it with his shotgun, which he happened to have with him as he had been out hunting rabbits. The Portuguese jeered and bent over turning his backside to the Galician, who quickly picked up his shotgun and blasted the Portuguese in the arse. The Portuguese let out a cry and fell down. The Galician, suddenly aware of what he had done – he was certain he had killed the Portuguese – ran back to his village and went to ask the mayor what he ought to do, since he had killed a Portuguese. The mayor asked him if the Portuguese had been shot in Spain or in Portugal. When the Galician replied 'In Portugal', the mayor is said to have told him 'Ah, then you needn't worry. Let the Portuguese bury him.' However, that is not the end of the story. Luckily, the Portuguese was not killed and managed to limp back to his village and was taken to hospital, where he was operated on and survived. He did nothing, however, about taking any legal action against the Galician. Here the explanations vary. Some say that his pride was more injured than his bum and he feared being made a figure of jest if he reported to the police what had happened. Others, on the other hand, emphasise the feeling that the legal consequences of any crime or misdemeanour committed in one country can easily be avoided by simply crossing the borderline. People tell the story of a man from the Galician village, a well-known smuggler, who simply popped into Portugal a few years ago when the police finally came for him when they discovered Portuguese coins in the scrap metal he had been claiming to be importing from somewhere else in Spain. The somewhat hastily 'retired' ex-smuggler later made his way to Brazil, where he is living happily.

This impunity provided by the border is illustrated by another story where the young men of the nearest of the Portuguese villages had got into one of the periodic stone fights – in fair weather, a regular Sunday afternoon custom, it seems – with the young men of the Galician village. The border guards generally ignored these fights. However, when a young Galician let off a few shots in the direction of Portugal with his father's pistol in the course of the usual Sunday skirmish between the youth of these border villages, this was a bit too much for the lieutenant of the Guarda Fiscal (the Portuguese border police) who came over to the Galician village to have a word with his Spanish colleague. The Spanish Guardia Civil lieutenant called all the rowdy young Galician men involved in the border incident to his office and gave them a stiff dressing-down in the presence of his Portuguese colleague. However, as soon as the Portuguese border policeman had left, the Spanish border policeman is reported to have told the Galician youths: 'Well done, lads, only next time hit them even harder'. This story also reveals one of the elements which is repeated in many of the stories – the ambivalent position of the border police in their relations both to their opposite numbers in the other country and to their own countrymen. While both the Guardia Civil and the Guarda Fiscal had power over aspects of villagers' lives, they were never really part of the village, since they were, in the case of the Guardia Civil always and in the case of the Guarda Fiscal nearly always, from somewhere else. As well, complain villagers, while ordinary people had difficulties in crossing the border and even greater difficulties in bringing anything with them, the border guards themselves could cross freely and bring back whatever they wished. Yet the life of a border guard could be a dangerous one as well. One man from the Portuguese village closest to the borderline told me how his grandfather, a Guarda Fiscal posted in his own village, had been killed on the raia. The grandson's story is that his *guardinha* grandfather had somehow managed to infiltrate himself into a smuggling group, but that when he tried to arrest them as they crossed the line into Portugal, he was overpowered and killed. It seems that many years after the event, a very old Galician, one of the gang of smugglers who had killed his grandfather, confessed to the Portuguese 'with tears in his eyes' that he had only hit the disguised border policeman in self-defence and had had no intention of killing him.

Villagers tell the story of one newly arrived border policeman who – incredibly – had refused to accept any bribes and had even tried to arrest some smugglers who had previously paid off his companion guards to look the other way as the contraband went through. His fellow guards – at the point of a pistol – quickly taught him the rules of the game. After that, he took his cut like the rest of them. Villagers tell the story with the clear implication that non-corrupt police are considered to be arbitrary and cruel to attempt to stop what is 'clean trade', whereas corrupt police are more human because they are more reasonable. The authorities are always to be distrusted, except when they can be shown to be human. The Galician villagers tell with glee the story of the time when some young men of their village stole the pistols of some drunken Portuguese border guards. Their Spanish colleagues 'with much mockery' returned the arms to the Portuguese.

The Galicians tell another story of the time one of their villagers was caught on the borderline by the Portuguese border guards, who suspected him of smuggling. With the excuse that he would show them where he had hidden the contraband, the Galician lead the Portuguese across the border straight into the arms of a patrol of the Guardia Civil, who sent the *guardinhas* packing, saying that the Portuguese had no right to be arresting anyone on Spanish soil. In this case, one authority was used to play off against the rival authority. Another story in which the border guards are made to look ridiculous was told me by a Portuguese woman about her great-aunt who was caught by the Guarda Fiscal bringing two dozen eggs from Spain. Taking her to the post to pay a large fine – it seems that one would be fined so much for each egg confiscated – the woman was thinking desperately how to get rid of the eggs. It was quite impossible to simply throw them away, since she had one guard walking ahead of her and one behind her. What she did was to take the eggs one by one, suck them, then crush the shells and drop the bits of eggshell in the tall grass along the path without letting the guards notice what she was up to. When the guards got her to the post, the woman was found to be carrying nothing and the *guardinhas* had to let her go without a fine.

These stories bring out what I think is one of the most salient points of inter-border relationships. That is, that while on the one hand people on both sides of the border can give excellent reasons for despising those of the other country – many define themselves as superior to an 'Other' regarded as 'inferior' – at the same time both sides have the same interests in outwitting the authorities. Since smuggling is, or rather was until very recently, so very profitable, the common distrust of authority brings together these people living on the border. People say that when there was *confiança / confianza* (trust) they were all good partners. They state that 'money would never change hands at the borderline'. The goods would be delivered and payment would be made later.

During the Second World War there was a mine near the Galician village that was used by the Germans as a cover in order to bring wolfram (tungsten ore), used in the making of bombs and aircraft, from Portugal to Spain. As Britain's oldest ally, Portugal was unable to export the wolfram directly to Germany, so the mineral was smuggled into Spain and then legally exported from Spain to Germany. At night, groups of from sixty to a hundred men would bring the sacks of wolfram loaded on donkeys and horses. The Portuguese would bring the wolfram to the border and the Galicians would then take it to the mine. The border police of both sides were bribed to look the other way (though only in a figurative sense; since the bribe was usually a percentage of the contraband, the guards would always count the horseloads). The following day, the sacks of mineral would be openly loaded onto lorries and shipped out. Villagers who worked in the mine at the time say that the amount of wolfram produced by the Galician mine was tiny in comparison to the amount of mineral shipped out as if coming from the mine.

This 'night work', as it is referred to, could be

very profitable for the villagers, but had its drawbacks. One of the local doctors confided to me that he has detected a higher incidence of cirrhosis among those people, especially those women, who worked for long periods as smugglers. The doctor puts this down to the quantity of brandy that they needed to drink to ward off the night chill while carrying out their smuggling operations.

Perhaps one of the most revealing stories is that of la banda de Juan (Juan's gang). This Juan was a Galician who had been a member of the Socialist party before the Spanish Civil War and had had to flee for his life to Portugal when Franco's forces took control of Spain. Juan and his band of anti-Francoist maquis – made up of both Galicians and Spaniards from other parts of the country, people are quick to point out – made their hideout in Portugal only a few hundred metres from the Spanish border, over which they would cross 'to rob rich fascists'. The Galician villagers speak of Juan as *una buena persona* ('a good fellow'). A bit of a Robin Hood figure, Juan is said to have escaped capture by the police any number of times by dressing as a woman. Ambiguous in more than one sense, Juan was admired as being able to move freely from one side of the border to the other, admired for being able to outwit the authorities of both countries. Eventually, however, his hideout was discovered. There was a tremendous shootout – which lasted two days, people say – until the Portuguese army brought in mortars and shelled the house. Most of the gang where killed, except for two who escaped from the house – Juan and a very young man called Enrique. Juan made for the border, but just as he got to the line was shot dead by the lieutenant of the Guardia Civil who had been lying in wait for him. Enrique was captured, spent a number of years in prison and was eventually released. Today, over eighty, he is a town councillor for the Spanish Socialist Party. Villagers all seem to agree that he is *una buena persona* ('a good chap').

Until very recently, people on both sides of the border were telling me that 'a Europe without borders' was something they felt they would never see during their lifetime. The border is a reality of their lives that they have always known, and have known as a politico-administrative reality imposed from outside. Only a few years ago it was nearly impossible to have an hour's conversation with anyone in these villages without the subject of the border coming up. When they spoke of their past, when they spoke of their present, when they spoke of almost anything, the border was always there somewhere. Today, however, the seemingly eternal vigilance of the border posts is no longer; the border guards – sometimes brutal and sometimes not, but always there – have gone; the chains across the roads have all been removed and what were once dirt tracks crossing the border are now proper roads surfaced with tarmac. One clear sign of the times was the recent wedding of a young woman from one of the Portuguese border villages with a young man from a nearby Galician border village and which was actually held on the very borderline itself!

There have been many obvious changes in a very few years, although not all of them can be considered to be positive from the point of view of the local people. Most obviously, despite all the inconveniences and the sometimes clear risks to life and limb attendant on living on an international border, was the fact that the very existence of the border provided villagers with their main source of income. The priest of both Portuguese villages, writing in the December 1992 issue of the monthly newspaper he edits, complained that the disappearance of the border would mean that his villages 'would lose their most important business and source of employment and wealth, which was smuggling'. Smuggling has all but disappeared, except for the movement of drugs such as heroine and cocaine, which most people regard as not at all like the 'clean trade' of the smuggling in the past. Another aspect of change is that neither economy is as insulated as before. This particularly affects the Portuguese, who had far less competition with a closed border, which permitted them to be less efficient than Spanish firms just over the border. For example, a man from one of the Portuguese border villages who owns his own small welding firm (he was trained as a welder in Germany, where he lived for a number of years) says he prefers to buy his material across the border in Galicia, not because the quality is any better, but simply because he finds the Spaniards to be 'more responsible' than his fellow countrymen. He says that the Spaniards deliver when they say they will, unlike the Portuguese, who don't even bother to deliver. He says you have to go to their shops in order to get what you want. He also complained that when he recently expanded his business and needed to take on two extra workers, he was unable to find any young men in the Portuguese villages in the area who were willing to work as apprentice welders and learn the trade. He had no trouble, however, in finding the two young men he needed in the Galician village just over the border. The welder's wife pointed out that now that her husband has Spanish, rather than Portuguese assistants, 'even his Portuguese clients take him more seriously', although she added that some people at their village are annoyed, 'because having hard-working Galicians coming every day shows up the Portuguese as being lazy'. More sinister were some of the rumours that were circulating in the Portuguese villages of the borderland shortly after border controls were removed in 1992. One, which was true to a certain extent, was that Portuguese girls from poor families of the *raia* were being tricked into going to Galicia with the promise of a job, would then be drugged, kept prisoners at some roadside brothel and forced into prostitution. The other rumour, for which no evidence was ever produced, had it that Spaniards 'in high-powered motorcars' were coming to Portugal to kidnap children 'for their organs'. The level of hysteria was such at one point that the priest of the Portuguese villages told me that he had stopped his car – admittedly a Mercedes, but with Portuguese number-plates – at another border village to talk with some children, when his car was suddenly surrounded by angry villagers armed with sticks. Luckily, the priest was recognised in time.

Eight centuries are not wiped away in a few short years. As my friend said: 'You may remove the door, but the doorframe remains.' While these borderland people admit that their relations with those on the other side are now much more fluid than in the past, there is *mais confiança / más confianza* ('more trust'), it is still clearly the case that national boundaries are markers of collective identity. Perhaps due to the fact that on this section of the Portuguese-Spanish border the concepts of 'nation' and 'state' coincide to a far greater extent than they do on the Basque and Catalan sections of the French-Spanish border. The nation-state, it would appear, is still 'the primary source of welfare, order, authority, legitimacy, identity and loyalty'. The inevitable conclusion would seem to be that the task of 'building Europe' or even a 'Europe of the regions' on this particular section of one of Europe's 'internal borders' may not be as easy or as rapid as some may hope – or others may fear.

# The Smuggler and the Beauty Queen

## The Border and Sovereignty as Sources of Body Style in Gibraltar

*Dieter Haller*

Haller, Dieter 2000: The Smuggler and the Beauty Queen. The Border and Sovereignty as Sources of Body Style in Gibraltar. – Ethnologia Europaea 30, 2: 57–72.

This article explores the relatively neglected topic of how borders influence the habitus and body styles of border populations. It extends notions of habitus and performativity to the field of national identification. Using data from the British Crown Colony of Gibraltar, it examines two contexts in which the dominant body styles of men and women are shaped as forms of resistence to political harrassment enacted by the neighboring country, Spain, at the colonies border: smuggling and beauty contests.
Smuggling is both economically lucrative and part of the Gibraltarians' struggle for political recognition and self-determination. The image of 'the smuggler' and his or her behaviour have become emblematic of this conflict. Related to the question of sovereignty and the border is the exclusion of Gibraltar from participation in many international events such as the Olympics and the Eurovision Song Contest. The only such event in which Gibraltar participates on an equal footing with other nations is the Miss World Contest, the preparatory heats for which have become major occasions in the Gibraltarian calendar, spawning a mass of local beauty contests. These examples illustrate not only how borders create and maintain national differences and distinctions, but also how such differences can come to be inscribed on the bodies of those who live at borders.

*PD Dr.habil. Dieter Haller, Department of Comparative Cultural and Social Anthropology, European University Viadrina, Große Scharrnstr. 59, D-15230 Frankfurt/Oder. E-mail: h0920cyt@rz.hu-berlin.de*

"You have to be very careful not to criticize. My wife always worries about me because she knows that I find it very difficult to keep quiet. When we had the double filter [a double control post at the border], we stopped going to Spain, but I have a daughter who is married and lives in Marbella [50 km away from Gibraltar], and she needed to have her insurance renewed, so we did it for her. Maribel said, lets take it over to her on Saturday. We went down there, no double filter. You know sometimes it was on, sometimes not. And I picked up the *Chronicle* [local newspaper] and I am reading it and it said that when you are an ordinary passenger car, you don't need the triangle. You know, they used to ask for the [warning] triangle, the first aid kit, for everything. And they said in the paper that they said with the RAC [Royal Automobile Club], that you didn't need to have it, because you could turn the flashes on. So I said to Maribel, 'look what they say here: they haven't got the right to ask us for the triangle. At that moment, they [the Spanish police] turned up: and we could see the double filter, and she said 'Look, we've only been in the queue for about 20 minutes, when we get to the front, let's go back, home'. I said 'why?'. She said, 'because I know what you are going to do and what will happen. Leave the queue'. I said 'I'm not going home. I'll give you money for the taxi, if you want to go home, I am going through and I am taking the paper to jail'. She said, 'if they ask for the triangle you tell them to sod of'. I said, 'I would'. As it happened, when we went through, it was alright. But that tension there...” (Informant Stephen Harding).

In the quotation above, Mr Harding talks about the insecurity he and his wife Maribel felt about crossing the border between Gibraltar and Spain in 1995. The trip to visit their daughter in Marbella activates a tension, that itself is heightened by this insecurity. Having decided to cross on hearing that there were no border controls, they once again discovered that crossing was not easy and unproblematic: Shortly before arriving by car at the border checkpoint, the Hardings realized that it had become effective again. The local newspaper had informed its readers that displaying a *triangle* was no longer necessary, but could one rely on this information? After all, experience taught border crossers that ‘they’ (the Spanish border guards) could not be trusted. Wasn’t Spain still laying claim to the Rock of Gibraltar?

Most Gibraltarians to whom I talked raised such topics. In their narratives the border is linked to bodily experience of tension, insecurity, impotence, and vulnerability. This experience is not presented as being peculiar to the Hardings or to other individual informants, but is thought to be the collective experience of all Gibraltarians. It has become commonplace to refer to Anderson (1983) and to Hobsbawm and Ranger (1973) when discussing matters of national identity. However, bodily experience is rather untheorized in their writings. I will argue that the body is a potent metaphor to naturalize national identity, and will show how bodies are related to sovereignty in Gibraltar.

The article is based on data collected during fieldwork between 1996 and 1997 in Gibraltar and especially on the border between the British colony and neighbouring Spain.

I point out the various ways in which the border is linked to bodily experience, both discursively and in practice, showing in particular how this bodily experience is used as a powerful resource to establish a Gibraltarian national identity. The aim of the article is threefold.

Firstly, I will expose the theoretical background of my approach, by focusing on the importance of habitualization and bodily performativity in national identification. I will show that the border situation, being one institution amongst others, generates the performance of a national habitus.

Secondly, I show that the very special make up of the Spanish-Gibraltar border makes visible processes which are not so easily discernible at many other national borders, especially within the EU. It is a border, where a state (Spain) enacts territorial claims (towards Gibraltar) via its border apparatus, which through intensive control measures inscribes cultural difference into the very bodies of Gibraltarian border crossers.

Thirdly, I will argue that the border is related in multiple ways to the differentiation of bodies outside the actual realm of border crossing itself. I will do so using two examples from my fieldwork: the popularity of the smuggler habitus amongst young men and the boom in beauty contests which have heavily influenced the bodily habitus of young women. Both examples will shed light on the indirect relationship between bodies and borders. It is not my intention, however, to explain both examples as effects of the border situation only – there are other aspects such as economical, status, and class which influence the popularity of these bodily styles. At the same time, their popularity cannot be understood without relating it to the border. As I will show, the particular resonance of both contexts in Gibraltar stems from their relationship to the border and national sovereignty, to which they are related as forms of symbolic resistance to the Spanish territorial claim: smuggling being more than just an economic activity (this ‘more’ being Gibraltarian ‘revenge’ for Spanish harassment, a weapon that can be used to harm the enemy); and the Miss Gibraltar contest, which because of the Spanish veto on Gibraltarian participation in other national sporting and musical contexts, is one of the few possibilities to represent the ‘nation’ as such on the international stage.

## Borders and Bodies

To name, discover, cross and recross cultural borders has become a hallmark of cultural anthropology. Borders create order and orientation in everyday life; they enable people to take a position in society, to identify with the known and to protect themselves from the unknown. This is not only true for symbolic borders of identity, but of many political borders as well.[1] Remarkably, unlike symbolic borders[2], political borders have long been neglected as a focus of anthropological research and theorizing.

In his groundbreaking book on the Spanish-French borderland Cerdenya, Sahlins (1989) has convincingly demonstrated that national borders are not passive, peripheral and receptive in the process of nation-building, but rather function as active and central agents. Sahlins revolutionized anthropological thinking about borders, by showing how the inhabitants of Cerdenya functioned not simply as the passive recipients of centralized national politics, but, by using national agents for their own aims, actively influenced the national politics of Spain and France[3]. Sahlins analyzed the national identification of the borderland population as mainly a strategic political act, limited by outer/institutional/socio-structural constraints only. His actors seem to have internalized these outer constraints on a cognitive level, thereby neglecting the importance of bodily habitualization of difference and its conscious or unconscious externalization via body styles. But borders, bodies and states are related in various ways.

First, the dichotomy inherent in the German distinction between *Körper* (as a carrier of signs) and *Leib* (as lived body) is reflected in different perspectives on national borders. The idea of borders as passive, peripheral and receptive is mirrored in the concept of the *Körper* as a readable system of signs only, while the idea of the border as permeable, central and as a source of power is analogous to the concept of the *Leib*.

Second, nations are often imagined as bodies and institutions of the state as its organs, as in Hobbes' *Leviathan*. The border, then, is the skin, which clearly demarcates an inside and an outside, and which distinguishes between insiders and outsiders. The border serves to canalize, to regulate and to control the exchange of insiders and outsiders and is often described as skin.

Third, the state's perspective on foreigners and of border crossers such as migrants and smugglers in particular often conceptualises their bodies in terms of threat and injury to the state.[4] For example, the organic analogy between body and state is decidedly expressed in the link between borders and the control of epidemics, ascribing to the foreign body a vital (or fatal) role in the carrying and spreading of diseases.[5] Just as skin and border are often associated, so too is the penetration of both and the sexualizing of border crossing.

Fourth, many European borderlands, such as Alsace, South Tyrol, Kosovo and Macedonia, are highly emotional spaces, deeply anchored in national narratives. Without doubt, the Rock of Gibraltar is a symbolic site for Britain (as a symbol of the perseverance of the Empire, British continuity and solidity, and national grandeur), for Morocco (as a symbol of Muslim expansion into Al-Andalus) and for Spain (as a symbol of the loss of empire and national decline); it is deeply burdened with emotion. Borders are cultural sites where the collective memory of national communities is represented and exposed via material artefacts (such as flags, fences, control posts, uniforms) and procedures (controls). Sometimes the physical appearance of borders and the borderland itself carries symbolic meaning.[6] From the point of view of the state, these artefacts and procedures are intended to be the central institution to divide insiders from outsiders and to transmit a different national habitus. Consequently, they are conceptualized as receptacles within which national memory is stored, or, as Jeggle (1997: 77) puts it: "What has been stored as resentments frequently 'comes up' at borders." This 'coming-up' can easily be understood in a physical sense, because what comes up may be physically experienced feelings of grandeur, fear, wrath or hatred; one may be deeply choked with emotion, contentedness or indifference. Even though feelings do not come up 'naturally', they are often perceived to be natural, because it is the body which reacts. As individuals only have direct access to their own physical reactions, these reactions are trusted to be authentic and true.

Of course, there is nothing inherently natural in these feelings, even in cases where we cannot control what's 'coming up'. Recent theories have shown that bodies are not natural either, but are always shaped by cultural forces.[7] Habitus is culture that has become naturalized. Bourdieu writes (1982: 308) that bodies function as a mnemonic aid for the "deep-rooted values of a group and [its] basic convictions". As a system of deeply spiritualized generative principles, habitus produces all physical action and behaviour of the individual. As far as habitus is basic to the relationship of the individual to his/her body, its effects are prevalent in "all activities and forms of practice... where the body is involved" (Bourdieu 1982: 339), including for example food habits, bodily hygiene, the way we deal with health, age, and sickness, as well as the "presumably most automatic poses and most insignificant body techniques – how to gesture and to walk, to sit or to sneeze, to move the mouth while talking or eating" (1982: 727, translated by the author).

Habitus is a powerful concept to explain cultural perseverance via its naturalizing effect. It is also able to explain why essentialist concepts are so attractive to many of our informants (and often to ourselves), and why situational-constructivist arguments are so seldom asserted by them: deconstruction is an act of violence, because so much energy has been invested in the acquisition of habitus (by naturalizing social reality).[8] Habitus is not only perceived as self-evident by those who acquire (e.g. children) it from others who teach it (e.g. parents), but by the latter as well. Transmission of habitus is therefore not exclusively based on verbal teaching of knowledge (do this, do that), but on mimetic performativity. Mimesis does not necessarily include verbalized or conceptual knowledge but is mostly based on unconscious perception, transmission and reproduction. According to Perl's gestalt-therapeutic theory (Dreitzel 1982), bodily performativities of a generation that physically experienced trauma, such as war, famine or, as in the Gibraltar case, isolation, can be perceived and reproduced by the following generation (even though it did not experience the trauma itself). This chain, if it proceeds unconsciously, is what I would call original sin.

The notion of habitus, however, has been forcefully challenged by performativity theory, for habitus acquisition presupposes a waxlike bodily matrix open to the inscription of hegemonic habitus-creating agencies, such as the family, class or ethnic We-groups, 'culture' and state institutions without allowing for the possibility that individuals can accept, affirm, resist, counteract, mock, manipulate or subvert these forces. The notion also presupposes stability, for habitus is often perceived as a product rather than as a constantly negotiated process. Connerton (1989) has shown that memories are not only cognitively recalled in rituals, but are also re-enacted and represented through ceremonial embodiment. Preformatted memory is "bodily memory, encoded in postures, gestures, and movements. Repeated re-enactment in such bodily practices entails the use of habit-memory, which consists simply in the capacity to reproduce a certain performativity without recalling how or when this capacity was acquired" (Foster 1991).

Butler (1998) has argued, that the acquisition of a sense of bodily naturalness (in her case: gender identity) is a regulated process of repetition, mediated via subtle mechanisms of power expressed in – often seemingly ephemeral – instructions and orders to behave, sit, eat etc. in the correct way. These discursive mechanisms achieve their goal if they generate the individual's desire to behave accordingly. Bodily memory therefore is not just "there", it can be activated or forgotten, manipulated, transformed and reinterpreted performatively, and it is communicated.[9]

It is the memory of the Spanish territorial claim over Gibraltar that is re-enacted and represented through the ceremonial embodiment of border control. Gibraltarians are convinced that border measures are enacted again and again to create a constant feeling of their helplessness, impotence and vulnerability. These feelings keep the claim alive, for they keep bodily memory alive. Every feeling recalls a chain of prior experiences at the border that were similarly unpleasant and creates the seemingly self-evident perception how reality is: Spain will never give up her claim and therefore will do the utmost to harass the local population of the Rock. Narratives about special border crossings are popular amongst Gibraltarians they often invoke prior experiences drawing on cognitive and physical memory alike and transforming the individual crossing into collective experience.

## The Border between Gibraltar and Spain

To understand why bodily experience is so prominent in narratives about the border, we have to take a closer look at history. In the War of the Spanish Succession Gibraltar was conquered by a British Admiral who fought for one of the pretenders, Archduke Charles of Austria. In 1713, when Charles was defeated and Philippe de Bourbon became Felipe V de España, the Treaty of Utrecht was signed and Gibraltar became part of Britain. The treaty is the basis of the present status of Gibraltar as a British colony (and therefore an important point of departure in any political argument about sovereignty over the Rock), but Spain has never given up her territorial claim which – notwithstanding several phases of cooperation between the two powers in the subsequent centuries in the area – resulted in several unsuccessful sieges of the Rock.[10]

On 8 June 1969, the Spanish government of fascist dictator Francisco Franco closed her frontier gates to the Rock, cutting Gibraltar off by land from its hinterland, the so-called Campo de Gibraltar, and isolating Gibraltarians from friends and relatives on the other side. The closure was a reaction against both the referendum of 1967, when Gibraltarians stated their wish to remain British and to the Constitution of 1969 which strengthened ties between the motherland and its colony. The gates were closed until 1982 when the border was opened for pedestrians. In 1985, it was opened for vehicles. Today, what Gibraltarians least desire is to become part of Spain.

Nevertheless, since the early 1980s Gibraltarians became increasingly disillusioned with Britain: they appreciate the constitutional guarantee which it grants but suffer from the progressive rundown of the Ministry of Defence (MoD), which until recently dominated the local economy and guaranteed full employment. In the political arena they decry the fact that Britain did little to counter-act the unpleasant Spanish checks and controls which Spain introduced when it reopened the border and which Gibraltarians interpret as harassment to make their life as miserable as possible. The Spanish authorities do not even recognize that there *is* a frontier between Gibraltar and La Línea. They call it *Verja* (fence) and do not use of the word frontier.[11]

Today, Gibraltar is still a British colony at the southern tip of the Iberian Peninsula. Through its links to Britain, Gibraltar is part of the European Union but it is not part of the Schengen Territory nor of the EU-Customs Agreement. There is a sense of political stalemate: Britain cannot leave the Rock, even if it wished to. It is subject to two treaties, the enactment of which is likely to be contradictory: the Treaty of Utrecht, which guarantees Spanish sovereignty after Britain leaves, and the colonies Constitution of 1969, which guarantees to honour the wishes of the Gibraltarians. Moreover, Spain still considers Gibraltar to be an essentially Spanish territory which is British only temporarily, until the Rock is decolonized, and even those Gibraltarians who favour self-determination or even independence from the UK cannot realize their aim, because if they were successful and Britain left the Rock, Spain would immediately demand its return according to the Treaty of Utrecht.

The government of socialist leader Joe Bossano (1988–96) was partly elected to counter such political and economical difficulties. His platform was to create an economy not vulnerable to Spanish actions and that countered the effects of the MoD-rundown. With regard to sovereignty, Bossano took a hard position, rejecting all forms of cooperation as long as Spain refused to recognize the right of the Gibraltarians to self-determination in regard to their future. Economically, the alternatives lay in the advantages offered by membership in the EC (but outside the customs union): Bossano's declared political aim was to create an international financial centre and a tax haven.

To back up his economic position, Bossano's strategy had to move in two directions: first, to reduce the importance of Britishness, and second, to increase national homogeneity. Gibraltarians had to be transformed from a pro-British colonial population into a nation. National symbolism and nationalist discourse became major features in Gibraltarian political discourse. Gibraltar being a tiny territory with a heterogeneous society, nationalist discourse had to be grounded in a common and creolized culture. Gibraltarians – who it was often said were more British than the British themselves – had to be persuaded to prioritize their Gibraltarian identity over their British one. In the 1990s, this resulted in a huge wave of cultural and national identity production.[12] Politically, the SDGG (Self-Determination for Gibraltar Group) was founded. This introduced the celebration of a National day and whose aim it was to enhance national symbolism, which included the increased use of the term 'national'. A national anthem was written, and *calentita*, a local chickpea-dish of Genoese origin, was declared the 'national dish'.

But Bossano's economic policy failed. The finance centre did not attract as many investors as expected, although Gibraltar's GNP benefited from this situation. And unemployment still remains a problem, mainly amongst unskilled youth.

## Crossing the Border, Controlling the Body

From a Gibraltarian perspective, the Rock's economic crisis is rooted in the Spanish territorial claim. This claim is enforced on several levels, but is most tangible through various measures at the border. That harassment continues has certainly helped to link actual experiences to the prior experience of border closure. Border guards often use physical gestures rather than words to issue commands (Drive right! Stop! Open back door! Go on!). Mere sight of their uniform can be enough to elicit anticipation of such directives – as my informant Samantha McNamara told me: "Even if they [Spanish Civil Guards] treat you friendly or correct... Whenever I see a Spanish uniform, automatically I recall all the bad experiences I made [with them] during all these years [of the closure]". During fieldwork I collected a number of examples of such "bad experiences":

- sometimes it takes up to six hours to cross from Gibraltar by car into Spain;
- sometimes regular Gibraltarian passports, identity cards and drivers' licences are rejected by the Spanish authorities;
- sometimes Gibraltarian citizens who enter Spain from other countries such as, for example, a Gibraltarian tourist returning from Italy who chooses to fly to Málaga or Barcelona, might be refused entry into Spain as a holder of Gibraltarian passport;
- when Abel Matutes became Spanish foreign minister in 1996 he even threatened to close the border again, recalling the closure that Spain did effect between 1969 and 1982.

The experience of the closure years is central to Gibraltarian narratives about their national identity. The closure, so the narrative goes, forced the 30,000 Gibraltarians, irrespective of their ethnic, educational or economic background to live on approx. 6 km$^2$. The closure is presented as the big equalizer, and common features caused by the closure are highlighted in narratives: such as the miserable housing situation with three or more generations of a family living tightly packed in a humble apartment; where young couples had no place of their own; where it was impossible to escape social control from family members, neighbours and acquaintances; where the only trip one could make by car was *skalestrics*, driving in circles around 'the island' without stopping, once, twice, three times, and always meeting the same people.

Border crossing demands physical and psychological strain, thereby activating feelings of tension, impotence and vulnerability. This is particularly true for those who cross by car (for pedestrians it is much less problematic to cross). The measures that create most physical and psychological strain are the queues, which are the result of the intensive regulation of personal and vehicle documentation (the so-called *double checks*). Queues are a particular problem in summer months; irritability is common, heart attacks not unknown, and sometimes even death due to the heat.[13]

Exacerbating the irritation is the fact that these checks are irregular. Sometimes it is possible to cross with regular identification, at other times, the same papers are rejected. Gibraltarians like Mr and Mrs Harding never know whether measure checks will be enforced or not.

Indeed, what might be interpreted as a mild nuisance to people who cross or live at the border in a bigger country, has a quite different impact on a territory the size of Gibraltar: border effects are everywhere:

- daily routine such as shopping in nearby Spanish towns, is structured by the degree of border controls; visits to the neighbouring country have to be planned carefully, especially if travelling by car;
- there is always uncertainty as to whether appointments can be kept, and this not only influences individuals, but also and to a much greater degree, the economy. Local politicians, trade unionists and the members of the chamber of commerce on both sides of the border lament the negative influence of time-keeping on economic development. Border restrictions are the main obstacle for foreign investment in Gibraltar, e.g. for the unsuccessful plan to attract enterprises after the handing over of Hong Kong to China;
- the second pillar of the economy, tourism, is also negatively influenced by Spanish border controls, since tourists from the Costa del Sol on a day trip to the colony would hardly wish to spend their day in a queue;
- internationally, Spain vetoes Gibraltar's independent participation in the Olympics, at sports competitions and at other leisure contests;
- what is going on at the border has become the central topos of public and political discourse, which is dominated by anti-Spanish sentiment;
- and, as already noted, people's bodily performativity is shaped by the border situation.

Individual tension, anxiety and impotence is shared by 'the community', because it is expressed in a collective code and communicated via language, symbols or mimesis. In Gibraltar, anti-Spanish sentiment and pronouncements encode these feelings towards what might possibly happen at the border.

## Resentments that 'Come up'. Heightened Emotions about Spain

Virulent anti-Hispanism is the result of the congruency between objective structures (here: border harassment) and incorporated habitus (here: physical expectation of harassment) (cf. Bourdieu 1977: 51ff). The primary experience of being subject to harassing and humiliating control leads to an identity crisis similar to what Rosaldo (1989: 28) called 'borderland hysteria'. Rosaldo examined the US-Mexican border, a highly controlled and politically hypersensitive region. For Rosaldo, borderland hysteria is the effect of a political border which functions as a barrier to wealth and accessibility to different material conditions of life. This economic barrier does not apply to the Spanish-Gibraltarian border. However, control mechanisms and the symbolic presence of the nation state are equally strong. In the Gibraltar case, it is the permanent performativity of humiliation at the hands of Spanish border agencies which is responsible for creating borderland hysteria. This primary experience is interpreted by Gibraltarians within the context of a long succession of different Spanish initiatives, as yet another attempt to subject them under a fascist regime.[14]

The doxical experience of the social world and the habitual patterns on which this experience is based (in this case: the nation-state as the hegemonic ordering principle of the globe) are confirmed and reinforced, or, as Donnan & Wilson (1999: 131) remark,

"the embodied knowledge of the border guard thus confronts the bodily demeanour of the border crosser in a meeting where the bodily dispositions and performances of the 'protagonists' are structured by the rules of the state and the attempt to evade them".

Anti-Hispanism as a form of permanent catharsis offers the possibility of evading the performativity of (Spanish) nationalism and at the same time reinforces the hegemony of nationalism as a central means of expressing difference.

Border controls and the modalities of border crossing can be described as rituals. Rituals classically have been theorized for the domain of religion; in the tradition of Durkheim as well as of Marxism, rituals have been conceptualized – as Driessen (1992: 11) writes – as *"epiphenomenal, circumstantial, and ephemeral"*. But rituals have their own form and they not only refer to power relationships of dominance and subordination.[15] With its phases of separation (waiting in queues), marginalisation (being controlled) and integration (leaving the control sector), border crossings show characteristics of secular rituals. Through instruction in rituals, initiands are made familiar with the rules and secrets of the new status. Often traumatic physical experiences such as mutilations or ritual death are part of the initiation, the new status being inscribed in the very body of the initiand.

Even if one disagrees as to whether or not border crossings may be compared to religious initiation, they can (if, for example, waiting in the heat is part of the process) stir deep emotions, similar to that of the candidate to initiation. Driver and ritual initiand are confronted with the uncertainty of what will happen during the process of crossing or 'on the other side'. Similar to the candidate to initiation, Gibraltarian drivers have no influence on the ritual procedures. But, in contrast to initiation, they are familiar with what possibly will occur. This enables them to take precautions before crossing to minimize the risk of being targeted: they can call the border hotline or select times for crossing that are considered 'safe'; they can carry all documents that possibly could be requested and carry along few and easily reloadable pieces of luggage. Yet contrary to the ritual initiand, precisely because border crossers know about the range of possibilities Spanish border guards might deploy, border controls are especially well suited to subject Gibraltarian drivers to the power relationship of dominance and subordination.

Unlike the ritual initiand, Gibraltarian drivers can never be certain of achieving, once within Spain, a status that safeguards them from harassment. On the contrary, while still in the area immediately adjacent to the border on the Spanish side, they have to expect special and additional controls by Spanish civil guards. It is the knowledge about the *possible* enactment of these measures, combined with their perceived arbitrariness and the incompleteness of integration, that converts border crossing into a ritual of humiliation and degradation, thereby reinforcing Gibraltarian identity and nationalist arguments as forms of symbolic resistance.

Uncertainty and tension as results of the specific border situation are repeatedly activated in the bodies of regular border crossers. This is mainly responsible for the virulence of borderland hysteria, present in anti-Hispanism. In addition to this direct relationship, bodies and borders in Gibraltar are also related in more indirect ways, as I will show in relation to two examples of resistance to the Spanish claim that foreground physical experience.

## Smuggling

My first example is exposing the bodily habitus of the smuggler amongst young Gibraltarian men. Smuggling of various goods – mainly tobacco – is an old and central activity in the western area of the Mediterranean,[16] enclosing Spain, Gibraltar and Morocco.[17]

Today, smuggling is not only an effect of economic and political history, but also of Gibraltar's special economic status within the EU (it is not a VAT area and is excluded from the Customs Union). Moreover, and this is a new phenomenon, it is discursively linked to the struggle for political representation and for self-determination (which is both a fight against Spain and Britain). The image of 'the smuggler', and its associated body styles and behaviour, has become a male icon for this struggle even amongst non-smugglers.

As one informant remarked:

"The other day I noticed that they [young local men] behave quite aggressively when parking their car in the parking lot. I could not help thinking of the smugglers, manoeuvring boldly with their pateras [speed boats] to escape the Spanish coast guard."

The behaviour of Gibraltarians is often interpreted in relation to smuggling, both negatively by Spaniards and positively by locals. The informant cited above emphasized her words with her hands mimicking the *pateras'* manoeuvres. Her interpretation of local driving habits indicates the ambivalence of the smuggling topos-expressing both admiration and indignation. Moreover, it reproduces and perpetuates the image of a society intimately tied to smuggling.

In Gibraltar, the smuggler has been an important social image for generations. Since the early 1990s it has been indirectly encouraged as an acceptable image for young men through the politics of Chief Minister Bossano. Bossano's tolerance towards smuggling was a way to counter the negative effects of unemployment among young unskilled workers. It was also consistent with Bossano's position on sovereignty and his refusal to accept and to participate in the regular Anglo-Spanish talks on Gibraltar's future. Rather than accepting a passive role towards the sovereignty question, smuggling was a means of expressing growing self-confidence in relation to both Britain and Spain.

This had several consequences for Gibraltar's civil society. Until the early 1990s, smuggling had been the preserve of a few specialists, but with the growing possibility of purchasing *pateras* through favourable credit, more and more people could participate. At the time immediately prior to fieldwork, about 2,000 people were directly or indirectly involved in smuggling (8 per cent of the population), a new development that I will call 'democratized smuggling'. It is not surprising, then, that, especially in the early 1990s, smuggling carried positive connotations. Conscience about its unlawful character was low, prestige – mainly for young men – was high. A sense of adventure, quick money, male bravado and the sense of harming an opponent imparted to the activity an irresistible aura of sex, money and success.

It is worth noting that, in contrast to many other borders, smuggling between Gibraltar and Spain is a one-way transaction. As a duty free zone, not only tobacco is smuggled into Spain, but also everyday goods, such as milk, cheese, sugar, alcohol and perfume. Smuggling at the border between Gibraltar and Spain is highly gendered. Whilst large-scale smuggling of tobacco and drugs is mainly controlled by young male Gibraltarians via sea, small scale-smuggling of other goods is dominated by Spanish women.[18]

It is popular among young Gibraltarian men to display the typical smuggler attributes of the cool Mafiosi so well known from Hollywood movies: sunglasses, muscle shirts, lots of golden chains and rings, earrings, tattoos, slick-backed hair. Many of these young men became rich in the early 1990s when smuggling activities were at their height and supported by the then local socialist government.

Initially, 'democratized' smuggling was "like a game", according to one smuggler informant.

"They brought tobacco into Spain, with rowing boats, and made 10,000, 15,000 or 20,000 pesetas a night. With the money they bought *pateras*, which were easily available on credit. Then, the game became serious. Six or seven kids were killed when pursued by the Spanish coast guards."

They bought spacious apartments, jewellery and big cars, with which in the evenings they paraded through the narrow streets of Gibraltar, noisy with ghettoblasters. Everybody knew their names, and their family background. Through the use of a device familiar from Mafia films as a means of concealing personal identities – tinted car windows – the smuggler scorned integration into the tight-knit web of local community. Without an integrative function, tinted windows symbolized something different: "we are the lords of the streets", which means the subordination of all other aspects of public life to the practice of smuggling.

The image of the smuggler is tied to class. As smuggling became more and more visible in public, middle-class Gibraltarians, especially such as merchants, accountants, lawyers and teachers, became increasingly concerned with Gibraltar's international reputation, which was already portrayed by the Spanish media in terms of smuggling and piracy. In combination with Bossano's refusal to co-operate with Britain on the question of sovereignty, the visibility of smuggling, interpreted not only as harmful to the colony's reputation, but also as a take-over of the public scene by lawless mobsters, were central topics, around which the then oppositional conservative (GSD) and liberal (GNP) parties organized. Both parties criticized the fact that Bossano's strategy towards smuggling would prevent the transformation of Gibraltar's economy into a service-based, off-shore and financial centre, an aim which was agreed upon not only by GSD and GNP, but by Bossano's own party as well.

The GSD in particular worried that Bossano's tolerance towards smuggling and the fact that smuggling had become the main pillar of the local economy, would result in Britain taking a tougher stance on Gibraltar. The parties were afraid that Britain, which the Spanish media portrayed as tolerating piracy in their colony, would introduce Direct Rule from Whitehall, removing Bossano's government and suspending Gibraltar's Constitution. Without that Constitution, which guaranteed the very existence of Gibraltar as a self-governed British colony, Gibraltarians would have no safeguard against Britain's talks with Spain, and, more importantly, no input into possible decisions on the question of sovereignty.

The GSD tried to persuade the public of their position by implicitly distinguishing between 'normal and acceptable, low quantity everyday' smuggling, carried out by almost everyone, from 'bad smuggling'. The latter was synonymous with 'democratized' smuggling. In 1995, under British pressure and the threat of Direct Rule, Bossano himself intervened against smuggling by expropriating most of the boats involved. His action led to local upheaval, the so-called "1995 riots". Nevertheless, under threat of Britain's direct intervention large-scale smuggling was soon brought under control.

When I arrived in Gibraltar in January 1996, there were hardly any *pateras* left with which large-scale smuggling could be carried out. However, the outer signs of democratized smuggling, remained.

To counter the dangers of smuggling by sea, many of the pious young smugglers had been tattooed with protective images of the Virgin. During the time of democraticized smuggling, such tattoos became popular even in those segments of society which did not actively participate in smuggling. Other public images of smuggling similarly persisted. A local designer produced T-shirts that showed a *patera*, followed by Spanish police boats. The smuggler in the *patera* had the face of a smiling shark. The sharklike smuggler is a local icon to counter Spanish discourse on smuggling. These T-shirts were extremely popular amongst young men at the height of smuggling in the early 1990s. When the GSD won the May elections of 1996, their first measure was intended to restore the old status quo of the non-visibility of smuggling by prohibiting the Mafia-like tinted car windows.

And again, even though any talk about smuggling with locals began with a condemnation, positive aspects of smuggling were still present discursively, especially when drawing connection between the border, bodies, and resistance, as the following quotation illustrates.

"It was a formula for economic subsistence which only damaged the all-powerful interests of the State, that mean stepmother who instead of protecting her children squeezed what she could out of them and, without recognising the revolutionary obligation of their citizenship, for many a century simply treated them as mere subjects. What did it matter robbing a State that was robbing one anyway? Contraband was the Robin Hood and the treasury the Sheriff of Nottingham."[19]

The evil and hostile Sheriff of Nottingham is, of course, a synonym for Spain: the noble smuggler, fighting successfully with male bravado, patience and a snare against an overtopping fascistic state machinery. In the Spanish version, the image is reversed: the noble bandit becomes a lawless and disgraceful criminal, whose persecution and punishment is the self-evident duty of any nation.

The Spanish media and officials often describe Gibraltarian smugglers as pirates in the sense of Sir Francis Drake. For example, César Brana, the civil governor of the Spanish province of Cádiz, turns the positive image of the 'noble smuggler's' into a negative one by comparing Bossano with Drake: like the raider of Spanish silver transports in the 17th century, Gibraltarians under Bossano attack Spain's economy with their speed boats, with drug-

smuggling and money-laundering.[20] Drake has positive associations in the British context, because symbolically he is the one who laid the foundation stone for the British Empire. The Drake metaphor offers a perfect vessel for associations of British maritime superiority, as he is thought of as the hero who successfully defeated the Spanish Armada. As in 1588, small British ships (= Gibraltarian speed boats) turn out to be superior to the big Spanish galleons. The Armada image also is evident in another metaphor often used by locals: Gibraltarians as David fighting against Goliath, who, by virtue of strategy, intelligence, smallness and the ability to outmanoeuvre quickly with their *pateras*, they manage to out-wit the sluggish Spanish police armada. This idea has become iconicized in a local series of postcards, amongst them one showing an ape (symbol for Gibraltarians) in a *patera* loaded with cartons of Winston tobacco and displaying its thumb as a symbol for the victory over Spain.

These metaphors and associations not only describe the tactics Gibraltarian smugglers perform with their speed boats, but, in a way, the tactics themselves become shaped according to these metaphors. Indeed a smuggler's speed boat action is described and rated by other smugglers as aesthetic or as non-aesthetic, as bravado or as timid. In this sense, metaphors materialize as behaviour.

In Gibraltar as well as in the hinterland, smuggling (with the exception of drug-smuggling) is considered a normal and a legitimate economic activity. Gibraltarians and Campo-people share this conviction with other borderlanders.[21] In local discourse, smuggling is considered a legitimate means of resisting Spanish policy which, as already mentioned, is believed deliberately to hamper the economic development. To Gibraltarians therefore, smuggling is one of the very few effective ways of harming the enemy.

James Scott (1990: 44) has suggested that subordinate articulate ideas and values that reverse and negate those generated by the dominant group, via what he calls a hidden transcript. Interestingly, and contrary to Scott, Gibraltarians do not resist dominant depictions of them as smugglers by countering those portrayals with alternative and oppositional portrayals of their own design. Although in fear of Spanish accusations, many Gibraltarians often negate the very existence of smuggling to the foreigner, but claim that 'everybody in the region, including the Spanish authorities, is involved in smuggling'; or when proudly displaying the image of the positive smuggler, they draw on precisely those notions and use them to their own advantage.[22]

## Beauty Contests

A second effect of the border on body and habitus is related to the boom in beauty contests in Gibraltar. Again, I will analyze these contests as a form of national identification and of symbolic resistance to the Spanish claim to Gibraltar.

Participation in beauty contests is extremely popular amongst little girls and young women, and, increasingly since the mid-90s, also amongst young men. In the first weeks of my research I was confronted with the fact that the appraisal of physical beauty through beauty contests is regularly reported in local newspapers and magazines. For example, in 1996 I counted 14 female beauty contests, amongst them the election of *Youth Princess*, *Miss Queensway Quay*, *Miss Nestlé*, *Miss Computec*, *Miss Star of India, Miss Casino*, *Miss Cover Girl*, *Miss Caleta Palace Hotel*, *Miss Security Express*, *Miss Newswatch, Miss Platter* and *Miss Radio Gibraltar*. Participants who do not win such contests can expect to obtain the title of *Miss Photogenic, Miss Personality* or *Miss Good Effort*. Moreover, Monique Chiara, *Miss Gibraltar 1995*, was almost omnipresent, now opening this fashion show, now smiling on that tourism fair, now presenting that variety programme.

Beauty contests celebrate a female gender ideal that lauds and reinforces classically heteronormative values, such as the beautiful but subordinated companion of men. Local female beauty standards are strongly influenced by the standards set in the contests. They are, nevertheless, interpreted in terms of their difference from Spanish (and also English) standards: whilst Spaniards are portrayed as flamboyant, exaggerated and colourful "*Bennetton adds on two legs*", Gibraltarian self-description tends towards unobtrusive, quiet and discreet colours. Burberry textiles are extremely popular, and locals are convinced that Burberry clothing sold in Marbella or in Seville is much more colourful than clothing of the same brand sold in Britain. But compared to British women, Gibraltarian women see themselves as more colourful and flamboyant, and more prepared to wear extravagant jewellery.

Female beauty contests in Spain and Britain are popular only amongst a small sector of society, and in general they have the reputation of being rather outdated and politically incorrect. In contrast, in Gibraltar girls and women participate as a matter of course, untouched by any feminist doubts. Local beauty contests in the 1990s are the result of a development that started in the 1960s, and that is closely linked to the border situation. Informants overwhelmingly portrayed closure of the border as a time when different social activities blossomed, mainly in arts, in entertainment, and in religion and spirituality. This was paralleled by an increasing preoccupation with the body, which men pursued in relation to sport, while women became more and more interested in beauty contests. Increasing preoccupation with the body was explained by boredom with life in the tiny and isolated community. Moreover, the limitations of living in what was then only 6 km$^2$ of space led to the need to expand at least physically and the need to self-experience.

Although the first beauty contests arose from a need to expand out of small-town boredom, this does not explain why the contests were still popular in 1996 at the time of fieldwork, 14 years after the border was opened, nor why they boom in Gibraltar today.

There are, of course, many factors operating here. Participants may have one set of motivations, their parents another, while participation itself may have very different significance to the different women involved. For example, the contests offer the possibility for a young woman to realize certain fantasies, such as to achieve reputation amongst peers, to become famous locally or to start an international career. It is important to keep in mind that one woman out of 1,840 (of the age cohort 15–24) will participate as *Miss Gibraltar* in the *Miss World-Contest* – there is hardly a better chance for a young woman in any other country to participate in this well-known international beauty contest. Preparation for contests generally involves all family members of the participants' kinship networks, their friends and neighbours. Mothers, aunts and grandmothers are involved in all kinds of preparations. In contrast to beauty contests in nation states, the organizers, the participants and their families are personally known to each other. Parental and familial control over a daughter's participation and the possible threats to her reputation is guaranteed. Contests reinforce family ties.

The many different local contests operate independently from the original (Miss Gibraltar) contest, for they have become an important source of income for the organizing modelling agency, which is run privately by Mrs G., an enterprising lady, who controls all local public-relations for the contest. Moreover, via her weekly column in the local paper (with the title *Life & Style*), she dominates local media discourse on all matters of gender relations as well as on (female and male) beauty. Even though the Gibraltar Government endows all participants in the *Miss Gibraltar Contest* with a certain sum of money, participants (with the possible exception of the winner)[23] hardly win financially, for participation in the various events which precede the actual contest is costly: taking different modelling courses to be prepared for the catwalk is a necessary prerequisite and has to be done in Mrs G.'s agency; a successful application to participate involves sitting a modelling-exam, which costs extra money; and the diploma has to be paid for extra, too. Once the diploma is obtained, modelling practice is necessary, again organized by Mrs G. Two possibilities exist: either, the young women 'job' as hostesses, for example during a conference or when a new shop is opened. The customers (e.g. hotels, shops) pay for hiring the young women, and the women themselves pay for the arrangement. Or, they may participate in other beauty contests (which are also organized by Mrs G.'s agency), which again costs money.

Yet, individual motivation, family cohesion and entrepreneurship do not fully explain why contests receive the high degree of local media coverage and the interest of local politicians. As I mentioned before, participation is not only a major event for the young woman and her family but for the community as a whole, as it offers the possibility of symbolic representation and of resistance to the enemy. Gibraltar's participation in international contests and competitions is almost always blocked by Spain. There are only a few international contests where Gibraltar is not vetoed by Spain, such as the world hockey championship and the Miss World Contest. Hence, symbolically, participation in the Miss World Contest offers a rare chance for Gibraltar to represent the community as a nation before a global audience. It creates the illusion that Gibraltar is on an equal footing with existing nation states. 30,000 people are represented alongside Miss India, that represents 900 million people. Participation offers the unique possibility of collective representation, which is a means to resist Spain and her claim over Gibraltar.

## Conclusion

The notion of the border is one of the basic metaphors of our discipline. Astonishingly, this has not led us to view borders between states as privileged sites to carry out research – a fact which is even more of a surprise given that state borders are places, where many central concepts of cultural anthropology, such as territory, identity and nationality, are exposed and performed, staged and negotiated. In this article, I have analyzed the border between Spain and Gibraltar as a productive element in the habitualization of a Gibraltarian national identity. I focused particularly on how the border influences bodily experience, and how this experience is linked in local discourse to national identification.

Anderson (1983) calls nations 'imagined communities', entities, within which the individual imagines a common 'national' bond with others. The cognitive approach reflected in 'believing' and 'imagining' has to be combined with the phenomenological approach of bodily 'feeling', bridging the gap between discourse and body. National identification, I would argue, is not simply a cognitive process, but can only be fully understood if we also consider the habitualizing effects of power (in this case: national power) on the bodies (and emotions) of individuals. Emotions as bodily experienced feelings, dislikes and obsessions, the feelings of emptiness and fulfilment, of arousal and indifference, of fear, happiness or hate are more than just expressions of individual experience; they are always embedded in culture and society and therefore able to establish closeness or distance, identification or lack of identification with others. Collective identification in Gibraltar is, as my examples show, strongly influenced by the physical experience of difference at the border. I tried to illustrate this in two ways.

Firstly, by showing how the border functions as a means through which Spain habitualizes the performativity of impotence by subjecting Gibraltarian bodies to constant humiliation, year after year. This border is a privileged site to show how (Spanish) national identity is made physically tangible to individuals, because it is here, that various controls, measures, and harassing experiences provoke emotions of uncertainty, tension, stress and the like. These emotions are communicated in narratives about border experience and in anti-Hispanic rhetoric. Both means of communication generate a feeling of solidarity and help to strengthen the development of a distinctive national identity.

Secondly, I tried to show that apart from being subjected to border controls, bodies, sovereignty and the border are also related in more indirect ways. Smuggling and beauty contests are not only linked to the border as effects of the conflict of sovereignty. They are also forms of resistance to the Spanish claim on Gibraltar, as they are arenas in which the enemy can be challenged and damaged: smuggling being both an important source of income and the very symbol of strength and independence, beauty contests being a means to present Gibraltar as a 'national' entity on the world stage and so undermine Spanish intentions to prevent such an attempts. Moreover, as physical expressions, they embody the very difference between Gibraltarians and Spaniards.

## Notes

I thank Andrew Canessa, John Borneman, Hastings Donnan, Michi Knecht, Dorle Dracklé, Lutz Jablonowsky, Barbara Ritchie, Joshua Marrache and Maya Nadig, who all helped to sharpen the focus in my article. The article is based on my research about the influence of political-economic transformation on the development of national and ethnic identities („Vom Aufmarschplatz zum Steuerparadies: der Einfluß politisch-ökonomischer Transformationsprozesse auf die Ausbildung nationaler und ethnischer Identitäten am Beispiel Gibraltars"). Fieldwork was carried out from Feb. -96 to Feb. -97. The Deutsche Forschungsgemeinschaft (DFG) and the Department of Comparative Cultural and Social Anthropology of EUROPA Universität Viadrina, Frankfurt/Oder supported field research in Gibraltar. I thankWerner Schiffauer for his support. The results of this research are published in Haller [2000]. Special thanks to Parvis Ghassem-Fachandi, my assistant in the field, and to Barbara Ritchie and Richard Gardner for their help with the translation.

1. Simmel 1992: 221ff; Girtler 1992: 11ff; Greverus 1969.
2. Consider e.g. the concept of ethnic boundary [Barth 1969: 10] or of the boundary of local communities [Anthony Cohen 1986]. See also Müller 1987: 28; Fernandez 1974, 1986; Van Gennep 1986; Turner 1967, 1969.
3. Also see Medick 1991, 1995; Ulbrich 1993: 139–146; Kotek 1996: 23.
4. Borneman [1998] about labelling Cuban Marielitos as 'bullets'. Also see Donnan & Wilson 1999: 129–151.
5. During the BSE-crisis in the summer 1996, Spanish border police legitimated stronger controls of Gibraltarian vehicles by referring to the possibility that they could illegally export British beef into Spain.
6. Wilson 1994.
7. Using Bourdieu's habitus theory, Bröskamp [1994] has argued that attempts to promote the participation of German and Turkish youths in sport as a means of integration often fail because they assume that bodies are culture-free and so a good basis for transcultural communication. According to Bröskamp, the reverse is true. He shows that bodies and bodily behaviour are culturally shaped.
8. Some further thoughts are offerd by Scarry [1985] who contends that torture is a technique that injures and harms the body with pain, just to destroy the naturalized and self-evident values and convictions with the aim of constructing a new habitus; violence in torture shows that much violence was invested in the acquisition of habitus.
9. See Nadig 1998.
10. The Treaty specified that whenever Britain

should leave the Rock, it must be handed over to Spain. The sandy istmus that separates Gibraltar from the Spanish border town of La Línea and which is now occupied by the Gibraltar airfield, Spanish Customs, parkland and housing, is not included in the Treaty of Utrecht.

11. It was Spanish Prime Minister, José María Aznar, who revealed in a Freudian slip that the *Verja* is in fact recognized as a frontier by mistakenly using the word 'frontera' shortly after his election in May 1996.
12. The *Gibraltar Heritage Journal* was founded in 1993 and a local boom in publications on Gibraltarian popular history and culture emerged, e.g. on the catholic church, the evacuation of WWII, biographies of great Gibraltarians, the sanitary system, the streets and quarters, theatre plays, aspects of local history and culture, histories and gossip.
13. Uproar after queue heart attack tragedy, in: *The Gibraltar Chronicle*, 17 May 1997.
14. Since Britain conquered the Rock in 1704, Gibraltar was subjected to various sieges by Spain in the 18th (most importantly the so-called Great Siege between 1779 and 1783), 19th and 20th centuries. These sieges are responsible for the emergence of a siege or fortress mentality amongst local civilians.
15. Bloch [1989, 1992], for example, shows that the ritual of the royal bath in Madagascar obtains its power through the fact that it was an extension of secular, everyday rites.
16. Jackson, W.G.F. 1987: 233.
17. Spanish historian Manuel Sanchez Mantero has argued that in the mid-19th century there were 100,000 smugglers who lived in the area surrounding the Rock of Gibraltar. In those days Campogibraltarenos could only legitimately be priests, infantry soldiers, minions of some Duke, or poorly paid fishermen. The rest, from notaries to muleteers and farm hands, lived directly or indirectly from that black economy which avoided tax, but which offered a good profit margin for the survival of the poor and the not so poor. Gomez Rubio, Juan Jose: Contraband, money laundering and tax avoiding. In: *The Times,* 3 March 1997.
18. About these women, the so-called *Matuteras*, see Haller 2000: 246f.
19. Gomez Rubio, Juan Jose: Contraband, money laundering and tax avoiding. In: *The Times,* 3 March 1997.
20. Hart, Robert: UK between the Rock and a hard place. In: *The Independent* 19 December 1994.
21. See Flynn [1997] for the borderland Shabe between Bénin and Nigeria.
22. Gibraltarians pursue a similar strategy of resistance to that used by Brazilian transgendered prostitutes who "oppose and resist hegemonic notions of gender and sexuality that degrade them by drawing on precisely those notions, and using them to their own advantage in their interactions with members of the dominant group" [Kulick 1996: 3], in this case: males who are perceived to be 'normal', heterosexual men.
23. The Government gives every participant £ 400. Additionally, the winner receives a prize of £ 2,000 as well as £ 1,500 for clothing. Second price is £ 1,000, and the third price is £ 500. *Miss Gib £ 2,000 prize*. In: *The Gibraltar Chronicle*, 25 March 1998: 1.

## References


Anderson, Benedict 1983: *Imagined-Communities – Reflections on the Origin and Spread of Nationalism*. London: Verso.

Barth, Fredrik 1969: *Ethnic Groups and Boundaries. The Social Organization of Cultural Difference.* London & Oslo: Allen & Unwin 1969 (also: *Process and form in social life. Selected essays of Fredrik Barth*, Volume I. London: Routledge & Kegan Paul 1981: 198–227).

Best, David 1978: *Philosophy and the human movement*. London: Allen & Unwin.

Bloch, Maurice 1989: *Ritual, History and Power: Selected Papers in Anthropology*. London & Atlantic Highlands, NJ: The Athlone Press.

Bloch, Maurice 1992: *Prey into hunter*. Cambridge: Cambridge University Press. pp. 24–45.

Borneman, John 1998: *Emigrees as Bullets / Immigration as Penetration: Perceptions of the Marielitos*, in J. Borneman: Subversions of International Order- Albany: State University Press of New York. pp. 249–273.

Bourdieu, Pierre 1977: *Outline of a Theory of Practice*. Cambridge: Cambridge University Press.

Bourdieu, Pierre 1982: *Die feinen Unterschiede – Kritik der gesellschaftlichen Urteilskraft*. Frankfurt/Main, Suhrkamp. p. 308.

Bröskamp, Bernd 1994: *Körperliche Fremdheit – Zum Problem der interkulturellen Begegnung im Sport*. St. Augustin: Academia.

Butler, Judith 1998: *Zur Politik des Performativen – Haß spricht*. Berlin: Berlin Verlag.

Cohen, Anthony 1986: *Symbolising boundaries – Identity and diversity in British culture*. Manchester: Manchester University Press.

Connerton, P. 1989: *How Societies Remember*. Cambridge: Cambridge University Press.

Csordas, Thomas J. (ed.) 1994: *Embodiment and experience – the existential ground of culture and self.* Cambridge: Cambridge University Press.

Donnan, Hastings 1999: Body Politics. In: Donnan, Hastings/Wilson, Thomas: *Borders – Frontiers of Identity, Nation and State*. New York/Oxford: Berg.

Douglas, Mary 1970: *Natural Symbols: Explorations in Cosmology.* London: Cresset Press.

Dreitzel, Hans-Peter 1982: Der Körper in der Gestalttherapie. In: Kamper, Dietmar/Wulff, Christoph (Hgs.): Die *Wiederkehr des Körpers*. Frankfurt/Main:

Suhrkamp. pp. 52–68.

Driessen, Henk 1992: *On the Spanish-Moroccan Frontier.* New York/Oxford: Berg.

Fernandez, James 1974: The Mission of Metaphor in Expressive Culture. In: *Current Anthropology*, Vol. 15/2 pp. 119–145.

Fernandez, James 1986: Persuasions and Performances – of the beast in every body and the metaphor *of* everyman. In: James Fernandez: *Persuasions and Performances*. Bloomington: Indiana Press. pp. 3–28.

Flynn, Donna K. 1997: "We are the border": identity, exchange, and the state along the Bénin-Nigeria border. In: *American Anthropologist.* 24 (2) pp. 311–330.

Foster, Robert J. 1991: Making National Cultures in the Global Ecumene. In: *Annual Review of Anthropology* 1991, 20: 235–260.

Geertz, Clifford 1973: *The Interpretation of Cultures*. New York: Basic Books.

Girtler, Roland 1992: *Schmuggler – von Grenzen und ihren Überwindern.* Linz: Veritas.

Greverus, Ina Maria 1969: Grenzen und Kontakte. Zur Territorialität des Menschen. In: *Kontakte und Grenzen*. Festschrift für Gerhard Heilfurth. Göttingen. pp. 11–26.

Haller, Dieter 2000: *Gelebte Grenze Gibraltar – Transnationalismus, Lokalität und Identität in kulturanthropologischer Perspektive*. Wiesbaden: Deutscher Universitätsverlag.

Hobsbawm, Eric/Ranger, Terence 1973: *The Invention of Tradition.* Oxford.

Jackson, Michael 1983: Knowledge of the body. In: *MAN* (18) pp. 327–345.

Jackson, Sir William G.F. 1987: *The Rock of the Gibraltarians – A History of Gibraltar*. Farleigh Dickinson U.P., Assoc.Univ. Press.

Jeggle, Utz 1997: Trennen and Verbinden. Warum ist es am Grunde des Rheins so schön? In: Jeggle, Utz/ Raphaël, Freddy: *D'une rive à l'autre – Kleiner Grenzverkehr*. Paris: Ed. de la Maison des sciences de l'homme. pp. 75–91.

Kotek, Joël (ed.) 1996: *L'Europe et ses villes-frontières*. Bruxelles: Editions Complexe.

Kulick, Don 1996: Causing a commotion – Public scandal as resistance among Brazilian transgendered prostitutes. In: *Anthropology Today* Vol. 12, No. 6, pp. 3–6.

McMurray, David A. 1998: *Recognition of State Authority as the Cost of Involvement in Moroccan Border Crime*, paper prepared for Stephanie Kane/ Phil Parnell, Ethnography of Crime.

Medick, Hans 1995: Grenzziehungen und die Herstellung des politisch-sozialen Raumes. Zur Begriffsgeschichte der Grenzen in der Frühen Neuzeit. In: Faber, Richard/Naumann, Barbara (Hgs.): *Literatur der Grenze / Theorie der Grenze*. Würzburg: Königshausen & Neumann. pp. 211–225.

Medick, Hans 1991: Zur politischen Sozialgeschichte der Grenzen in der Neuzeit Europas. In: *Sozialwissenschaftliche Informationen* 20 (3), pp. 157–163.

Müller, Klaus E. 1987: *Das magische Universum der Identität: Elementarformen sozialen Verhaltens*. Frankfurt/Main & New York: Campus.

Nadig, Maya 1998: Transkulturelles symbolisches Verstehen in Übergangsräumen. Ein Beispiel zur Bedeutung der Körpererfahrung im Feldforschungsprozeß. In: *Kea*, Nr 11, pp. 195–206.

Popp, Herbert 1998: EU in Nordafrika – die spanischen Enklaven Ceuta und Melilla. In: *Geographische Rundschau* (50), 6 pp. 337–344.

Rico, Gumersindo 1967: *La Población de Gibraltar (sus origenes, naturaleza y sentido)*. Madrid: Editorial Nacional.

Rosaldo, Renato 1989: *Culture and Truth: The Remaking of Social Analysis*. Boston: Beacon.

Sahlins, Peter 1989: *Boundaries – The Making of France and Spain in the Pyrenees.* Berkeley: University of California Press.

Scarry, Elaine 1985: *The body in pain – The Making and Unmaking of the World*. New York: Oxford University Press.

Scott, James 1990: *Domination and the Arts of Resistance – Hidden Transcripts*. New Haven: Yale University Press.

Simmel, Georg 1992: *Soziologie des Raumes*. In: Schriften zur Soziologie. Berlin[Frankfurt/Main: Suhrkamp (4.Aufl.) 1992: 221–243].

Turner, Victor 1967: Betwixt and Between: The Liminal Period in Rites de Passage. In: *The Forest of Symbols.* Ithaca: Cornell Univerity Press. pp. 93–111.

Turner, Victor 1969: *The Ritual Process: Structure and Anti-Structure*. Chicago: Aldine.

Ulbrich, Claudia 1993: Grenze als Chance? Bemerkungen zur Bedeutung der Reichsgrenze im Saar-Lor-Lux-Raum am Vorabend der Französischen Revolution. In: Pilgram, Arno (Hg.): *Grenzöffnung, Migration, Kriminalität*. Baden-Baden: Nomos. pp. 139–146.

Van Gennep, Arnold 1909: *Les Rites de passage. Etude Systématique des Rites*. Paris [dt. 1986].

Wilson, Thomas M. 1994: Symbolic Dimensions to the Irish Border. In: Donnan and Wilson (eds.): *Border Approaches. Anthropological Perspectives on Frontiers*. Lanham, MD: University Press of America. pp. 101–118.

# Saint Martin

## Communal Identities on a Divided Caribbean Island

*Ank Klomp*

Klomp, Ank 2000: Saint Martin. Communal Identities on a Divided Caribbean Island. – Ethnologia Europaea 30, 2:73–86.

The Caribbean island St Martin, with a land area of about 90 km$^2$, is divided by an international border.[1] The northern part forms an integral part of the French Republic, the southern area belongs to the Netherlands Antilles, an autonomous constituent of the Dutch Kingdom. Despite the partition which exists already for 350 years, St Martiners conceive themselves as one people. A people which shares a language (English), an national anthem, and many interests. In my paper I will describe St Martin as a special borderland case. Special because in this small demarcated space, centre and periphery overlap. The whole of St Martin may be conceived as a borderland. On the other hand St Martin does not stand on its own, each of the two sections of the island forms part of a larger country. In this respect St Martin is like other borderlands, which are the peripheries of larger entities. I will indicate what makes St Martin a unity, and I will indicate that differences between the French and the Dutch part. It will become clear that the impact of the attachment to the centres, the two European states, forms a threat to the unity of the island. This impact increased concomitantly with the move towards unification in Europe. Luckily there are countervailing forces of which the awareness of the local population forms one of the elements.

*Dr Ank Klomp, Department of Cultural Anthropology, POB 80 140, NL-3508 TC Utrecht, the Netherlands. E-mail: A.Klomp@FSS.UU.NL*

'It's Dutch, it's French, it's Caribbean', a tourist slogan once proclaimed. The message is still true: the island Saint Martin is Dutch, French, and Caribbean. The northern area is an integral part of the French Republic, while the south belongs to the Netherlands Antilles, an autonomous constituent of the Dutch Kingdom. However, Saint Martin's most interesting characteristic is its shared 'Caribbean' identity: for notwithstanding a division of more than three hundred and fifty years Saint Martiners still see themselves as one people. They are proud of their unity, 'We are an example to the world' a self-conscious Saint Martiner will say referring to the long-standing peaceful coexistence and not without justification given the fate of other divided islands. But not all Saint Martiners are content with the present situation, some are in favour of a united independence.

International borders have recently received much attention. The reason is clear: they are no longer perceived as fixed and impermeable. The border is inextricably bound up with the fate of the nation state and the nation state is nowadays often confined to the dustbin of history (Creveld 1999, Hobsbawm 1990). Not all agree about its demise, however. Wilson and Donnan (1998:2) stress the continuing importance of the state in shaping the lives of its subjects. According to their viewpoint, "the new politics of identity is in large part determined by the old structure of the state." They propose the development of an anthropology of international borders, an attempt to "integrate seemingly divergent trends in the study of power and culture." They argue that "[T]heir integration in an anthropology of borders resides in the focus on the place and space of visible and literal borders between states, and the symbolic boundaries of identity and culture which make nations and states two very different entities."[2]

Saint Martin is a good case for illuminating

the debate on international borders. On the one hand the border on Saint Martin is like other borders discussed in the literature (Donnan and Wilson 1994, Wilson and Donnan 1998, Rosaldo 1989). The border on Saint Martin, this "twin dependency of other dependencies, [this] double appendage of other peripheries" (Badejo 1990:120), is on the political margins of two (large) states. The French and Dutch governments regulate the daily lives of their subjects on their respective parts of the island. The two Saint Martins are constructed as separate communities by the interventions of the core state to which they belong. The ties which bind each side of Saint Martin to the metropolis create barriers to the unity of the island. This became particularly evident when each metropolitan power stepped up its concern for this distant outpost of the realm concomitant with the process of European unification.

On the other hand Saint Martin is an island, and as an island, and as a (semi)colonial island, it has some specific characteristics. An island is a clearly demarcated space, and in the case of Saint Martin, this is a very small demarcated space indeed, about 90 km$^2$ altogether. Donnan and Wilson's (1994:3) assertion, "that all borders, by their very historical, political and social constructions, serve as barriers of exclusion and protection, marking 'home' from the 'foreign'," does not apply to Saint Martin: the border between French and Dutch Saint Martin does not carry this exclusionary significance. As will be seen below, Saint Martiners do share *'communitas'* and *'societas'* with those at the other side of the border.

This article begins by providing a brief historical background to Saint Martin. I then discuss those elements which are shared by the two Saint Martins and focus on the centripetal tendencies in Saint Martin society. The second part addresses the differences between the two island parts and considers the centrifugal forces. In the third part I review the unity of Saint Martin and speculate about the future.

## Historical Background

The division of Saint Martin dates from the early involvement of the French and the Dutch in the Caribbean. A treaty signed in 1648, giving France the slightly larger portion (56 km$^2$) still forms the basis of the relationship today. Nowadays the border is marked by little more than a hump in the road and friendly signs, written in French on the French side and in English and Dutch on the Dutch side[3], welcoming the visitor. A small monument reminds the visitor of the long friendship between the two sides. There are no border controls. This is remarkable, as the border is an outer EU border: French Saint Martin, as an integral part of France, forms part of the EU, while Dutch Saint Martin, which belongs to the autonomous Netherlands Antilles, is only an associated member. The customs barrier was scrapped when Saint Martin became a free port in 1939.

Although Saint Martin was a plantation island in the past, the climate was too dry for successful agriculture. "Salt, not sugar [—] was king here" as Badejo (1990:121) puts it. But salt was never economically important enough for the island to prosper. After the abolition of slavery (in 1848 on the French part and in 1863 on the Dutch part), plantation agriculture practically ceased and the land was divided up for subsistence farming. The majority of the population are descended from African slaves, most white plantation owners left the island after the abolition. Often people had to go elsewhere to earn a living. The most significant destination for Dutch as well as French Saint Martiners, were the oil refineries, established on Curaçao in 1918 and on Aruba in 1927. The tide turned towards the end of the 1950s, when the opening of the first modern hotel in 1955 marked the beginnings of a tourist boom. In 1994 the island had more than 7,000 hotel rooms, nearly 733 cruise ships dropped their anchor at its harbours, and 627,406 persons passed through the airport (La Guadeloupe 1993:120, and 1996:91–93). Consequently, the population grew rapidly (see Table 1).

Table 1. Population of *Sint Maarten* and *Saint-Martin* (1954–1992).

| *Sint Maarten* | | *Saint-Martin* | |
|---|---|---|---|
| 1954 | 1,597 | 1954 | 3,364 |
| 1972 | 7,807 | 1974 | 6,191 |
| 1981 | 13,156 | 1982 | 8,072 |
| 1992 | 32,221 | 1990 | 29,505 |

Source: Hartog 1981: 123; Census of *Sint Maarten* 1992: 45; Census of *Saint-Martin* 1990: 20.

At the end of the 1950s many Saint Martiners[4], who had migrated to Aruba or Curaçao, returned home, accompanied by their children born on one of the Dutch Leewards.[5] Other migrants began to arrive as well and in large numbers as the figures in table 1 suggest. As a result in 1992 only 30 per cent of the population on *Sint Maarten* was born on the island and only 47,9 per cent was Dutch (Census 1992:47–48). On *Saint-Martin* 45 per cent of the total number of registered inhabitants were French subjects, and of these only 28 per cent are born on *Saint-Martin* (La Guadeloupe 1996:89). On both *Sint Maarten* and *Saint-Martin* most of those without either a Dutch or a French passport come from Haiti, the Dominican Republic and the nearby 'English' islands.

In 1995 two hurricanes struck Saint Martin, causing heavy material damage. This disaster also effected the composition of the population, however this cannot be illustrated by figures.

## Unity, Co-operation and Shared Experiences

The French and Dutch who carved up Saint Martin in 1648, ruled over an empty land. The people who came or were brought to the island over the years were a heterogeneous group, but the mixture was almost identical on both sides. Hartog (1981:130) writes that the population was "ethnically the same in the French and in the Dutch part." Among the whites there were many people of British descent, who came to Saint Martin by way of an English island. The slaves came from Curaçao, St Eustatius, or Guadeloupe, but quite a few also arrived via English islands or North America. Given the anglophone origin of many inhabitants, and the contacts with the surrounding 'English' islands, English of a Creole variety became the mother tongue of all Saint Martiners.

The 'English' influence is also clearly discernible in the religious orientation of Saint Martiners, the majority of whom belong to a Protestant church (Richardson 1996:62). These churches have an all-Saint Martin organization. The Roman Catholic Church is now the largest on both *Sint Maarten* and *Saint-Martin* as most newcomers are Roman Catholics. This church is not organized on a cross-border basis. However the split is, or never was, that serious. French priests with sufficient command of English to preside at mass were difficult to find so Dutch priests were often appointed on the French side. This co-operation on the personal level continues till the present time, irrespective of the national origin of the incumbents. The shared ethnic background, the language, and the religion make Saint Martin in many respects a cultural unity. This cultural unity is expressed in the 'national' anthem: 'Sweet Saint Martin's Land', which is common to both sides. Most political rallies are opened and closed now with the communal singing of this song.

There have always been flourishing social and economic contacts across the border. The treaty of 1648 stipulated that the natural resources of the island should be placed at the disposal of all inhabitants, and that people should be allowed to move freely from one side to the other. These opportunities were well used, in ways foreseen by the treaty, but also by less conventional activities: Saint Martiners became adept at skirting the border.

The exodus to the Dutch Leeward Islands also furthered the mixing of *Sint Maartenaren* and *Saint-Martinois* both through their common experience as *'Ingles'* on Curaçao or Aruba, where Papiamentu is the vernacular, and because the French Saint Martiners send their children to Dutch schools and often obtained Dutch nationality. Most Saint Martiners preferred to go to Aruba because English was spoken at the American EXXON (ESSO) refinery whilst Dutch was spoken at the SHELL plant on Curaçao.

In the 1950s the oil refineries introduced automation and many jobs were scrapped. Luckily on Saint Martin the tourist boom was just about to begin. The Dutch side took the lead and for twenty years dominated touristic developments. The explanation for the difference between the two sides lies in the views of Saint Martin's local leaders. *Sint Maarten's* political leader, the late Dr Claude Wathey, was a staunch advocate of development, of any kind of development. He admired the U.S. and hoped to attract American capital and American visitors. In both respects he was successful. Wathey's counterpart on the French side, Dr Hubert Petit, had other ideals. He wanted to transform *Saint-Martin* into a luxury resort for the privileged few, a *'Petit St.Tropez'* as it was called at the time. His development policy was more restricted and employment opportunities were fewer than on the Dutch side. Consequently, Saint Martiners who returned to the island, be they originally French or Dutch, tended to settle on *Sint Maarten*. Therefore many Saint Martiners who now live on the Dutch side have a 'French' background.

The departure of many to work in the oil refineries and the subsequent economic boom on the Dutch side of the island had other repercussions for the inhabitants. Many *Saint-Martinois* crossed the border to fill the gaps in the *Sint Maarten* labour market or to profit from the newly created jobs. In 1978 about 40% of the French work force was employed on *Sint Maarten* (Bakhuis Report 1978:102).

*Saint-Martin* did not remain oblivious to tourist developments. The Lowlands, the scarcely inhabited Western triangle of the island, was parcelled out for luxury villas. Movie stars, famous singers, and other members of the international jet set bought houses in this area and gave Saint Martin a welcome touch of glamour. Restaurants offering excellent French cuisine opened up in Marigot, the capital of the French side, and especially in the village Grand' Case.

In the 1980s, *Saint-Martin* opened up to large scale tourism and underwent a complete metamorphosis. In 1990 hotels had been built with a total capacity of 3,000 rooms (the Dutch side had a capacity of about 4,000 rooms at that time) and luxurious shopping precincts and large residential areas were constructed in Marigot. The binational character of the island could now be exploited to the full. In the wording of a recent slogan, 'Twice the Vacation, Twice the Fun'. The fact that English is spoken everywhere and the dollar is the most common currency means that language and money problems, which a simple Dutch-French situation might present, simply do not exist. Altogether it is a ticket that makes the island very appealing to the (anglophone) tourist.

The social and economic ties between the two sides can be illustrated in many ways, but one example summarizes it all. Mr Fleming, the present mayor of *Saint-Martin,* was a building contractor before he became *Saint-Martin's* local leader in 1983. As a contractor most of his income came from the Dutch side where the tourist industry began. The mayor still owns two building firms both of which are located on the Dutch side, with a subsidiary branch on French Saint Martin. Mrs Fleming stems from a French Saint Martin family, but she was born on Aruba, where her parents had migrated to work at the EXXON refinery. She studied in Aruba and in the Netherlands (and later in the U.S.A.). With her teaching certificate she returned to the island of her parents, and found a job at the Dutch side, becoming the headmistress of a school there. The Flemings used to live on the Dutch side, but they moved across the border before the municipal elections of 1989, as the mayor had been criticized for his living 'abroad.'

## Foreign Immigrants

As mentioned earlier, Saint Martin harbours a substantial number of foreigners (i.e. people who have neither French nor Dutch nationality). Table 2 sets out the growth of the most numerous groups.[6]

Table 2. Origins and numbers of the largest groups of foreigners on *Sint Maarten/Saint-Martin*.

| | *Sint Maarten* | | *Saint-Martin* | |
|---|---|---|---|---|
| | 1981 | 1992 | 1981 | 1990 |
| Dominican Republic | 124 | 4,111 | 144 | 3,046 |
| Haiti | 462 | 3,871 | 631 | 7,157 |
| Dominica | ? | 1,590 | 222 | 1,099 |
| St.Kitts/ Nevis | ? | 1,487 | 168 | ? |

Source: *Sint Maarten,* Census 1992; *Saint-Martin* Monnier 1983: 56, Census Guadeloupe 1990.

As we see, the same immigrant groups predominate on *Sint Maarten* and *Saint-Martin*. Timmer (1994:15,17) notes that both the Haitians and those from the Dominican Republic intend to stay for more than ten years on the island. This makes them look like permanent residents, who will probably follow a transnational lifestyle (Basch, Glick Schiller and Szanton Blanc 1994). Both these groups have their own associations on the island and membership is organized on a cross-border basis. Dominicans and Kittians are also organized and I presume that the pattern of interactions with regard to the border will not differ from those of the Haitians and Dominican Republicans.

The foreign immigrants play a crucial part in Saint Martin's economy. They supply the hotels, restaurants and other tourist facilities with cheap labour and provide a welcome solution to Saint Martin domestic problems, cleaning the homes and minding the children. Altogether it seems not too far-fetched to conclude that the foreign immigrants help to bind the two Saint Martins together. The one proviso to this relates to the large number of Haitians on the French side. This point will be addressed later in the section on differences.

## Americanization

Saint Martin is one of the most americanized islands in the Caribbean, being not so very different from the U.S. Virgin Islands. Americanization has been an uneven and protracted process, affecting Saint Martiners in different ways and at different times. We can distinguish at least four aspects of this process.

First, there is a history of migration from Saint Martin to the U.S. In the first half of the 20th century a considerable number of Saint Martiners settled permanently in the U.S. Many of them were sailors who found a job on shore. Migrants from the French side often retained their French nationality, even though they may have lived many years in the U.S. and have acquired American citizenship. Some still vote in *Saint-Martin* elections either in person or by proxy. The main candidates for *Saint-Martin* always visit the U.S. and American Saint Martiners help to run the campaign. There exists an American-*Saint-Martin* friendship society, i.e. a club which unites the emigrants with the people on their island of origin. Such intensive organized contacts do not exist on the Dutch side, but Dutch Saint Martiners have other vital links with the U.S. as many do their advanced studies there.

Second, there is the fact that following the opening of the EXXON refinery on Aruba in 1927 many Saint Martiners have been employed by an American company. On Aruba Saint Martiners underwent an important learning experience in what they understood the U.S. to stand for: modernity, efficiency, wealth.

Third, U.S. citizens and companies played a very important role in the development of tourism and in the 'hospitality industry' in general. The boom in the 1960s and 1970s on *Sint Maarten* was mostly based on American investment. Both sides have American residents (Monnier 1983:56, Timmer 1994:23,24). According to Timmer, on the Dutch side nearly 50 per cent of the Americans are managers and business owners, the highest proportion of any other group on the Dutch side.

Fourth, there is the general phenomenon of U.S. cultural hegemony. As the U.S. cultural influence grew across the globe, its popularity was reflected in Saint Martin. Dutch Saint Martin even applied for the Puerto Rican status of 'free associated state' of the U.S., a request which was politely ignored (Badejo 1990:139). Today most of the news on Saint Martin comes from U.S. sources. Large transistor radios can pick up the U.S. stations, and satellite television enables Saint Martiners to follow popular U.S. programmes. As the majority of the tourists stem from the U.S., they tend to set the scene as far as style of dress and hotel culture is concerned, especially on the Dutch side. The importance of the dollar was mentioned already.

The long and positively evaluated association with the U.S. helps to bind the two Saint Martins culturally. To be called 'American' is generally liked on Saint Martin, it makes one feel good, it stands for money and modernity. (Being identified as 'English' does not have such a positive connotation, being associated with the impoverished Caribbean 'English' islands.)

While Americanization has gone further on the Dutch side, *"l'insidieuse américanisation,"* (Monnier 1983:46) has not left *Saint-Martin* untouched. Monnier, an Euro-French geographer, visited *Saint-Martin* before it turned to large scale tourism. He expresses concern about the Americanization of French territory, not only because of cultural factors – Monnier (1983:114,120) recommends *"[L]a qualité, le bon goût français"*, as a remedy to *"[la] banalisation de l'île"* – but also because of what he perceives to be lost economic opportunities for France. He would certainly be more at ease with changes in the 1980s when metropolitan France rediscovered *Saint-Martin*. In the 1990s the European Dutch also intensified their interest in *Sint Maarten*, not so much because they worried about 'good taste,' no matter how defined, but because they were concerned about 'good governance,' and thought that *Sint Maarten* could use a metropolitan push in the right direction.

## Differences and Centrifugal Forces

Saint Martin has been advertised as 'Delightfully Dutch' and 'Fantastically French', but nowadays it is 'A Little European' and 'A Lot of Caribbean': to stress Frenchness and Dutchness is no longer fashionable. The question arises of just how French and Dutch is each part of Saint Martin? In answer, one can say that the French side is notably more French than the Dutch side is Dutch. This is a reflection of the difference in administrative status, but historical chance also plays a part in explaining this dissimilarity. The economic efflorescence of southern Saint Martin began at a time when the Netherlands was not much interested in the last remnants of the colonial domain. By contrast *Saint-Martin* began to develop its tourist industry in the beginning of the 1980s, a time when metropolitan interest in the island was increasing. There is more to explain the uneven impact of the two metropolises. Globally France and the French language have more prestige than the Netherlands and Dutch. In the popular imagination it is more *chic* to be French and to speak French, than to be Dutch and speak Dutch. Furthermore France pursues an explicitly nationalistic cultural policy, of which the promotion of the French language is an important strand. This concern for cultural and linguistic purity is not found in the Netherlands.[7]

The cultural differences between the two metropolitan powers and its implications for local identities were already noted in the 1950s. The Keurs write: "It is notable that if one asks the native of French Saint Martin what he is, he will say, 'French,' but the Dutch are more likely to say, 'a St.Maartener'. When any conflict arises, however, he is proud to be 'Dutch' (Keur and Keur 1960:274).

### *Saint-Martin, the Relationship with France and Guadeloupe*

*Saint-Martin* forms part of the department of Guadeloupe, one of the overseas departments of the French Republic. The tie with the metropolis is reflected in several ways. Marigot, with its *Hôtel de Ville* and *Palais de Justice* is "unmistakably Gallic" (Block 1991:193). French is the sole official language on the French side and the sole language of instruction. English is only taught as a foreign language at high school level. This means that only a tiny minority of the *Saint-Martinois* learns to write English, the mother tongue of the population. For higher or specialized education *Saint-Martinois* go to Guadeloupe or to European France.

France was never much interested in this 'speck on the map', where people neither spoke French nor 'proper' English. French interest amounted to little more than sending out a few officials to run the place, and a handful of private citizens who opened restaurants. The main changes came in the 1980s. Albert Fleming, who became mayor in 1983, aimed to develop *Saint-Martin* as a tourist resort just as *Sint Maarten* had become. Fortuitously, in 1986 the metropolitan French government introduced a tax incentive programme to stimulate French investment in the DOM-TOM, the *départements* and *territoires d'outre-mer*. This programme, which was intended to stimulate DOM-TOM economy, fulfilled another aim as well. When the borders of the EU member states were opened to all EU citizens on the 1st January 1993, French metropolitans (*métros*) were already well-established in the overseas territories. This new policy was a great success on *Saint-Martin* and is reflected in the pervasive French economic and cultural influence. *Métro* investments helped to build the new *Saint-Martin*. A few big business names are *Saint-Martinois*, as are the largest landowners, but nearly all the new hotels are in the hands of *métro* companies, as are many of the new shops. The *métros* are also found in the professions and in the administration. Competition from *métros* is particularly keenly felt by the smaller local enterprises for not all French incomers are well-to-do. Some spent their last penny to settle on the island. One wonders whether there is a group of *'petits blancs'* in the making.

In 1990 about 8 per cent of the French subjects on *Saint-Martin* were born in metropolitan France (La Guadeloupe 1996:89). There are however more *métros* on *Saint-Martin* than the figures show. Not all metropolitans are registered on the island, some because they see their stay as temporary, while others commute between Europe and the Caribbean. Nor are the statistics an accurate measure of influence. While there may be only a handful of *métros* in the whole administration, this handful occupies pivotal positions. For instance, the developments in the 1980s were steered by SEMSAMAR (*Société d'Economie Mixte de Saint-Martin*) the *Saint-Martin* development company. SEMSAMAR was led by a *métro*.

The *Saint-Martinois* are ambivalent about the increased presence of the European French on their island. Most French Saint Martiners have never been attracted to independence. For many, the connection with France means being part of a big, modern and democratic country and is felt as a form of security. Belonging to France also means financial help and better opportunities for higher education. Moreover 'France' stands for culture and glamour: to be French, to speak French, elevates one's status. The policy which stimulated the arrival of the *métros* also brought new opportunities, progress and modernity to *Saint-Martin*. France, for its part, did not question the existing relationship: the departments of Guadeloupe, Martinique and Guyana are part and parcel of the French Republic. Nevertheless, there are signs of unrest on northern Saint Martin as seen in the associations which have sprung up to protect the interest of local businessmen, and local people and culture in general. The main association is SMECO which stands for 'Saint Martin Educational and Cultural Organization'. SMECO is in the first place a cultural organization, but a subject like '*Saint-Martin* identity,' cannot be separated off from a discussion of the position on the labour market of the 'sons and daughters of the soil.' The main issue addressed by SMECO is the tie with France and the resulting influx of *métros*. The right of free entry to *Saint-Martin* of European French citizens, and after 'Schengen' of other EU citizens is greatly resented. When asked to reach a final assessment however, the verdict of the *Saint-Martinois* is clear: Mayor Fleming, who is seen as the main instigator of developments, has been re-elected twice.

The *métros* are not the only French subjects on *Saint-Martin*, about 9 per cent of the French citizens originates from one of the other French Antilles (La Guadeloupe 1996:89). Among them the Guadeloupeans form the large majority. At the beginning of the 1980s Guadeloupeans formed the target for local action groups, who charged them with taking jobs and houses away from *Saint-Martinois*. This charge was later dropped as the focus shifted to new groups of competitors, such as *métros*. *Saint-Martin's* administrative subjugation to Guadeloupe is another matter. This relationship is disliked, perceived more as a hindrance than as a help, and many people would prefer to have a direct line to France.

Another group of francophones, the Haitians, have already been referred to and identified as one of the unifying factors on Saint Martin. That is certainly not wrong, however in Euro-French eyes they are perceived differently. In the government report on the hurricanes (Ouragans Luis et Marilyn 1995:14) their contribution to *Saint-Martin's* GNP and to the recovery effort is singled out for praise. The report continues: "They are without doubt the cause of the revival of the French language on the island, whereas only a few years ago English was mostly used" (my translation). It is not implausible to interpret the official acceptance on *Saint-Martin* of more than 7,000 Haitians as part of the French policy to strengthen the position of the French language on the island. It means the Haitians play a double role in defining identity. They not only make the French side more French, but by building bridges with Dutch Saint Martin, they contribute towards the maintenance of an island-wide identity.

*Sint Maarten: Relations with the Netherlands and the Netherlands Antilles*

Since Aruba left the federation (1986), the Netherlands Antilles consist of five so-called 'island territories': the Windward Islands of *Sint Maarten*, Saba and St Eustatius, and the Leeward Islands of Curaçao and Bonaire. The autonomy enjoyed by the Dutch Antilles has a real significance. For instance, the Netherlands Antilles and Aruba are not integrated in the EU, but are associated members. Another important point concerns the regulations relating to settlement: Euro-Dutch persons need a residence permit for the islands, this notwithstanding the fact that inhabitants of the Antilles with a Dutch passport have free access to the Netherlands.

With respect to cultural identity, it is rather hard to define what is Dutch about the Dutch side. There is not anything which could be characterized as a Dutch atmosphere on *Sint Maarten* and the Dutch language is rarely heard. A 'dead language' in the opinion of Saint Martin linguist Richardson (1983:64). Indeed, *Sint Maarten* is more American than Dutch, having "given itself wholeheartedly to American tourist culture" (Block 1991:193). Normally the Dutchness of *Sint Maarten* is only invoked to attract tourists. A shopping centre, constructed in the 1980s, has gables (painted in pink and yellow), and squares and streets are given such names as 'Rembrandtplein', or 'Van Goghstraat'. A windmill has long formed one of *Sint Maarten's* attractions.

Both Dutch and English are officially used, as on the sign for the local government in Philipsburg: '*Bestuursgebouw*/Administration Building.' Dutch is used in all official correspondence, especially where Willemstad (Curaçao) or the Hague are involved. At the local level English is normally used. Dutch is the official language of instruction, at least after the two first classes of the elementary school. But over the last twenty years the use of English has increased in schools and some schools teach only in English. English is taught as a (foreign) language in all schools. For further studies people go to Curaçao or to the Netherlands. Those who can afford it often send their children to the U.S.A. and the *Sint Maarten* administration also provides scholarships for the U.S. This means that there are well-educated *Sint Maartenaren* who have hardly any knowledge of Dutch or the Netherlands. Recently, however, Dutch has been regaining ground. In 1994 one elementary school reintroduced Dutch as the sole language of instruction in all classes.

The fluctuating fortunes of the Dutch language on *Sint Maarten* reflect the fluctuating relationship between the Netherlands towards its overseas territories. At the end of the 1960s Holland proposed independence to the Antilles, in line with its view that 'colonies' were a thing of the past. However, this proposal was not well-received in the 'colony' itself and delaying tactics were successfully applied. In 1989 the Hague declared that independence was no longer on the agenda. This U-turn was never really explained but the EU may well have played a part. As was the case in France, the Netherlands may have realised that within the context of the common market, the Antilles could become an asset rather than a liability. The islands are often referred to as a stepping stone to the Latin American continent. The sudden benevolence had a price: a larger voice for the Netherlands in local affairs. For instance, the access of Euro-Dutch in the Antilles had to be enlarged or no longer subject to restraint. More influence of the Netherlands is not what the Antilles see as in their interest, they want to remain as autonomous as possible. At the time of writing, nothing has been decided yet concerning the future relations within the Kingdom.

The new involvement of the Netherlands had a decisive influence on *Sint Maarten. Sint Maarten* had a bad name, being linked to drug-related crime, and its administration being accused of corruption, and misgovernment. The complaints dated from the 1970s, but no action was ever taken. In 1992, however, *Sint Maarten* was put under a form of legal restraint, the most extreme form of intervention provided in the regulations of the Kingdom. After *Sint Maarten* became a ward of court, the Hague sent police officers, tax officials, judges and other personnel to improve administrative proceedings.

According to the latest census (1992), 5,6 per cent of the Dutch subjects on *Sint Maarten* are born in the Netherlands. The majority plans to leave after a short stay on the island (Timmer 1994:22). The number of metropolitan Dutch on *Sint Maarten* has always been small. They include a handful of business people, among whom were one or two big names, and others like teachers, who took up jobs for which local people were not then available. How the latest developments influenced the figures could not be established.

In the past most *Sint Maartenaren* were pleased to have Dutch citizenship, which was perceived as a guarantee of legal security and political stability, opportunities for higher education and financial support. This situation has not changed, but the number of people who are dissatisfied with the present situation has increased and support for independence is growing. In 1998 15 per cent voted in favour of independence compared to 6.24 per cent in 1994 (Oostindie & Verton 1998:161). There are several reasons for this change of heart. Many people experienced the intervention by the Netherlands (and Curaçao as its representative) in 1992 as an insult, even if a few people believed the charges to be unfounded. These recent events are grist to the mill of people already dissatisfied with the status quo. Some time before the Euro-Dutch intervention in *Sint Maarten* an organization 'We fo We' was set up to protect the interests of the local people, especially business people. 'We fo We' condemned the imposition of legal restraint as colonialism. These are not the only signs of discontent. Lasana M. Sekou (the pseudonym of H.H. Lake) a *Sint Maarten* or better Saint Martin poet and newspaper editor is the driving force behind a group of people from both sides of the island who are struggling for an independent and united Saint Martin. Lasana's position is ideological: 'colonies' belong to the past and the colonial border has to disappear (Sekou 1996, Sekou, Francis and Gumbs 1990). Due to his efforts Saint Martin now also has its own flag.

*Sint Maarten's* connection to Curaçao has only been mentioned in passing and the presence on southern Saint Martin of many Curaçaoans has not been referred to at all. The bond between *Sint Maarten* and Curaçao resembles the relations between *Saint-Martin* and Guadeloupe. Curaçao has always been the most important island of the Netherlands Antilles, so it played something of the role of a metropolis to the other islands. Unlike the situation on *Saint-Martin*, the low profile of the Euro-Dutch until recently meant that the brunt of local resentment of external influence was borne by Curaçao and the Curaçaoans. The presence of Curaçao is felt directly as 2,100 people on *Sint Maarten* were born on Curaçao (Timmer 1994:14), by far the most numerous group of immigrants with a Dutch passport. For Curaçaoans *Sint Maarten* is their own country, they do not need anybody's permission to come and go. Papiamentu is often heard in the streets of Philipsburg and also in offices, at the banks, and other enterprises, as many Curaçaoans hold jobs in the civil service and in other white collar employment. They also figure prominently in the police force. Curaçaoans are generally better educated and better paid than *Sint Maartenaren*, educational facilities being more advanced on Curaçao than on *Sint Maarten*. Timmer also found that 39 per cent has the intention to stay more than ten years on *Sint Maarten*.[8]

In general the Curaçaoans are not liked on

Saint Martin. Amongst other negative stereotypes, they are seen as arrogant. The problem lies in the division of roles. When Saint Martiners lived on Curaçao they generally belonged to the lowest stratum of Curaçao society. Yet now on their own island, the Curaçaoans are seen to have the upper hand and *Sint Maartenaren* to be subordinate to them.

In recent years *Sint Maarten's* relationship with the Netherlands Antilles has been the subject of debate as it has been many times in history. *Sint Maartenaren* did not like the idea of being subjugated to Curaçao without the Dutch umbrella. The Dutch decision to retain ties with the Antilles has modified the situation somewhat. Nevertheless, in 1994 only 60 per cent of *Sint Maartenaren* voted in favour of a continued relation with the Netherlands Antilles, i.e. Curaçao. This was not a very positive result, especially when it is borne in mind that part of the electorate is from Curaçao. At the end of the 1990s the number of people in favour of the Netherlands Antilles had dropped even further to 41 per cent (Oostindie & Verton 1998:161).

## The Border Redefined

Saint Martin's economic development has an important implication for the island: it served to redefine and enhance the border. The accompanying influx of Dutch subjects to southern Saint Martin, and the French subjects to northern Saint Martin had the effect of strengthening the different cultural identities on each side of the border. These changes are more evident on the French side where the use of French has increased considerably, and where some parts are predominantly white and French speaking. A Dutch Saint Martiner experiences these new *métro* precincts as a foreign country.

Turning to the Dutch side, the division opened up by the inflow of Dutch subjects, particularly those from Curaçao, is also apparent. The dislike of *Sint Maartenaren* for the Curaçaoans is shared by the *Saint-Martinois*. When asked about the Dutch side of the island, *Saint-Martinois* will immediately tell you that they do not like all those Curaçaoans, who treat them like strangers and with whom they have nothing in common. The Euro-Dutch are less visible than their Euro-French counterparts as they usually speak English, do not dominate business, and are not concentrated in specific residential areas.

The attitude of the *métros* and Guadeloupeans towards the Dutch side, depends partly on their level of ease with the English language. They do not cross the border very often. Some only make use of the banks on the Dutch side, and then insist on having an interpreter when doing business there.

For those from Curaçao *Saint-Martin* has always been experienced as 'abroad,' a feeling which has intensified the more French it has become. Only the very sophisticated among them will pluck up the courage to enter the *métro* enclaves. The Euro-Dutch perceive French Saint Martin in terms of a holiday resort, somewhere where you go for a shopping spree or a nice dinner. They know as little or as much about the French side as people usually know about their vacation destination.

Recent developments still had an other effect. In the past it has always been the Dutch side which was economically better off, *Saint Martin* was the dependent partner. French involvement in *Saint-Martin* has changed that and nowadays *Sint Maarten* and *Saint-Martin* are almost at equal footing. Only in a few respects *Saint-Martin* is still dependent on *Sint Maarten*. *Saint-Martin* has only a very small airstrip so nearly all tourists land at the international airport on the Dutch side. The large cruise ships, whose passengers disperse over the whole island, nearly all anchor in *Sint Maarten's* Great Bay. Yet *Saint-Martin* has some advantages over *Sint Maarten*. Whilst *Sint Maarten's* development followed the 'free play of market forces,' careful planning in *Saint-Martin* left some rural areas unspoiled, creating a beautiful natural backdrop to the more urbanized localities. Furthermore, the new architecture has an attractive West-Indian appeal. When the many development plans are fully realized, it is not inconceivable that the pecking order between the two sides of the island will be reversed. That will put the relationship between the two Saint Martins to the test, in a situation where not only because of the immigration of Dutch and French 'nationals' the two Saint Martins are growing somewhat apart, but also because population growth as such made each side more self-supporting in the social and technical sense.

## Unity Reconsidered

Saint Martin, that "curious anomaly from the colonial past" (Block 1991:193) is remarkable for its long sustained cultural and social unity. What makes this island different from other divided islands?

Common sense would lead one to think of its small size as an explanation. Certainly smallness removes practical barriers to unity. Saint Martin's relative global marginality – a factor not unrelated to size – has also played a role. A more active colonial interest in the past might have resulted in widening the gap or abolishing the border altogether. Yet smallness in itself is not sufficient, for after all people also quarrel in mini arenas.

We have to look to history to understand how Saint Martin has evaded the fate of some other divided islands: its shared 'ethnic' background, the benevolent partition treaty, and the accident of English becoming the vernacular. Being the tongue of neither of the two colonial powers, it served as a neutral vehicle for communication. Its position on the island is strengthened both by the global status of English and of the U.S., a country which is most admired on both sides of the border. As the U.S. never exercised formal political control over Saint Martin, no (past) colonial connections complicate or cloud the relationship.

The relationship between Saint Martin and its respective metropolitan and regional powers has been described as the main centrifugal force on the island. There can be little doubt about this effect. Yet one might wonder what the situation would be without the 'external' powers. May be their influence is more contradictory: two independent Saint Martins might have more difficulty sticking together. Now they are never (completely) responsible for the decisions made, there are always others to blame.

Wilson and Donnan (1998) analyze international borders as a tool with which to discriminate state from nation. Normally it is the nation not the state which is the elusive entity.[9] What would being a nation mean for Saint Martiners? It is clear that this feeling excludes France and the Netherlands, Guadeloupe and Curaçao: their interference is always felt as the interference of outsiders. The kind of emotion aroused by 'nationhood' does express something of the feelings Saint Martiners have for their island, notwithstanding their 'moving roots' (Richardson 1997), and their eschewal of independence. In fact the loyalty is more established now that Saint Martin is able to feed the 'sons and daughters of the soil.' Of course for Dutch Saint Martiners *Sint Maarten* is more 'home' than French Saint Martin and the other way round, but this does not harm the idea of a community which includes the whole island.

Saint Martin is one of the many cases which challenges the territoriality of the state (see the other articles in this collection and i.a. Donnan and Wilson 1994 , Wilson and Donnan 1998). We have to learn to understand the territoriality of the state as a relative notion. Saint Martin also shows that this state of affairs has already a long history, which cannot be simply attributed to such modern phenomena as globalization.

It is interesting to speculate about how many 'imagined communities,' to use Anderson's (1991) term in a somewhat liberal way, will co-exist in the future, three as in the past? Two, given the renewed interest in the island by France and the Netherlands? Or one, born from a unified Saint Martin? Certainly the political unity of Saint Martin is not on the cards for the time being. As neither *Sint Maartenaren* nor *Saint-Martinois* want to become independent the border between French and Dutch Saint Martin is likely to remain. There will continue to be two Saint Martins, but what about the third dimension, the shared cross-border identity? Paradoxically, we saw that the unification of Europe had the effect of emphasizing cultural differences between the two sides of the island.

Will the emancipation of the French side, which came about by the injection of *métro* investment, destroy the harmony between them? It seems unlikely. In the first place because there are no old scores to settle, French Saint Martiners like to be equal to the Dutch side, but there are no ill feelings about the past. Secondly, the business advantages to be gained from the present situation do include Euro-French enterprises. The foreign migrants were mentioned. Many of the newcomers already have a residence and a work permit. Over time many will acquire full civil rights, and then continue to link the two parts of the island.

With respect to the impact of Americanization, this global cultural influence is likely to grow and affect both sides of the island. Officially and unofficially English is gaining in importance, despite the presence of Euro-French on *Saint-Martin* and the passage of the *loi Toubon* (see note 7). Paradoxically, we saw that the unification of Europe had the effect of emphasizing cultural differences between the two sides of the island. Competition within the EU regional bloc is real, yet there is also evidence of co-operation between enterprises from different member states. Co-operation between France and the Netherlands with respect to Saint Martin barely exists. Yet agreement between France and the Netherlands on the status of Saint Martin has been made necessary by the terms of the Maastricht and Schengen treaties. *Saint-Martin* is part of the single European market and thereby an area where people and goods from Europe can circulate freely, while *Sint Maarten* with its autonomous status can still restrict the entrance of migrants and goods from Europe. If *Saint-Martin* were to be included in a EU tax regime, the differences with freeport *Sint Maarten* would create substantial inequalities. Moreover the border should have to be controlled, which is inconceivable on present-day Saint Martin.

Formal cross-border co-operation is as yet not much developed. As far as organizations such as SMECO and 'We fo We' are concerned, co-operation is generally restricted to cultural affairs, such as joint musical, theatrical, and literary meetings. Yet, there are examples of joint action, and one concerns the very symbol of unity on Saint Martin, the border monument. It happened in 1989. The border monument, a simple pillar with an inscription, was erected in 1948 to commemorate three hundred years of friendly coexistence. It is located at the frontier on the western road connecting Marigot (*Saint-Martin*) with Philipsburg (*Sint Maarten*). To the south of the monument a new tourist attraction was planned. The project included the construction of an eighteen hole golf-course, with sixteen holes on the Dutch side and two holes on the French side. Presumably it was thought that the idea of hitting a golf ball from the Netherlands Antilles into France would inspire many a golfer. However, putting this plan into practice meant replacing the border monument. This proposal caused such indignation throughout Saint Martin that a protest march was organized. It was a great success: the monument remained and the golf-course had to be redesigned. It was a remarkable protest: the symbol of Saint Martin's unity should not be touched. It shows exactly what Saint Martiners want: continued peaceful coexistence.

## Notes

1. Fieldwork on Saint Martin took place in 1984, 1998, and 1990. The author, Euro Dutch, stayed in the French part in 1984 and 1989, and in the Dutch part in 1990. She would like to acknowledge the support of the University of Utrecht in funding this research. She is also grateful to Paul van der Grijp, Wim Hoogbergen, Diana Kay, Dirk Kruijt, Françoise Marsaudon, Bill Maurer and Bonno Thoden van Velzen for their helpful comments on an earlier draft.
2. The idea of an 'anthropology of borders' was first proposed in an earlier publication (Donnan and Wilson 1994).
3. Not all Saint Martiners approve of the terms 'French' and 'Dutch Saint Martin' as they sound too colonialist for their liking. They prefer 'northern' and 'southern' to distinguish the parts. In this article I will use the different terms indiscriminately, besides others such as the French *Saint-Martin* and the Dutch *Sint Maarten*. I will ignore the often employed description 'St.Maarten/ St.Martin' for the whole island and simply use 'Saint Martin.'
4. In this article the figures relating to Saint Martiners refer to people born on Saint Martin and with either French or Dutch nationality (or both). Needless to say, these 'statistical' Saint Martiners do not exactly overlap with those who feel they are Saint Martiners and are considered to be such by others. My discussion refers to these ethnic Saint Martiners and the statistics are drawn only to give some indication of their number. Also see note 8.
5. I have followed local usage here, 'Leeward' includes Aruba, Curaçao and Bonaire, and 'Windward' Saint Martin, Saba, and Saint Eustatius.

6. These figures underestimate the number of foreign residents on the island. Whilst the *Sint Maarten* census aims to include all inhabitants, whether documented or not, this does not ensure that all the residents are counted. On *Saint-Martin* only legal residents are counted.
7. One exemple serves by way of illustration. In France the 'loi Toubon,' which was passed in 1994 and named after the Minister of Culture and Francophonie, aims to protect the French language from corruption by foreign, especially English influences. Around the same time in Holland the Minister of Education proposed that university courses should be taught in English. Although the proposal was not accepted, there are no strong objections against the use of English (or other languages) for teaching purposes.
8. There are also quite a few Arubans among the Papiamentu speakers on Sint Maarten. In 1992 they numbered 1,900 (Timmer 1994:13). Among these are many people who are ethnic Saint Martiners, being the children of Saint Martin parents who migrated to Aruba at the time the EXXON refinery created many jobs. Other Arubans arrived in the 1980s after the EXXON refinery island closed down and independence loomed. The people who are born on Aruba surpass the Curaçaoans when it comes to education and pay and are only inferior to the Euro-Dutch in this respect.
9. I am assuming here that Sint Maarten belongs to the Dutch state, an assumption which is debatable. The Antilles are no longer recognized by the UN as being colonial.

## References


Anderson, B. 1994: *Imagined Communities. Reflections on the Origins and the Spread of Nationalism.* London: Verso.

Badejo, F. 1990: Sint Maarten: the Dutch Half in Future Perspective. In: Sedoc-Dahlberg, B. (ed.) *The Dutch Caribbean. Prospects for Democracy.* New York etc.: Gordon and Breach: 119–151.

Bakhuis, D. 1978: *Rapport van de commissie van onderzoek Bovenwindse eilanden.* Voorzitter: D. Bakhuis.

Basch, L., Glick Schiller, N. and C. Szanton Blanc 1994: *Nations, Transnational Projects, Postcolonial Predicaments and Deterritorialized Nation-State.* Australia etc.: Gordon and Breach Publishers.

Block, A. 1991: *Masters of Paradise: Organised Crime and the Internal Revenue Service in the Bahamas.* New Brunswick, New Jersey: Transaction Publishers.

Census *Sint Maarten* see: Volks- en Woningtelling.

Census *Saint-Martin* see: Recensement et Résultats.

Creveld, M. van 1999: *The Rise and Decline of the State.* Cambridge: Cambridge University Press.

Donnan, H. and T.M. Wilson (eds.) 1994 *Border Approaches: Anthropological Perspectives on Frontiers.* Lanham: University Press of America.

Guadeloupe, La 1993, 1996: Rapport Annuel. Paris: Institut d'Emission des Départements d'Outre-Mer.

Hartog, J. 1981: *History of Sint Maarten and Saint Martin.* Sint Maarten, N.A.: The Sint Maarten Jaycees.

Hobsbawm, E. 1990: *Nations and Nationalisms since 1780s: Programme, Myth, Reality.* Cambridge: Cambridge University Press.

Keur, J.Y. and D.L. Keur 1960: *Windward Children. A Study in Human Ecology of the Three Dutch Windward Islands in the Caribbean.* Assen: Royal Van Gorcum LTD.

Monnier, Y. 1983: *"L'immuable et le changeant", étude de la partie française de Saint-Martin.* Bordeaux: CRET et CEGET.

Oostindie, G. & P. Verton 1998: *Ki sorto di Reino? What kind of Kingdom? Visies en verwachtingen van Antillianen en Arubanen omtrent het Koninkrijk.* Den Haag: Sdu Uitgevers.

Ouragans Luis and Marilyn 1995: Rapport de mission 17 au 23 septembre 1995. Ministère du Logement. Direction de l'Habitat et de la Construction. Direction Départementale de l'Equipement. Guadeloupe.

Recensement général de la population de 1990. 1990 Evolutions démographiques 1975 – 1982 – 1990. Départments – arrondisements, communes – unités urbaines. Départments d'outre-mer. Paris: Institut national de la statistique et des études économiques.

Richardson, L. 1983: The sociolinguistic situation in St Martin. In: Carrington, L.D. (ed.) *Studies in Caribbean Language.* Society for Caribbean Linguistics: 63–70.

Richardson, B. 1996: Ancestor. Une Etude d'Histoire & d'Anthropologie Culturelle de l'île de Saint-Martin. Unpublished Thesis. Paris/Saint-Martin.

Richardson, B. 1997: Interview in *The St Maarten Guardian.* July 25–26.

Rosaldo, R. 1989: *Culture & Truth. The Remaking of Social Analysis.* Boston: Beacon Press.

Sekou, L.M. (ed.) 1996 (1990): *National Symbols of St. Martin. A Primer.* House of Nehesi Publishers. St. Martin, Caribbean.

Sekou, L.M., Francis, O. and N. Gumbs 1990: *The Independence Papers. Readings on a New Political Status for St Maarten / St Martin.* House of Nehesi. St. Maarten, Caribbean.

Timmer, M. 1994: Ethnicity on St Maarten: Key or Obstacle? Research into the Ethnic Organization of a Timesharing Resort on St. Maarten *N.A.* Undergraduate Thesis. University Utrecht.

*Volks- en Woningtelling.* 1993: Derde Algemene Volks- en Woningtelling Nederlandse Antillen. Toestand per 27 januari 1992. Willemstad: Centraal Bureau voor de Statistiek.

Wilson, T.M. and H. Donnan (eds.) 1998: *Border Identities. Nation and State at International Frontiers.* Cambridge University Press.

# Crossing the Spanish-Moroccan Border with Migrants, New Islamists, and Riff-Raff

*Ninna Nyberg Sørensen*

Sørensen, Ninna Nyberg 2000: Crossing the Spanish-Moroccan Border with Migrants, New Islamists, and Riff-Raff. – Ethnologia Europaea 30, 2: 87–100.

Practices of movement between Morocco and Spain have for centuries been a common economic, social and political livelihood strategy for thousands of individuals and families inhabiting the border area of Tetuán/Yebala, Morocco. However, only few studies have approached the border as object for anthropological inquiry. This essay analyses the Spanish-Moroccan border from the perspective of three male crossers, as well as from the perspective of Spanish and Moroccan ethno-landscaping in Tetuán. I argue that the common Tetuáni ambivalence towards Spain as well as towards the Spanish Protectorate era must be understood within the wider context of the impress of the Moroccan state on Northern Moroccan identities.

*Ninna Nyberg Sørensen, Senior Researcher, PhD, Centre for Development Research, Gammel Kongevej 5, DK-1610 Copenhagen V, Denmark. E-mail: nns@cdr.dk*

In a 1998 article, Henk Driessen points to the celebration of 1992 – including the celebration of the European integration process, the commemoration of the 1492 discovery of America, and the remembrance of the 1492 fall of the Muslim kingdom of Granada – to highlight the irony of the fact that 1992 became the year in which North African clandestine migration to Europe broke all records (Driessen 1998). Since 1992, however, much effort has been put into controlling Europe's southern sea-border and border towns on the southern shore. In 1993, the European Union decided to build an 8 kilometres long defensive wall around Ceuta, the Spanish enclave in northern Morocco, consisting of two parallel wire fences, 2.5 metres high, 5 metres apart, and with a line of sensors between the wires. Although this defence line is no more than a term in the same game that sets clandestine migrants against wealthy countries further North ... that has to be reached and surmounted (Harding 2000), it has become exceedingly difficult and expensive for North Africans to cross the border to Europe. Those who manage to beat European border controls find themselves in steadily deteriorating working and living conditions in Europe. At the same time a growing number of persons who had hoped for better lives elsewhere find themselves stuck in Morocco.

In this essay I wish to analyse the Spanish-Moroccan border as seen from Tetuán, a northern Moroccan city. I will use the narratives of three male border crossers to reflect upon past and recent changes in this particular borderland. Together with the large majority of Tetuán inhabitants, these young men share a critical view on Spain and Spaniards, simultaneously as their symbolic resistance towards the Moroccan state and the former King Hassan II is expressed by reference to Spanish ethno- and urban landscaping (terms I advance to refer to traditions and architecture), especially to the former Plaza España, which in 1988 was reconstructed and re-named Plaza Hassan II by the King. I will argue that the common Tetuáni ambivalence towards Spain as well as towards the Spanish Protectorate era (1912–56) must be understood within the wider context of the impress of the Moroccan state on Northern Moroccan identities. My argument is based on the assumption that public discourse and whispered narratives about the Plaza and the surrounding social space are expressions of various power struggles over spatial and social control.

I have chosen to examine the everyday effects of the Spanish-Moroccan border in terms of the tensions between state power and mobile livelihood practices. In doing so, I focus on the agency of migratory subjects and attempts by the states in question to regulate their activities and identities. My larger goal, however, is to redirect the study of contemporary migratory processes beyond the geo-political frontier separating Europe from Africa or Spain from Morocco. Inside Moroccan territory other boundaries prevail.

The analysis that follows is divided into four parts. Part 1 provides a broad historical overview of the region. This overview makes apparent that the Spanish-Moroccan border has varied in terms of permeability over time. In Part 2, I describe the foundation of the city of Tetuán, its inhabitants, historical as well as contemporary movement in and out of the city, and finally the recent changes in the urban space. In Part 3, I present the narratives provided by the three male border crossers in extracted form. Their migratory experiences are distinct, both because of their different socio-economic backgrounds and their different forms of encounters with the border. The final part of the essay offers a theoretical discussion of the relationship between the seemingly nostalgic imagery of the urban landscape of the past, the current ambivalence towards Spain and the persistent critique of the Moroccan regime, prior to the death of King Hassan II and the subsequent democratic openings in 1999. This discussion gives rise to my suggestion that we need to be more precise as to which kinds of borders we are talking and writing about, as well as to what kind of global processes we refer to. It is often assumed that territorial state and cultural borders are coterminous. But as my analysis of the northern Moroccan borderlands will show, it is possible for borders to be erased in terms of culture without being erased in terms of state effects.

## The Mediterranean: Bridge or Frontier?

The Mediterranean region is marked by a continuous movement of people from both sides of the sea border. Historically, the area now known as Morocco was populated by various groups of pastoralists, who were later to be known as Berbers. Their local forms of mobility were bound up with the search for pasture. Together with the rest of the Maghreb region, their various territories were at different times invaded by foreign intruders (e.g. Phoenicians, Romans, Byzantines, Arabs, Iberians, and so forth), of which the Arabs perhaps made the strongest impact with the establishment of the Western Islamic Empire (consolidated in 710). I shall not dwell long on these historical movements or early global processes, but point to some of the links of importance for present-day identity politics in northern Morocco and for the identifications that the inhabitants of Tetuán often employ.

After 710, the Western Islamic Empire expanded into the Iberian Peninsula and subsequently consolidated Muslim power in Andalusia (Al Andaluz). This movement was later countered by the Spanish expulsion of the Moors and Sephardic Jews[1] (in 1492 and 1609), followed by the movement of European colonials to Northern Africa. In the Moroccan case, Ceuta was incorporated into the Iberian Kingdom in 1415, Melilla in 1497, and the two islands Peñon de Vélez de la Gómera in 1508 and Peñon de Alhucemas in 1673. Spain took effective control over Western Sahara in 1900. In 1912, the European states met at the Algeciras Conference and shared out Africa between them. Morocco was divided between France and Spain, the South to France, the North to Spain. In 1913 Spain occupied Tetuán and made the city its colonial capital (Miège et al. 1996, Ruiz Manzanero 1997). French and Spanish protectorates over Morocco lasted until Moroccan independence in 1956. Ceuta, Melilla and the Peñons still remain Spanish enclaves or EU territory in Africa.

From the beginning of the 20th century, these movements were once again reversed. During the First World War, thousands of Moroccans fought for the French or worked as replacement labour in the French industry and agriculture. During the Spanish Civil War (1936–39), Franco recruited 60,000 Moroccans (primarily from the northern Riff region) to fight in Spain for the nationalist cause (Collinson 1996). At the same time thousands of oppositional Spaniards fleeing Franco's oppression found a safe refuge in Morocco.

From the early 1960s, Moroccan movements towards Europe began to be conceptualised as labour migration. Until 1965, the number of Moroccans in Europe was still very modest, estimated at some 70–80,000 persons. The overall majority of these 'guest workers' or migrants were young men from rural areas, generally married, who left their families behind and remitted large parts of their European salaries back home. Although the EEC countries restricted entrance in the early 1970s, family reunification programmes made it possible for Moroccans to continue travelling to various European countries. Deteriorating economic and political conditions in Morocco as well as established family networks in various European countries made migration to Europe both attractive, conceivable and feasible. According to official estimates, 1.1 million Moroccans entered Europe between 1971 and 1982 (ib.).

In comparison with pre-1970 Moroccan movements to Europe, these migratory movements were characterized by a progressive incorporation of new sending regions, especially the Atlantic Coast and the interior. People from larger urban areas such as Casablanca, Rabat, Fez, Meknés, Kenitra, Marrakesh, Agadir, Tangier and Tetuán also began to add their numbers – and experiences – to what was formerly understood as a rural labour migration (Colectivo Ioé 1994). At the same time economic adjustments and a restrictive university reform produced a massive abandonment of advanced Moroccan students. Many of them chose to migrate to Europe, often to new destinations such as Spain, other Maghreb countries and the Persian Gulf, which became added to the traditional EEC countries.[2] Others were forced into exile by their oppositional political beliefs and conduct.

As hopefully stands to reason after this shortcut summary of more than 1 200 years of back and forth population movements, the Mediterranean has at various points of time shifted from serving as a bridge, defined by inclusion; a boundary, defined as a symbolic divide between groups; and a frontier, defined as a political and legal divide adjacent nation states. According to Henk Driessen (1996, 1998), the Mediterranean Sea never acted as a barrier between Europe and North Africa. It was rather a river that united more than it divided by making a single world out of North and South. It was not until the beginning of the 16th century, and the final expulsion of Moors from the Iberian Peninsula, that the Strait of Gibraltar became a political frontier; and only by Spain's incorporation into the European Union in 1986 that the southern border of Spain was transformed into a frontier of major concern for Western Europe. This frontier is not only a political and economic divide, but also an ideological and moral frontier, increasingly perceived by Europeans as a barrier between democracy and secularism on the one hand, and totalitarian and religious fanaticism on the other (Driessen 1998:100).

For many Moroccans, the Strait of Gibraltar has lately converted into a Wall, which they can only pass legally with a visa in their pocket. If Europe was once seen as a continent of opportunities, it is now increasingly seen as a force that will employ all means to keep Moroccans from entering. Still, Moroccan perceptions of Europe, although ambiguous, tend to be more nuanced than European perceptions of the North African migration threat, neatly summarized below: "In the North you find democracy, prosperity and freedom from tradition. Also individualism, violence and fear. In the South authoritarianism, the hard struggle for the Dirham and a separation of the sexes. But also solidarity, the sweet life and patience" (Valenzuela & Masegosa, 1996:27).

When we direct our attention to the former centre of Spain's colonial administration in Morocco, Tetuán, the perceptions become even more complex. Paraphrasing Anne Michaels we could say that the search for facts, for places, names, influential events, important conversations [...and] political circumstances account to nothing if you can't find the assumption your subjects live by (Michaels 1997:222). Border landers tend to live by complex and ambiguous assumptions. Recent changes in European conceptions of the southern border, *la ultima frontera* (the ultimate frontier) to the African continent, have not made assumptions less ambiguous.

## Tetuán: City on the Border of Things

The city of Tetuán[3] is located in the north-western part of Morocco – some 42 kilometres south of the Spanish enclave of Ceuta, 54 kilometres south-east of Tangier. For more than 40 years, Tetuán was the capital of the Spanish Protectorate, but the city's Andalusian heritage has a much longer history. Around 710 and the following centuries, a small village was founded between the natural barriers of two mountain chains, Djebel Dersa and Djebel Ghorghiz. These mountains still supply Tetuán with gentle summer breezes and chilling winter winds. In the years 961–962 (at the time of the Caliphate of Córdoba), the village gained status as a city. This city was destroyed somewhere between 1399 and 1437, but with the expulsion of the Moors in 1492 it rose again to a thriving city, *hijuela de Granada, soeur nonchalante* (little daughter of Granada in Spanish, nonchalant sister in French) (Ruiz Manzanero 1997). You may ask any contemporary gold or silk salesman in the Medina about the trades history and soon the sighs of the Moorish past resonate between old and damp walls.

The first Andalusians arrived around 1483–84. For years they fought over the rights to the city with the inhabitants of the Kabila de Beni Hozmar, a dispute that was not settled before the Sultan of Fez sold the area in and around Tetuán to the Grenadinians for the sum of 40,000 mizkales. Grenadian Jews arrived together with the Andalusians, and their presence influenced the economic, commercial and cultural development of the city profoundly (ib.).

The local Berbers, Andalusians, Moors and Jews were governed by the Grenadian Captain, Sidi Al Mandari. When he died in 1511, first his son and later the son's wife, Sit al Horra, continued to govern Tetuán independently from the Sultan of Fez. The second half of the 16th century was characterized by a series of civil fights over power. From the mid-16th century to 1688, the al-Naqsis family – descendants of the Beni Ider tribe – won power over the city and managed to keep the city free and independent from outside domination for more than 40 years. From 1688 and until the war between Morocco and Spain was declared in 1860, various families (the Rifis, the Ash-ashs) held power over the city. The entire period, however, was dominated by a strong Andalusian influence. An influence characterized by ambiguous relations to Europe, by at the same time hostility and persistent nostalgia toward the places left behind (Miège et al. 1996, Ruiz Manzanero 1997).

Tetuán received more than 40,000 Moors in the primary phases of expulsion from the Iberian Peninsula. Their numbers increased considerably during the successive centuries. By the end of the 19th century, however, some of their descendants had moved on to other and more important urban centres in Morocco. Still, both their numbers and their cultural influence remained profound. The Muslims exiled from the Granada, the indigenous Berbers, the Hebrews, and the Christian Spaniards have all contributed to a local form of speech, a special Tetuáni dialect. Today, Spanish is perhaps the strongest influence. A bag is called a *borsa* (bolsa in Spanish), a kitchen is a *kuchiniia* (cocina in Spanish), a cracker is a *bexquittu* (bizcocho in Spanish), and so on. But when I was invited to participate in an upper-middle class wedding in August 1997, I was given an Arab-style party-dress by one of my male informant's sister to wear during the night fiesta. By good fortune I decided to wear my own European dress. Luckily, because the rest of the party guests were all dressed up in Al Andaluz party-wear.

In 1912, prior to the Spanish protectorate era, circa 20–25,000 Muslims, 7–8,000 Jews, and 1,000 Europeans lived in Tetuán. In the rest of the 20th century, Tetuán experienced a considerable demographic growth. In 1940, the city had approximately 70,000 inhabitants, in 1950 80,000, and in 1960 101,000. In 1971 the number of inhabitants had grown to 139,000, in 1981 to 213,000, and in 1991 to more than 300,000. 12,228 Riff-migrants of rural origin (from the provinces of Alhucemas, Chauen, and Nador) moved to Tetuán between 1975 and 1982. In the same time-span, Tetuán received

11,648 migrants of urban origin, of whom 25 per cent originated in the urban centres of Alhucemas and Nador (calculated from Ruiz Manzanero 1997 and the Tetuáni local government statistics 1997). From the early 1980s, poor and landless peasants from all over the country moved into the city, a mass influx that several of the old families of Tetuán conceive of as a ruralization of the city. At the same time, the majority of the state servants in the city are Arabic speaking southerners from the Atlantic plains, installed by King Hassan II after years of public unrest culminating with the riots in 1984.[4]

In the late 1990s, Tetuán had grown to a city with over 300,000 registered inhabitants. The city centre, Place Hassan II, links the old Medina to the new city added by the Spaniards, where even now you can buy a *bocadillo*, where expatriate Spaniards flock to the Cathedral on Place Moulay el-Mehdi on Sundays, and where local people speak Spanish more than any other foreign language – a fact referring as much to the city's colonial heritage as to the local populations dissociation from southern Moroccan authorities who do not have Spanish but French as their second language. Local food and goods are sold in markets in the Medina and the great Bazaar just outside the old city walls. European and other foreign products – including everything from soap to towels, plastic sandals to kitchen utensils, synthetic sexy underwear and radio cassettes – are smuggled in from Ceuta and sold on almost every street corner and side walk without much notice from the authorities. And discarded goods collected from the garbage cans in Ceuta are sold or bartered among the poorest of the poor in the narrow and dark passages in the very heart of the old Medina.

It is also to the heart of the Medina, long the place for transactions of the greatest diversity, that would be migrants, who lack the means to buy forged papers and a flight ticket across the Strait of Gibraltar, will turn. The bodies of hundreds of Moroccans who during the last ten years have washed up on Spanish and Moroccan shores reflect how much some are willing to risk crossing el Estrecho, the Strait. Outside the Medina, in the fancier coffee and tea houses around Place Hassan II and Place Moulay el-Mehdi, middle-class business men complain that even they now need a visa to go on a business trip to Europe. Quite a few have experienced to have their visa application turned down. How in Allah's name can you run a business under these conditions?

Until the recent death of King Hassan II, July 23, 1999, and the new democratic measures promised by his son and contemporary ruler, King Mohammed VI, Morocco has been essentially an absolute monarchy, a fact that among other things could be read by King Hassan II's omnipresent image in all public places, including bazaars and cafés. During my fieldwork I found the King depicted with a receiver in his hand in phone offices, in post offices with a letter or a pen, and in the cafés he gazed down from the walls sipping a steaming gilt-edged glass of mint tea. It was in the cafés around Place Hassan II that I first noticed that a photostat of an old Spanish Plaza more often than not was hanging next to, or right below, the King's picture. On inquiry I learned that the plaza depicted was the old Plaza de España constructed during the Spanish protectorate but razed to the ground in the mid-1980s in order to give space for the construction of a new palace for the King and a new Islamic architecture Place in front of the Palace.

I shall return to this and the ways in which Tetuánis express resistance through wall decoration in a short while. Before venturing into the public discourses and whispered narratives about the Plaza and its social surroundings, let me introduce the three male border crossers from Tetuán. Their experiences and narratives are of course individually specific. However, like de Certeau I consider individual narratives the locus of a plurality of social relations (De Certeau 1984:xi). Seen in this perspective, individual narratives may serve to make the common visible through the specific.

## Crossing the Border with an Old Yellowed Picture and Conflicting Travel Stories

During the summer of 1997, I spent quite some time together with three young men, whom I in the following shall refer to as Maruf, Haddú, and Mohammad.[5] I knew Mohammad from an earlier visit in Spain, Maruf and Haddú were new acquaintances.

Informal gathering with Maruf and Haddú usually took place in cafés or during late afternoon city and Medina walks (not curtailed by café-walls with ears). As confidence grew, our conversations began to move into the house of Maruf's parents, a tiny two-room inner-city apartment, housing not only Maruf's old father, mother and himself, but also his younger brother – a taxi driver – and his newly divorced sister and her one-year old son. I was never invited into the home of Haddú, who temporarily lived in the apartment of his grandparents – a, seen from the outside, gloomy apartment in the inner city. Mohammad several times invited me to his family's duplex city house located in the new suburban housing sectors of Tetuán. I was also invited to either of the family's two beach houses outside Tetuán a couple of times. When our conversations took place in public spaces, Mohammad made sure that other persons were present. He attached great importance to not ruining my – and his own – reputation. Haddú had lived in Denmark in the early 1990s. Our relationship was to a large extent a consequence of my citizenship (Danish) and the potentiality of discussing Danish immigration policy as well as using my expertise to sort out the papers and letters related to Haddú's deportation, Haddú's Danish visa re-applications, and the refusals given by the Danish Consulate in Rabat. Maruf was a friend of Haddú. He remained slightly reserved and uncomfortable with my research.

All their differences not withstanding, conversations with Maruf, Haddú and Mohammad often slipped into the genre of border-talk, a discursive form based on comparisons between lives lived in different places; in Morocco, behind the border to Ceuta, in Spain and the rest of the continental Europe. A genre Schade Poulsen defines by its capacity to identify and mirror socio-moral concerns about the kind of life a citizen ought to live (Schade Poulsen 1997:167). Such concerns have to do with absence as well as presence, future-oriented activities and expectations as well as accomplished ones.[6] Border talk is comparative in nature. It centres around the good and the bad in different places. It is to some extent based on stereotypes, but to the extent that the narrator has been to the places talked about, it is also based on experience. When experience from abroad is used to criticize local forms of practice, border conversations often take the form of counter narratives.

When our conversations took place, Maruf was 36 years old. He is of Berber and migrant origin. Both his parents moved to Tetuán before he was born. He grew up in Tetuán, was trained as an electrician in Malaga, Spain, but returned to Morocco shortly after his apprenticeship was served. Through family networks he got himself to France, where he worked illegally as an electrician for six months, before he decided to go back and make himself a life in Morocco. Back in Tetuán he found a job at a factory, but was laid off because of problems between his family and the family of the factory owner. According to Maruf, the factory owner – a newcomer from Casablanca – wanted all the factory positions for his own family and friends. Local workers of Berber descent were gradually fired, always on the grounds that they were troublemakers. Maruf admitted that he at times did kick up a row, for example when he refused to take part in friendly turns and bribery arrangements. After a few months of unemployment he once again went to Spain. He entered on a tourist visa and worked any odd job for two years before he heard about better luck in northern Europe. Why not?, he thought, and entered Denmark illegally in 1990, married a Danish woman and was subsequently granted a residence and work permit. The marriage turned out to be more troublesome than anticipated. The Danish wife appeared to be a drug addict and when the domestic disputes passed beyond reasonable limits, Maruf moved to a friend's apartment. His wife still asked him for drug money, but when he one day refused to give her any, she reported him to the foreign police (on the grounds that they no longer lived together and that Maruf's residence permit was no longer grounded on marriage). Unfortunately the wife was killed in a car accident before the case was solved. Five days after her death, the foreign police presented him with an order of deportation. They told him, that if he left voluntarily, he could apply for a new visa in Morocco without any trouble. This was of course a lie. By the time I met Maruf, he was desperately trying to get a new visa for any European country after having his Danish visa application turned down.

Haddú was 35 years old, of Berber origin and in the summer of 1997 he had been unemployed for nearly a year. He is the fortunate holder of a Spanish passport, a valuable document he has obtained through family contacts working in the Spanish consulate. His grown-up life has been spent circulating between mainland Spain, Ceuta and Tetuán. During his time in Spain, he has typically been employed in the agricultural sector, lately as well in the service sector. His latest job in Spain was in a restaurant in the winter resort of Sierra Nevada, a real good job he had to quit because he couldn't take the cold weather. To Haddú, work and employment is associated with being outside of Morocco. He could, if he wanted to, find employment in Tetuán, yes, but the wages are too low compared with the earnings you can have on the other side of the Strait of Gibraltar. In addition to differences in wage levels, finding a job in Tetúan has nothing to do with qualifications but everything to do with connections. If you do not have access to such connections, forget it ... you might as well go to Europe right away. To cope with these conditions Haddú has developed a strategy based on 2–3 months of work in Spain, 2–3 months of rest in Morocco, and, while in Morocco, occasional trips to Ceuta to buy products for distribution among the street vendors in Tetuán. An activity which in legal terms is to be termed smuggling but which in Haddú's and most other Tetuani small-scale businesspersons' perception is doing business. During my time in Tetuán, Haddú was time and again moving around Tangier, Ceuta and Tetuán. His explanation for these short trips (2–3 days) was always that he was going to find out if he could get himself a working contract in Spain. As time went by, he got more and more nervous and less communicative as to what his business trips were all about. I got the picture, however, when he one day told me – in his awkward and typical Tetuáni way – that too many Moroccans are drowning on their way to Spain these days. The boat business is low.[7]

At the age of 28, Mohammad was slightly younger than the other two. After the recent death of his father, Mohammad, being the eldest brother, has taken over as the male head of his mother's household. In reality, he is only given this role in the dispute about the succession to property with his father's family. Inside the nuclear family, his mother is taking the decisions. Her side of the family is among the better off families in the region. They run a wholesale business with offices in Ceuta as well as in Tetuán. His father's side of the family has several smaller businesses in Tetuán, but the father himself was an intellectual who never made any big money. Both parents studied in Spain, a family tradition Mohammad has taken over. Neither he nor his family consider his stay abroad migration. He will return as soon as he has obtained his PhD- degree. Local bribery and the system of having to know the right people are among several reasons for getting his PhD abroad. According to Mohammad, you will never get a scholarship at the local university unless you bribe the university authorities. One of Mohammad's younger brothers failed his university exams in 1996. He passed during my stay in 1997, most probably because the family presented his professor with a brand new moped. Mohammad's family has both Berber and Arab ancestors. They are serious religious practitioners of Islam, and Mohammad has joined an Islamic student organisation in Spain. While in Spain, Mohammad prays the prescribed five times a day and makes sure to go to the mosque every Friday. In Tetuán, his religious practice is more relaxed. After all, he is on vacation. During the summer of 1997, Mohammad was travelling back and forth between Tetuán and Barcelona. In Barcelona he made the final preparations for his thesis while at the same time buying equipment for a sandwich bar he and his family were planning to establish next to the beach house. Each time he came back to Morocco, the family went to Ceuta to pick up not only him but also loads of kitchen hardware for the sandwich bar. Such things are indisputably cheaper in Spain but, as the family reluctantly admitted, they are also of a better quality than similar Moroccan products ... and young Moroccan costumers attach higher symbolic value to European style restaurants.

The above descriptions of the local circumstances in which these three border crossers found themselves are by no means complete. I do hope, however, that they may give some context to the following analysis of narratives and discourse.

Café talk in Tetuán is often border talk. Sitting in a café with Maruf, Haddú or Mohammad, conversation would often start with the café wall decoration, just below King Hassan II, right in the middle of the old yellowed picture of Plaza España. Oh, wasn't it a beautiful Plaza, they would sigh, and addressing me they would continue: "Look at the small gardens with high palm trees giving shade to the burning sun, notice the pavilion in the middle ... many a concert was given there." Mohammad, who beside his admiration for the Plaza also has an academic interest in the Spanish Protectorate era would go into detail: "Notice the elaborate mosaics covering the entire Plaza, all the small coloured stones forming the complicated patterns of ancient carpets ... a work of real art. The Spaniards may have thought of this as Spanish handicraft, but we know that they learned it al from the Al Andaluzes." What a shame, what a pity (Haddú), what a provocation (Mohammad), what an act of terror (Maruf) to demolish it.

Praise would often be followed by severe criticism of the new Place Hassan II, constructed after a French architect's designs in 1988. Vocal tones would change from soft nostalgia to something in between the harsh and painful; from audible voices to barely perceptible whispers. One day, while crossing the Place with Maruf, he said: "The King had all the trees cut down, and yes, I know, to be able to control that nothing hides from his gaze." Another day Mohammad took me to the end of the Place. "Look at the Palace, one can neither enter nor cross its premises. And this is so although the King never comes to stay in Tetuán. He did once, in the late 1980s, but somebody threatened him and he never came back after that. He probably never will. He is not welcome here." Yet another day Mohammad told me, that large parts of

The colonial Plaza España.

Tetuán's University were moved out of the city after the 1984–85 riots – a move intended to prevent the students from demonstrating in the city. On various occasions they would all point to the enormous amount of money used to construct the Palace and the new Place, often comparing the sum to how many workplaces could have been established instead. Haddú and Maruf both saw a close relation between the region's links to wider spaces in Morocco as well as to Spain. "The King doesn't care about the North of Morocco ... all the revenue is transferred to the South ... there is no development here, no future ... no wonder everybody attempts to get to Europe."

From Plaza-talk conversation would inescapably slip into travel stories. Manuf would tell about his hardships in Europe, encounters with the police, racism, and so forth, but also about the sweet life he lived with European women (in Spain and in Denmark), women who did not demand gold jewellery, clothes and expensive gifts from their male partners, but simply based relationships on love and bodily desire. Outside the wedding palaces of the old Medina, both Manuf and Haddú would comment on the enormous amount of money Moroccans spend on weddings. "Lots of gold, all these women want is gold. After the wedding (and all of the money invested in the celebration of the wedding) many marriages turn into divorce. – Women demand and demand. They do not understand that a man needs to be left alone once in a while, to have some peace and quiet. Upon divorce, all your money is lost."

One of the reasons why Haddú and Manuf are still unmarried is – according to themselves – that they cannot afford a wedding. But on top of that they would also prefer a mutual love relation with a Europeanish woman. A decent one, not a prostitute, Haddú would often make clear to me. "Oh yes, I had my experiences with prostitutes in Barcelona. They too want your money." In the same breath Haddú and Maruf would sometimes comment on the young Tetuáni women who cross the border to Ceuta or mainly Spain: "Most certainly prostitutes, at least the great majority."[8]

The new Place Hassan II.

Maruf would also tell stories about the Moroccan police, of how they beat up decent local Tetuánis on no solid grounds. Haddú, who on several occasions has been charged with illegal (but widespread) street wending of kif (hashish) lost four of his teeth in a beating in which it turned out that he did not possess any kif in his pocket. "You know the ordinary police officers by their uniform ... but who knows if the secret police is involved with the contraband mafia (basically controlling the trade in tobacco and alcohol) to trap people. What you do know is that the great majority of the police officers are not local. They are brought up by the central authorities to control us, the northern rebels. Local policemen are different. I know of several cases in which a Tetuáni police officer has covered up for a hometown boy. As long as you get incarcerated in Tetuán ... they may treat you all right. If you are transferred to Rabat or Casa, forget it. You won't be able to walk out of there, not after the torture they put you through."

Mohammad's narratives, although of a different kind, would also be very ambiguous. They would occasionally concern the beach rubbish, which he would claim to be dumped in the sea in Spain and Ceuta (no matter how many Arabic consumer labels on the driftage I would be able to point to). On baddish days he would tell the story about how his youngest brother was killed in Spain by incompetent doctors who deliberately did not give him the proper treatment for a harmless diarrhoea. How his father after that experience had chosen to get medical treatment in Morocco, no matter his means to cover the expenses in a European hospital. About Europeans who trust any Moroccan to be a fundamentalist terrorist when many – though not many enough – are just pious practitioners of Islam. But also narratives about the King's failed policy in northern Morocco. About the regime's transfer of development funds from the Yebala region to dubious projects in the south, not least in Sahara. During the 1997 local government elections he would tell me why he wouldn't make a fool of himself by voting. "Al Adl Wal Ihsan (the semi clandestine Islamist movement) is banded by the King. The movement's leader, Abdesalam Yasín, has been in house arrest in Salé since 1989. Other political parties of the opposition will probably get more votes than the King's supporters. But your vote doesn't matter, the King will win anyway. That's the only thing you can be sure of in Morocco."

The socialists actually won the local elections in Tetuán. The Islamists, who were not allowed to put up candidates, marched the streets as soon as the election result was publicly known. They were spread with truncheons by the more than 1,000 extra police officers stationed in Tetuán during the elections.

## The Moor's Last Sigh or a Silent Cry of Resistance?

"Translation is a kind of transubstantiation; one poem becomes another. You can choose your philosophy of translation just as you choose how to live; the free adaptation that sacrifices meaning to exactitude. The poet moves from life to language, the translator moves from language to life; both, like the immigrant, try to identify the invisible, what's between the lines, the mysterious implications" (Michaels 1997: 109).

According to James Clifford, thinking historically is a process of locating oneself in space and time. Such analytical processes of location should be seen as initiaries rather than bounded sites – as series of encounters and translations in which the use of comparative concepts or translation terms work as approximations. Given the historical contingency of translations, there is no single location from which a full comparative account can be produced (Clifford 1997:11). Seen in this perspective, café conversations around the old Plaza España in Tetuán can be seen as a privileged site for border-talk among inhabitants of Tetuán. In such conversations people translate feelings of old empires lost, ambiguous feelings of belonging to more than one nation state, as well as feelings of not belonging to the nation state in which they hold at least nominal citizenship.

On another level, Plaza-conversations become the condensed site from which other sites for socio-moral concerns of the good and the bad life can be constructed. The divide between

Berber and Arab ethnic groups in Morocco, and the Berber's feeling of exclusion from national politics could be one example; aversion against local bribery practices as well as ingrained patterns of friendly turns and merchant-like social relations could be another; and conceptions of femininity, masculinity and gender relations on both sides of the border could be yet other examples.

Border crossing subjects from Tetuán – whether travelling in thought (through imagining and critically debating their own and other worlds), or in space (from one location to another) – expose their capacity of imagining lives transnationally but maybe less a capacity of forging and sustaining simultaneous multistranded social relations that link together their societies of origin and settlement than predicted by Basch and Glick Schiller (1995:48). In this process they engage in dialectics of belonging, opposition and resistance to the hegemonic logic of their own nation-state as well as to the nation states in which they occasionally live their lives. Their practices may not be self-consciously resistant toward their state of citizenship (although they often are), nor even loosely political in character understood as leading to collective organization against oppression) (Smith and Guarnizo 1998). They are, however, counter narratives to a state from which they are excluded on ethnic, regional, economic, political, religious, or gender grounds. It is in this sense that the public discourses and whispered narratives about Plaza España and the surrounding social space can be understood. Understood as expressions of resistance to the regime's spatial and political control. The very act of hanging up the picture of Plaza España below the obligatory picture of the King in public places is a direct challenge to state control. The state may decree the display of the King in public places, yes, but it cannot control what is put up right next to him, nor can it control the meaning attached to the additional wall décor. At the same time the discourses and narratives are expressions of a divided nation, speech acts through which a boundary to state power is defined. While the public discourses and private narratives can be read as simultaneous ambivalent feelings toward both Spain and Morocco south of Yebala – as experiences of real frontiers that not only divide adjacent nation states but also nations within states – they do at the same time function to establish a bridge over the river that once united North and South in Al Andaluz.

Mobility and fixity in place are aspects of border societies which have a bearing on the people who live there, for example by helping to define the strengths and weaknesses of communities, nations and states at their juncture on the borders. As such, the anthropology of borders is simultaneously one nation's history and of one or more states frontiers (Wilson & Donnan 1998). Among the border landers in northern Morocco, the Strait of Gibraltar has at times been less an important border than the various boundaries established towards southern sultans and kings or the Spanish/European frontier around Ceuta. Representations of the former Plaza España and the present Place Hassan II are part and parcels of this. But as Chris Hann states (quoted in Wilson and Donnan 1998), "... local experiences of the state and resistance to it cannot be limited to the imaginative consequences of the actions of states for local populations" (Hann 1995:136).

Concrete material consequences are (un-)fortunately easy to deduce from the border talks I had with Maruf, Haddú, Mohammad and other persons in Tetuán in 1996 and 1997. Lack of development and development funds, the government's transfer of resources from Yebala to the south and the transfer of state servants from the south to Yebala, fraud, bribery practices, and close-knit networks of personal relations, are integrated in the discursive framework in which Tetuánis articulate their opposition to national identity politics. Experiences of vulnerable labour market conditions in Spain and other European countries, of increasingly closed borders to Fortress Europe, of being met not only with xenophobic reactions but also accusations of Islamic fundamentalism and terrorism if you actually manage to beat the border, with apprehension and repatriation and subsequent family setbacks in Morocco, if you are caught in clandestine attempts at landing on European shores, feed into yet other feelings of abandonment.

## Epilogue

On January 31, 2000, my phone rings. The call is from Morocco, from Tetuán. It is my friend, the scribe, who has spent good parts of his grown-up life in imprisonment charged of anti-state political activities. His addiction to sports and health food cannot conceal the result of prison treatment. His eyes are forever out of focus, his row of teeth only the faintest memory of his childhood smile, his fit body disfigured by marks of torture. Through the lisping I cannot fail to notice the joy in his voice. "So what's up, Abdellah?", I ask, "What can I do for you." – "Nothing", he answers, "absolutely nothing. That's the reason for my call." Silence, then laughter. "You heard about the death of Hassan II, right? I just call to say that you do not have to do your research in Morocco anymore. Democracy has finally reached Tetuán. Why would people want to leave, then? "

## Notes

1. Sefarad means Spain in Hebrew.
2. Migration researchers often point to a diversification of demographic characteristics in the Moroccan migration process, in which single men began to migrate toward the new destination countries, whereas women and children continued to travel toward the EEC countries (through family reunification).
3. A note on spelling: The city is called Titauin in Berber, Tétouan in French, and Tetuán in Spanish. I stick to the Spanish naming and way of spelling, since this was what most local people used when I conducted field work in and around Tetuán in the summers of 1996 and 1997. This local spelling practice is of course significant for the argument I attempt to make.
4. Analyses of the 1984 riots in Morocco tend to emphasize immediate price increases as the most important catalyst of the riots and to neglect the more complex causes specific to a region or a city, like Tetuán. Of direct relevance for the Tetuán case, but based on findings in and around Melilla, Mc Murray argues that the little noticed IMF-inspired anti-smuggling measures taken in Morocco in August 1983 were more inflammatory than the price rises that followed. For while prices ate into all Moroccan household economies, the anti-smuggling border tax destroyed the incomes of the mass of lumpen smugglers outright (Mc Murray 1992:158).
5. In accordance with 'Maruf', 'Haddú', and 'Mohammad', I have changed their real names for pseudonyms and slightly blurred their identity.
6. Schade Poulsen's study is concerned with the departure culture among young men in the Oujda region who have not yet managed to "beat the border". He therefore talks about absence rather than presence, future-oriented activities rather than accomplished ones.
7. Ferrying people across the Strait to Spain for money has been a lucrative trafficking business in northern Morocco. According to Harding, this business has in the later years been substituted with drug trafficking, an incomparable better business. 15 passengers on a fishing smack, paying around $1,300 each, cannot match the earnings of a drug run (Harding 2000:22).
8. During my work among Moroccan migrants in Spain I have found the percentage of Moroccan women in prostitution to be very low, compared to other migrant groups. Most Moroccan women – be they single, married or divorced – work in the domestic sector.

## References


Basch, Linda & Nina Glick Schiller 1995: From Immigrant to Transmigrant. In: *Anthropology Quarterly*: 48–63.

Clifford, James 1997: *Routes*. Cambridge.

Collectivo Ioé 1994: *Presencia del Sur: Marroquíes en Cataluña*. Madrid.

Collinson, Sarah 1996: *Shore to Shore. The Politics of Migration in Euro-Maghreb Relations*. London.

de Certeau, Michel 1988: *The Practice of Everyday Life*. Berkeley.

Driessen, Henk 1996. At the Edge of Europe: Crossing and Marking the Mediterranean Divide. In: L. O'Down & T. M. Wilson (eds.): *Borders, Nations and States: Frontiers of Sovereignty in the New Europe*. Aldershot: 179–199.

Driessen, Henk 1998: The New Immigration and the Transformation of the European-African Frontier. In: T. M. Wilson & D. Hastings (eds.): *Border Identities: Nation and State at International Frontiers*. Cambridge: 96–116.

Hann, Chris 1995: Subverting Strong States: The Dialectics of Social Engineering in Hungary and Turkey. In: *Daedalus:* 133–153.

Harding, Jeremy 2000: The Uninvited. In: *London Review of Books* 3 February 2000: 3–25.

Mc Murray, David Andrew 1992: *The Contemporary Culture of Nador, Morocco, and the Impact of International Labor Migration.* Dissertation from the University of Texas at Austin. Michigan.

Michaels, Ann 1997: *Fugitive Pieces*. London.

Miège, Jean-Louis, Mohammad Benaboud & Nadia Erzini 1996: *Tétouan: Ville Andalouse Marocaine*. Rabat.

Ruiz Manzanero, Cirilo 1997: *Tetúan Es Mi Ciudad*. Tetuán.

Schade Poulsen, Marc 1997: Men and Migration in

Morocco: Towards European Borders. In: F. Wilson & B. F. Frederiksen (eds.): *Livelihood, Identity and Instability*. Copenhagen: 157–166.

Smith, Michael Peter & Luís E. Guarnizo 1998: The Locations of Transnationalism. In: M.P. Smith & L. E. Guarnizo (eds.): *Transnationalism from Below*. New Brunswick: 3–34.

Valenzuela, Javier & Alberto Masegosa 1996: *La Ultima Frontera: Marruecos, El Vecino Inquietante*. Madrid.

Wilson, Thomas M. & Hastings Donnan 1998: *Nations, State and Identity at International Borders*. Cambridge.

# Fifty Years, Five Crossings, More to Come

## The Kirad Bedouins of Galilee and the Israeli-Syrian Border, 1948

*Dan Rabinowitz*

Dan Rabinowitz 2000: Fifty Years, Five Crossings, More to Come: The Kirad Bedouins of Galilee and the Israeli-Syrian Border, 1948. – Ethnologia Europaea 30, 2:101–110.

The post 1948 history of the Kirad Bedouins of the Hula valley in Northern Israel is a series of forced mass border-crossings between Israel, Syria, Jordan and Lebanon. These migrations came concurrently with a staggered process of dispossession, in which the Kirad lost ownership of their ancestral lands, and ended up as a diaspora scattered over four states. The upheavals experienced by the Kirad are historicized and analyzed as a 'small scale diasporic situation'. This, I argue, is an exceedingly widespread situation in a world characterized as 'glocalized', in which powerful globalizing trends combine with ethno-national fervor that accentuates territoriality and state borders. The Kirad's own perception of their world, fragmented and disturbed beyond recognition by impermeable and often hostile state borders since 1948, is contextualized in terms of the analogy between the recent, vivid past, and ancient history, only vaguely remembered and invoked. Wolfe's (1982) notion that world systems are by no means new phenomena, the place of diachronic reckoning and subjective historical perceptions, and the place of fate and repetition in the Kirad's identity inform the theoretical trajectory of the analysis.

*Dr Dan Rabinowitz, Department of Sociology and Anthropology, Tel Aviv University, Ramat-Aviv, Tel-Aviv, Israel. E-mail: drabinowitz_il@yahoo.com*

## Fragmented Kin Groups

Abu-Uthman, born ca. 1935, currently a resident of the Palestinian village Sha'ab in West Galilee, spent most of his adult life separated from his older sister. She has lived in Syria since the family's forced migration from the Hula valley during the 1948 hostilities. While acutely aware of the traumatic significance of family disunion, he is nevertheless convinced that blood ties do and will prevail. The illustration he recently chose to stress this point was somewhat unexpected. In his words:

"A mountain can never meet a mountain. But people can come together. There was this Jewish guy I knew, a Russian Jew. We worked together for seventeen years in construction, all over Israel. They say that people who live together and are close have salt and bread together. Well in our case you could say that over the years we had between us a whole sack of flour.

Anyway, he had come here from the Soviet Union at the age of thirteen, before the Second World War. Then the war broke out, and he lost contact with his family in Russia. Time went by, and fifty years later he suddenly had contact with them again. A letter from his sister arrived one morning, and by evening he was in Italy to meet her. They met in a street, amongst many strangers, but immediately recognized each other. He says their identical foreheads gave them away."

"The same happened between my sister and me. In 1948 we were chased by the Israelis into Syria. She stayed while I later returned to Israel. I never saw or talked to her for more than forty years. Then a few years back we re-established contact, and made an appointment to meet in Mecca, during the Haj. She was with her son, whom I recognized before I even saw her. That's the way it is with *dam*."

*Dam*, literally meaning blood, also denotes physical appearance. In Abu-Uthman's view, it is blood – both the person's external looks and their inner essence – which binds him to members of his family despite forced separation across impermeable political frontiers. The Syrian-Israeli border, an immensely powerful border structuring the lives of all Kirad Bedouins, thus becomes a yard-stick against which strengths of kinship, group solidarity and endurance can be measured.

Abu-Uthman is the third of five siblings. His eldest sister, who lives in Syria with her many offspring, is some seven years older than he. She was born in or around 1928. Two younger brothers live like Abu-Uthman in Sha'ab, while a fifth sibling died as an infant in the 1920s. Roughly a quarter of Abu-Uthman's immediate agnatic relations are thus in forced exile as refugees in Syria. The remaining three-quarters of the agnatic group – himself, his two siblings and their offspring in Sha'ab – are in a different predicament. While displaced from their ancestral home like their sister, they live within the state of Israel, only a few hours' travel from the village. They can visit the ruins relatively easily. Their status as citizens of a state purporting to be a democracy, where the rule of law prevails, gives them a semblance of political leverage and a faint hope of return – a vision their cousins in Syria cannot dream of.

The picture is even more fragmented in the generation of Abu-Uthman's father, Ahmad. Born around 1900 in the Hula as one of seven siblings, Ahmad died in 1964 in Sha'ab, near his

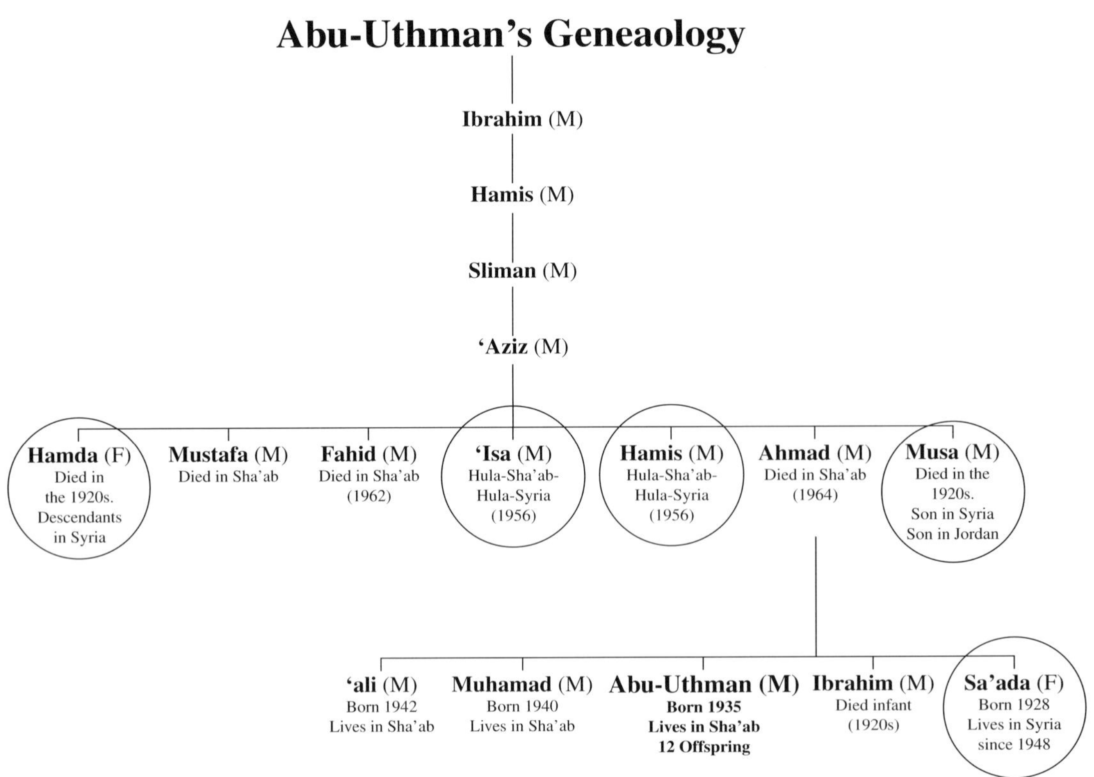


Encircled: branches of the family living in Syria

three sons. Four of his six siblings, however, had become refugees in Syria – some in 1948, others later. Sixty per cent of Ahmad's agnates are thus refugees in Syria.

A second case is that of Um-Nader[1], who was separated from her agnatic kin in 1951. Her agnates, having managed to return like other Kirads from an initial period of exile in Syria, were displaced for the second time (below). Like Abu-Uthman and others, Um-Nader and her husband moved to Sha'ab too. Her six siblings, on the other hand, moved to Syria, where they and their descendants have been living since. Her husband's agnatic family did more or less the same, and by the mid-1950s the couple found themselves with no immediate kin near them in Sha'ab or, for that matter, anywhere else in Israel.

Um-Nader's husband died young, leaving her with a son – Nader – and a daughter, Hamida. Hamida soon married 'adnan, a member of a large family most of which now live in Galilee. Hamida's union became a lifeline for herself, her mother and her brother. It provided them with alternative kin and a new social focus. Hamida and her brother, for example, took to calling 'adnan's elder brother Muhammad 'father', although he is no member of their agnatic kin. Curiously, Muhammad is not even the senior sibling in his own family: he and 'Adnan have an elder brother, Sa'id, a refugee in Syria.

A third example is Salim, now in his seventies. Salim named some of his children after pivotal events in his life. His eldest daughter, born in 1948, carries a name that means in Arabic 'predicament' or 'hardship', commemorating the family's forced departure from the Hula valley in 1948. Another daughter, born in late 1951, carries a name that means 'migration', after the second forced migration of the same year. Over the years Salim had pictures of his sisters and of their descendants, all of whom now live in Syria, passed on to him through Europe or Jordan. He keeps the pictures in a special case, presents them proudly, and knows the names of most of those who feature in them, none of whom he ever met. Having retired from work, in the mid-1990's he spent much time and energy obtaining permission for two of his sisters to come and visit him in Sha'ab. The month or so long visits eventually took place in 1994 and 1995.

## Historicizing Removal and Return

Prior to the war of 1948, the Kirad Bedouin had found themselves along with 20 other Palestinian, Bedouin and Arab Villages in the Hula valley at the forefront of a tough contest against Zionism over settlement and territory. Their immediate *dira* (assigned tribal territory) and its environs at the southern tip of the valley, had a number of Zionist settlements established in it, including Mishmar Hayarden (founded 1890), Yisud Hama'ala (founded 1883), Ayelet Hashahar (founded 1918) and Hulata (founded 1936).

The Kirad were forced out of their two villages for the first time on April 22nd 1948, two days after the flight of the inhabitants of adjacent al-'Ulmaniya and al-Husaniya (Morris 1991:172). Morris, who does not record direct expulsion or even occupation on the part of the Jewish forces against the Kirad villages, suggests that the Kirad's departure resulted from the fear of impending Jewish attack and of being caught in the crossfire of an approaching Syrian offensive (ibid.).

Most Kirad members fled eastwards, taking temporary refuge in and around Arab villages in the southern section of the Golan Heights, particularly al-Sanabir, some 10 km from their villages of origin. The circumstances of the flight were probably not extreme, since many managed to transport their herds – their major source of livelihood – with them. Some returned later for their livestock and removable belongings, while other items were stored in and around the villages in the hope of future return. By the time a Syrian ground attack into the Hula valley began in early June 1948, the twin Kirad villages, like other Arab villages in the valley, were empty. At cease-fire, the villages were part of 19 km$^2$ west of the Jordan river controlled by Syrian troops.

The General Armistice Agreement signed between Israel and Syria on July 20th 1949 (the last one to be signed by Israel and an Arab state as part of the Rhodes Armistice Accord), gave Israel control over most areas where Israeli army (I.D.F.) troops were present. This included parts that had not been designated in the UN Partition Plan of 1947 as part of Israel, but were nevertheless conquered by the I.D.F. during the hostilities. This was a bitter blow to all dispossessed and dislocated Palestinians. Having fled to neighboring Arab states, the refugees remained in waiting, hoping to return to their communities and properties and to restore the lives they once had there.

The disappointment was naturally harsher for those whose homes and properties had been in areas not designated by the 1947 Partition Plan as part of the Zionist state. Had the General Armistice Agreement disregarded the military situation on the ground at cease-fire, and turned the wheel back so that only territories assigned to Israel in the Partition Plan were in fact included within it, the return of hundreds of thousands of refugees would have been facilitated.

Most Hula refugees who fled to Syria or the Lebanon were hoping to return to their old homes in spite of the fact that the Hula had been designated by the UN Partition Plan as part of Israel. However, the General Armistice Agreement, which consolidated Israeli sovereignty over the Hula, was soon followed by Israeli actions to effectively seal-off the border, thus preventing Palestinian refugees from returning. Hope of restoration of the pre-1948 situation quickly eroded.

The General Armistice Agreement designated a number of tracts on either side of the Israeli-Syrian border as Demilitarized Zones (DMZ's). One such area was the 19 $km^2$ west of the Jordan, where Syrian troops were present at cease fire, in which the old Kirad villages are located. In return for the Syrian agreement to withdraw from this tract, Israel agreed to keep it demilitarized.[2]

The General Armistice Agreement included an important provision, which soon proved fateful to many of the Kirad. It empowered the Chairman of the Joint Israeli—Syrian Armistice Committee, a UN official, to authorize the return of civilians to villages and settlements within the DMZ.[3] This pertained to seven villages (Morris 1991:323), two of which were Kirad Bakkara and Kirad Ghannama. In the following months the Kirad, along with residents of al-Samara, Nuqeib and al-Hamma (villages located in other DMZ's on either side of the border) were in fact allowed to return. This move was obviously part of a Syrian attempt to maintain some presence in the Hula after the evacuation. The Syrians equipped the Kirad with official travel documents which allowed them to travel between Syria, the Hula valley and Lebanon, and hoped to maintain them as loyal representatives of Syrian interests in the Hula DMZ.

It was at that stage that Abu-Uthman lost contact with his sister. While he and his two brothers seized the opportunity to return to their old homeland, his sister and her husband went the other way. They lingered in the Golan, eventually finding their way to a Palestinian refugee camp near Damascus, where they and their descendants have been living since.

The presence in the Hula DMZ of Kirad returnees officially equipped with Syrian documents became significant again in 1951, when Israel began to execute a long standing plan to drain the Hula wetlands.

The drainage of the Hula was the major development and economic project undertaken by the state of Israel during the first decade since statehood. A major engineering feat by any standards, it was managed by a joint ministerial committee, fuelled by Jewish National Fund money, boosted by international know-how and executed by state of the art machinery chartered in Western Europe and the USA. In early 1951 earth began to move, signaling a multi-staged operation that was carried out at various locations over almost seven years.

Ground could have been broken almost anywhere in the valley. However in February 1951 Israel decided to start digging only a stone's throw away from the twin Kirad villages, inside the Demilitarized Zone. The first bulldozers were deployed in early March 1951 in two adjoining spots. One was west of the Jordan River, on private land that had belonged to Arab refugees. Israel was fully aware that Syria regarded the owners as Syrian citizens, and purported to represent them. The other spot was east of the Jordan River, near the Bridge of Banat Yaacub. It was within the 100 m wide strip assigned as part of Israel in the original UN Partition Plan of 1947, only a few hundred yards away from Syrian frontier posts overlooking the river.

The choice of both spots was anything but accidental. The drainage project itself was designed to attain political objectives, including an assertion of sovereignty inside the Hula DMZ (Shalev 1993:51–52). The significance did not escape the Syrians. In March 1951, soon after Israeli bulldozers began work, plain-clothed Syrians began shooting at them. Heroic attempts by UN officials to contain the tension and prevent an outbreak were to no avail, and the tension spilt over to other DMZ's along the Israeli-Syrian frontier east and south of the Sea of Galilee. The border crisis threatened to catapult the two states into a war neither of them wanted.

All this proved fateful for the Kirad Bedouins. On March 30th, following the breakdown of UN mediation on the drainage project, a meeting took place in Prime Minister Ben-Gurion's office, yielding a resolution to 'carry out actions whose purpose is to maintain our sovereignty in that zone' (Shalev 1993:70). These measures were to include distribution of Israeli ID cards to all residents of the zone so as to sever their attachment to Syria, the transfer of as many Arab civilians from the zone to other parts of Israel outside the DMZ, and tighter control of the border in an attempt to prevent movement between the DMZ and Syria (ibid.).

Israeli security forces moved swiftly. On the 30th and the 31st of March, they chased the residents of al-Samara and Nuqeib, two villages east of Lake Tiberias, from their homes and into Syria (Shalev 1993:71). Then, on the night of March 31st, 785 residents of Kirad Bakara and Kirad Ghannama were forced to embark on trucks and buses assembled by the government and were transferred westwards. Their destination Sha'ab is a Palestinian village whose original inhabitants had been dispossessed during the 1948 hostilities, and whose empty houses were used by Israel to resettle various groups of displaced Palestinians.

Abu-Uthman, who was 18 years old at the time, remembers: 'The army came, and encircled the whole village with barbed wire. Then they summoned the elders to the *bayadir* (thrashing ring) and told them: 'there are problems between us and the Syrians, so we want you out'. The elders asked: 'Is it only us you want out of the zone, or the Jews (from newly established Kibbutz Gadot within the DMZ, D.R) too'? 'They asked that because Kibbutz Gadot was still in tents, and they were afraid that it would take over Kirad land and property. The officers replied that this was none of the Kirad's business, and the elders understood that only us, the Kirad, are about to go. So they told the officers: 'We are not going. Either you transfer everybody out, including the Kibbutzniks, or we stay'. At that stage one of the officers suggested to the others, in Hebrew, to shoot some of the elders and thus scare us all into fleeing. Some of the younger people, who knew Hebrew from having worked in Kibbutz Ayelet Hashahar as kids, heard and understood him. They warned the elders, and the decision was made to consent and go in peace. Also, one guy – he was married to my cousin – went out of the barbed zone, and was shot dead on the spot. So we were scared."

The trucks came that night, and the officers and policemen gave the Kirad only minutes to pack and board. The Kirad had very few possessions, having migrated thrice in as many years. They boarded the trucks, traveled all night and got to Sha'ab in the morning. The herds were brought on foot, escorted by armed police, and took two more days to arrive.

Upon arrival in Sha'ab, the Kirad were offered a choice between relocation in the village and exile in Syria. Most elected Sha'ab, where a substantial number of them still live to date. Others went to Syria. A few families were allowed to return to their homes in the Hula valley DMZ.

The ultimate migration from the valley came five and a half years later. On October 30th 1956, the second day of the Suez crisis, in which Israel collaborated with France and Britain against Egypt, General Yitzhak Rabin, then CO of Israel's Northern Command, made a move. Using emergency regulations many believed were in force due to the war against Egypt[4], Rabin assumed the authority of Military Governor and issued an order forcing the last remaining

Kirad to leave their homes and cross the Syrian border into the Golan[5]. The Bedouins, displaced for the third time, sought their relatives – those who having been chased from their village in 1948 declined to return in 1950. They found them in refugee camps near Damascus, and settled in with them.

The two forced evacuations from the old Kirad villages, that of 1951 and that of 1956, sealed the fate of many Kirad families, including those of Um-Nader and of Salim. The Kirad, who currently number approximately 5,400, are now scattered across Israel, Syria, Jordan and Lebanon.[6] Their twin villages have been empty and ruined since.

## Deep Chronology: Kurdish Origins

The prefix 'Kirad' rings of distant lands. Most writers on the region agree it is the plural form of the singular Kurdi, denoting origins in Kurdistan (Dabagh 1988:168, Zakariya 1923:654). The earliest evidence of the presence of Islamic peoples in the Hula is that of the 10th century chronicler Mukaddassi, who mentions agriculture and artificial irrigation in the valley (Le Strange 1896). Al-Jubir, who wrote in 1185, describes the valley as a prosperous area, where Muslims and Franks share pastures and cultivation (cited in Bakhit 1990:104). Le Strange (1890) likewise cites Yakut's 1220 description of the valley as 'one with many villages'. There are references to early presence of Kurdish groups in Hula, but none conclusive. Bakhit (1990) cites primary sources which indicate that in the 15th century some Kurdish Arabs paid waqf (religious endowment) property taxes to the Ottoman region of Safad. Cohen and Lewis (1978:155) indicate that in the 16th century some Kurdish individuals lived in Safad, a town some 12 km west of the Hula valley[7], as do other sources. Hutteroth and Abdulfatah (1977:27) likewise suggest that 16th century Eastern Galilee had groups, which claimed Turkish, and Kurdish roots. A book published in 1572 by the Safadi qabalist Hayim Vital, entitled *Gate of the Incarnations* cites the existence of a Kurdish quarter in the town (*Ariel Encyclopaedia of the Land of Israel*). Vital also cites a 1865 piece in the Jewish periodical *Hamevaser*, featuring a 'Kurdish' group in Galilee strong enough to have successfully engaged in armed conflict with local Arabs (ibid.).

Shim'oni (1947:108), who does not cite his primary source, suggests that Kurds came into Palestine in trickles rather than in a specific wave. He assumes that some came in the 12th century with the conquest of Palestine by Salah al-Din al Ayubi, himself an issue to a dynasty of Kurdish origin. Shim'oni identify three communities in northern Palestine, which claim Kurdish descent: residents of a Kurdish neighborhood in Safad; the Krad of the Hula valley; and the Bashatwa near Beisan. Dabagh (1988:168) summarily states that the Kurds of Krad Al-Khait in Hula arrived in Palestine 'in the Middle Ages'.

These bits of evidence regarding the Kirad must be seen within the wider context of Bedouin migration into Galilee at large. Fallah (1990:402) puts forward the plausible argument that the Kurds, like other nomadic and semi-nomadic groups in the periphery of Palestine, arrived in Galilee as the result of forced migration. He suggests, after Lewis (1955:52), that strong tribes such as the 'Anizeh from Arabia, who since the 17th century periodically invaded Syria, continuously dispossessed weaker groups, pushing them off their lands, forcing them to relocate and seek new Dirah (tribal territory) in more marginal areas. Tyler (1994) likewise describes the population of the Hula valley as an amalgam of tribes and splinter groups originating in and associated with groups in Lebanon, Syria and elsewhere in the Middle-East, largely dominated by and dependent on local and regional powers outside the valley.

The Hula valley – a hot, humid, uncomfortable and inhospitable depression lying at an altitude of 100 m below sea level, is precisely such a region – at least in recent centuries.[8] Tribal elders of the Kirad in fact cite a battle between their ancestors and the Bedouin tribe of 'Arab al-Fadel of the Golan Heights which, they claim, took place '200 years ago or more'.

Whatever the population influx that may have taken place in Hula in the earlier Ottoman period, a number of sources indicate that by the turn of the 19th century the valley had very little in the way of permanent settlement. Karmon

(1956:60) cites a number of British and German sources attesting to this – mostly travelers who visited the area between 1806 and 1850. This may well be the basis for Sawa'id's (1995) claim that the Kurds of Eastern Galilee first settled in the north of Palestine as late as the 1850s. Sawa'id goes on to assert that the Kirad came at the invitation of the Ottomans, who imported them to curb the influence and power of the local big-man turned peace-keeper Akili Aga.

Registration of land, which began in Palestine following the 1858 Ottoman land reforms and the establishment therein of a real-estate market, encouraged villagers and other tenure holders across Palestine to issue titles to land and settle. Khawalde (1995) indicates that members of the Kirad began registering parcels to their names as early as the 1870s. Within the next five decades the Hula Bedouins – Kirad and others – had founded a few dozen villages in the valley, many consisting of permanent stone houses or wooden huts. This had been the situation on the eve of the 1948 war.

The personal and familial post-1948 history of the current members of the Kirad is thus a sinister, ironic analogy to the mythologized collective chronology of the tribe as a whole. Uprooted, displaced, forced to migrate and then resettled according to the priorities and interests of political powers beyond their control, the living Kirad recreate with their persons, property and heritage a movement similar to that which dominates their group identity.

Two precautionary remarks are in line here. One is that the political predicament that has literally sent the Kirad packing three times within as many years must not be obfuscated in anyway by the stereotypical image of Bedouins as nomadic pastoralists. Elsewhere (Rabinowitz 1985) I show how the essentialist image of the Bedouins as 'children of the desert' – herders leading a nomadic lifestyle that suits their 'nature', 'identity' and 'social structure' – collapses in the face of properly historicized diachronic evidence. In Sinai, herding and other livelihoods connected to natural desert resources transpire as options selected only once other economic opportunities are not available. Nomadism, even cyclical transhumance movement, is not the option of choice on the part of 'sons of the desert'. Rather, it is the default choice taken by impoverished and marginal peasants, a last resort involving hardship and poverty, turned to at specific moments in their economic histories. In a similar vein, the Kirad, who have been settled since the late 19th century, should not be presumed in any way to be 'accustomed' to migrations such as those their recent history brought upon them.

The deep sense shared by the Kirad of being a people who have survived forced migration from Kurdistan to Palestine some centuries ago is quite a different matter here. In fact Abu-Uthman's deep-seated conviction that *dam* (blood) is sometimes stronger than the indeterminacy and hardship brought by displacement and separation is a much more relevant sentiment here than is the propensity towards nomadic life so fondly imagined by European observers.

Those Kirad who remained in Israel after the 1948, 1951 and 1956 events, reestablished themselves as best they could as culturally and economically marginal communities within Palestinian towns and villages in Galilee, predominantly Sha'ab and Shafa'Amer. The elders still dream of return or remuneration, and visit the old ruined villages whenever possible.

Peace negotiations between Israel and Syria since 1995 brought all DMZ's – not least the Hula DMZ – into focus once again, as both Syria and Israel would like to include them in their territories. The Kirad, for their part, realize that reconciliation between Syria and Israel may bring the status of their homeland and its future prospects to the negotiation table, and may start a process that could eventually facilitate their return.

The hopes of possible recuperation of their rights and property triggered new sensitivities amongst the Kirad regarding genealogy and kinship (Rabinowitz and Khawalde, forthcoming). While prior to 1948 the Kirad community tended to be hierarchical and dichotomized between the core 'Kurdish' segments on the one hand and those believed to be descendants of client families, serfs, outcasts and other recent additions to the Kirad on the other, dispossession and exile bred a more egalitarian Kirad identity [9], including a higher frequency of marriage unions between original Kurdish sub-groups and other, more inferior sub-groups (ibid.).

Social and familial reckoning is naturally linked to land tenure, hence also to the prospect of return. Land ownership in the old homeland was restricted to the 'Kurdish' Kirad alone, largely excluding other groups within the Kirad. If return – or, for that matter, remuneration for lost property – transpires as a realistic option, the 'Kurdish' Kirad will have to make a choice: either stand by the more recent inclusive Kirad identity forged in exile and find a way to share whatever yield the process brings with all other Kirads. Or revert to re-inventing the old exclusive cleavages, safeguarding property rights for the 'authentic' Kirad alone, thus ensuring a non-egalitarian spread of revenue (ibid.).

The issue becomes even more complex once we incorporate the exiled members of the tribe – both 'Kurdish' Kirad and members of more peripheral sub-groups – who now reside across the border, mainly in Syria, into the reckoning picture. The current political and social horizons of both communities seem wide apart. Moreover, for members of the tribe now residing in Syria the issue of rights in the ancestral territory is vague and hardly relevant. This, however, may be altered once a real breakthrough in Israeli-Syrian relations actually happens. It is at such junctures that the power of blood ties is likely to be invoked again, perhaps to form an automatic, 'natural' parity between relatives across the border. And it is in such situations that the specific histories of various sections of the tribe, including the histories of those who became refugees, become significant in ways not easily overseen.

The Palestinian citizens of Israel can be defined as a 'trapped minority', an individual case of a national minority (Rabinowitz and Khawalde forthcoming). Trapped minorities stretch across territorial borders in ways traditional concepts of states and nations fail to acknowledge, let alone theorize. Citizens in states which are hegemonized by groups they are excluded from, members of trapped minorities are alienated from political power and cannot influence the definition of public goods or determine who enjoys them. Having no part in their mother nation's national project, which takes place in other territories, they are marginal twice over: once in their state of residence and citizenship; and a second time within their mother nation.

Entrapment is a dramatic development. A space initially perceived to be safe is subject to sudden external interference leading to confinement: a door is closed, a fence erected, a wall cemented. The space becomes a dangerous enclosure, the subject is suddenly incarcerated. Most homeland minorities are trapped in two distinct but complimentary dimensions. The first one is historical, pertaining to the sequence of undesirable events that brought about their current predicament as a minority within an alien state. The other denotes entrapment between contemporary entities, and in particular between their host state and their mother nation.

The Kirad are not a national minority to themselves. The history they share with the majority of Palestinian communities has ironed out most of the differences and distance that may have existed between them and mainstream Palestinians before 1948. Many Kirad in fact identify themselves as Palestinians, feeling a shared fate. But when it comes to an analysis of the group by itself, the Kirad, like other Bedouins, can be subsumed under the definition of 'Fourth world' (Manuel and Posulns 1974). They are a small scale, marginal group whose territory and other vital resources were overtaken by an alien state.

They are spread, since 1948, over four states, that suggests analogies between their situation and that of larger national minorities in a similar predicament. Like trapped minorities, the Kirad have to negotiate between their state of citizenship and their mother group. But in addition to the scattered mother Palestinian nation, the Kirad have an additional entity – the bifurcated tribe, historicized as an important focus of identity and essence, to reckon with.

The result is what I wish to call 'small scale diasporic situation': a diaspora created by a hostile frontier running through the middle of a small scale. Like other diasporas, that of the Kirad too has a cradle territory – the Hula valley – and those who have been forced away and now live elsewhere. Unlike normal diasporic situations, however, small scale diasporas are personal, immediate and concrete. The central idiom is the border, not the world at large, and the imagination is of a linear trajectory – a line between the homeland and the place of exile – rather than a sphericone in which the world at large serves as the alternative to home.

It is no wonder that in such a predicament kinship transpires as a central unifying symbol. More than the nation, citizenship or other types of generalized affiliation, kinship is, for Bedouins, an idiom that unites the most important elements that form the sense of home and of belonging. The ever important blood ties dictate solidarity (Abu Lughod 1986), rights in land (Marx 1977), allegiance (Evans-Pritchard 1940, Peters 1965) and the place and legitimacy of individuals in a significant social web.

## Notes

1. Um-Nader and all other names specified in connection with her are not the actors' real names.
2. See Shalev 1993 for a detailed account of the central DMZ in the Armistice Regime, 1949–1955.
3. Security Council (UN) (1949) *Communication dated 20 July 1949 from the UN Acting Mediator on Palestine to the Acting Secretary-General transmitting the text of the General Armistice Agreement Between Israel and Syria. Document s / 1353 / Rev. 1, Official Records, Fourth Year.* (Article 5, paragraph 5 sub-paragraph e).
4. In the event, a state of emergency was never officially declared during that conflict.
5. Rabin, Yitzhak (1979) *Service Record.* Tel-Aviv: Maariv (in Hebrew).
6. Khawalde's field survey of the Kirad in Northern Israel in 1997 has found 1,859 members: 877 in the village of Sha'ab in western Galilee, the rest in the town of Shafa'amar and the villages of Tuba, Kufr-Yasif, Jdaidah and Abu-Snan in lower Galilee. A further 3,500 Kirad are estimated to live as refugees abroad – mostly in Syria, some in Jordan, a handful in Lebanon. An earlier survey conducted by Khawalde in 1990 indicates that at the time the total number of the Kirad in Galilee was 1,599. Sha'ab had 737, Shafa'amar 579, and the rest resided in smaller numbers in other villages (Khawalde 1994:133).
7. Turkman tribes inhabiting the Valley of Esdralon are mentioned by a number of writers, some of whom cite the name 'Theishat. See Ashkenazi (1938:240), Shimoni (1947:100–103).
8. Since irrigation is a major limiting factor, ancient irrigation schemes may have had the valley more fertile and productive in earlier times.
9. A similar process is known amongst the 25 or so Bedouin tribes and splinter groups of the Negev, which Israel systematically dispossessed and relocated in the early 1950s in an attempt to gain full control of their ancestral land. Uprooted and forcefully transferred to a triangular zone located between Beer-Sheva, Dimona and Arad and pushed by powers beyond their control into becoming tenants on land historically belonging to another Bedouin coalition, the 'Dulam, the newly arrived Bedouin were – and still are – in a dubious position. The military government under which they found themselves in the 1950s dictated total dependency on recognition by the government for purposes of work and travel permits, social security and grazing rights. Such recognition would only be extended through an intricate system of patronage, carried out by co-opted Bedouin Sheikhs. The newcomers thus had to find protection and official representation with their reluctant Bedouin hosts, or suffer the dire consequences of nonrecognition by the state.

## References


*Ariel, Encyclopaedia of the Land of Israel*. Jerusalem: Ariel.

Ashkenazi, Tuvia 1938: *Tribus Semi-nomades de Ia Palestine du Nord*. Paris.

Bakhit, Muhammad A. 1990: Safad et sa region d'après des documents de Wagfs et des titres de propriété 1378–1556. In: *La Revue du Monde Muslamane et de la Mediterranee No 55 / 56,* 101–123. P. 104.

Cohen, Amnon and Bernard Lewis 1978: *Population and Revenue in the Towns of Palestine in the Sixteenth Century.* Princeton: Princeton University Press: 155.

Dabagh, Mustafa Murad 1965: *Biladina Falastin (Our Land Palestine).* Beirut: (in Arabic).

Falah, Ghazi 1990: The Evolution of Semi-nomadism in Non-desert Environment. The Case of the Galilee in the 19th Century. In: *Geojournal* Vol. 24 no. 4:397–410.

Hutteroth, Wolf-Dieter and Kamal Abdulfattah 1977: *Historical Geography of Palestine Transjordan and Southern Syria in the late 16th Century.* Erlangen: Geographische Arbeiten Nr 5.

Karmon, Yehuda 1956: *The Northern Hula Valley: A Chapter in the History of the Landscape of the Land of Israel.* Jerusalem: Magnes Publishing House (in Hebrew).

Khawalde, Sliman 1995: Changes among Krad al-Kheit tribe at the Galilee, from 1858 until 1994. *Notes on the Bedouin* No. 27:24–39 (in Hebrew).

Le Strange, Guy (Translator) 1896: *Mukaddissi's* (985) Description of Syria, including Palestine. London.

Le Strange, Guy 1890: *Palestine Under the Moslems.* London.

Lewis, N.N 1955: The Frontier of Settlement in Syria,

1800–1950. In: *International Affairs Journal* Vol. 21 no. 1:48–60.

Manuel, George & Michael Posluns 1974: *The Fourth World: an Indian Reality.* New York: Free Press.

Marx, Emmanuel 1977: The tribe as a unit of subsistence: nomadic pastoralists in the Middle-East. In: *American Anthropologist 79*:343–363.

Rabinowitz, Dan 1985: Themes in the economy of Sinai Bedouin in the 19th and 20th centuries. In: *International Journal of Middle East Studies* 17:211–228.

Rabinowitz, Dan & Sliman Khawalde (forthcoming) Demilitarized Then Dispossessed: The Kirad Bedouins of the Hula Valley in the Context of Syrian-Israeli Relations. In: *International Journal of Middle East Studies.*

Sawa'id, Yusuf 1995: The Sheikhs' Regime in the North of Palestine: The Example of Akil Agha, 1840–1870. In: *Notes on the Bedouin,* Vol. 27: 40–57 (in Hebrew).

Shalev, Aryeh 1993: *The Israel-Syria Armistice Regime, 1949–1955.* Boulder, Colorado: Westview Press (JCSS study no. 21).

Shim'oni Ya'acov 1947: *'Arviyey Eretz Yisrael (The Arabs of the Land of Israel)* Tel-Aviv: Am-Oved: 100–103.

Tyler, W.P.N 1994: The Huleh concession and Jewish settlement of the Huleh valley, 1934–1948. In: *Middle Eastern Studies,* Vol. 30. No. 4, October: 826–859.

Zakariya, Ahmad Wasfi 1923: *'Asha`ir al-Sham (The Tribes of Syria).* Damascus: Dar al-Fiqr (in Arabic).

# Borders and Emotions

## Hope and Fear in the Bohemian-Bavarian Frontier Zone[1]

*Maruška Svašek*

Svašek, Maruška 2000: Borders and Emotions: Hope and Fear in the Bohemian-Bavarian Frontier Zone. – Ethnologia Europaea 30, 2: 111–126.

The paper argues that the emotional aspects of identity construction at international borders, and the ways in which different feelings and sentiments affect border people's perceptions and actions, have in the main remained an underexplored field of research. The analyses focuses on the Bohemian-Bavarian frontier zone, and shows that the inhabitants' perceptions of 'those on the other side' have been strongly affected by memories of the horrors of the Second World War and the post-war Sudeten German expulsion. Emotional displays and discourses of emotions have been actively used in the negation of social reality in the first post-Cold War decade. Introducing an analytical distinction between 'evoked', 'remembered', and 're-experienced' emotions, the paper outlines how emotionally complex memories can become a political force, weakening or strengthening both national and transnational identities.

*Dr Maruška Svašek, School of Anthropological Studies, The Queen's University of Belfast, BT7 1NN Belfast, Northern Ireland, UK. E-mail: m.svasek@qub.ac.uk*

"While [emotions] are subjectively felt and interpreted, it is socialized human beings – that is, thinking human bodies – who are feeling them in specific social contexts" (Leavitt 1996: 531).

## Introduction

In the past six years, Hastings Donnan and Thomas M. Wilson have sketched the outline of an anthropology of frontiers that perceives borders as 'domains of contested power, in which local, national, and international groups negotiate relations of subordination and control' (Wilson and Donnan 1998: 10). This perspective focuses on the problematic relations of power and identity at international borders, and examines the ways in which border inhabitants deal with state power, and face transnational economic, environmental, political, and social problems (cf. Donnan and Wilson 1999: 156).

An important theme in the anthropology of frontiers is the construction of multiple identities in changing socio-economic and political contexts. Numerous scholars have convincingly shown that border peoples in different parts of the world demonstrate ambiguous identities because they are pulled in different directions by political, economic, cultural, and linguistic factors (see, for example, Cheater 1998; Kearney 1998; Douglass 1998). Other scholars have examined the ways in which political processes such as cross-border migration, the creation of new state boundaries, and the end of the Cold War have partly shaped border inhabitants' perceptions of themselves and others (see, for example, Borneman 1998; Driessen 1992, 1998; Green 1998).

Even though much valuable work has been done that has provided a better understanding of identity construction at international borders, the emotional aspects of this process, and the ways in which different feelings and sentiments may affect border people's perceptions and actions, have in the main remained an underexplored field of research.[2] In my view, a focus on emotions is essential because 'emotions are, in many societies, a critical link in cultural interpretations of action' (Lutz and White 1986: 420). One should however, not limit the study of emotions by simply regarding emotions as cultural constructions. As Margot Lyon (1995: 258) noted, emotions have 'social consequences', and 'social relations themselves may generate emotions', and it is therefore necessary to acknowledge 'the importance of social relations in the genesis of emotions' (ibid. 249). John Leavitt similarly argued that it is necessary to recognize the social nature of emotions.[3]

Inspired by writings by Spinoza and the Russian psychologist L.S. Vygotsky, he noted that emotions should be regarded as: 'experiences learned and expressed in the body in social interactions through the mediation of systems of signs, verbal and non-verbal' (Leavitt 1996: 526).

In my view, an anthropological approach to emotions must also deal with the way in which emotions are embedded in contexts of changing power relations (Svašek 1995: 115–116; Svašek 1999: 45–47). After all, power struggles are inherent to social life, and instances of emotional 'navigation' are part and parcel of political processes (Reddy 1999: 271; cf. Wikan 1990). This article will demonstrate that, in post-Cold War border areas, emotions have helped to shape political identification processes in particular ways.

In general, it is interesting to examine the dynamics of politics and emotion in frontier zones. In these areas, people's social life is at least partly affected by the proximity of the state border, and problems specific to border regions may stir up people's emotions and force them to take specific political actions. Emotional discourses may, for example, empower particular border communities to challenge the power of state centres or to make political demands that increase or decrease regional autonomy. Furthermore, particular shared sentiments may both reinforce and undermine national, regional, or transnational identification processes.

This article will argue that emotional displays and discourses of emotion have been actively used in the negotiation of social and political reality in the first post-Cold War decade in areas that used to be the outer territories of the Capitalist West and the Communist East. The analysis particularly focuses on the emotional reactions of the inhabitants of the Bohemian-Bavarian border area to the disappearance of the Iron Curtain in 1990, and on the ways in which local politicians, priests, and interest groups have tried to evoke and control emotions in an attempt to influence border inhabitants' perceptions of 'those on the other side'.

## Initial Euphoria

On the 23rd December 1989, the West German Minister of Foreign Affairs Hans-Dietrich Genscher and his Czech counterpart Jiří Dienstbier symbolically ended the Cold War relations between their countries. Just outside the village of Nové Domky, not far from the border crossing Waidhaus-Rozvadov, they ritually cut through a fence of barbed wire that, for a period of over forty years, had formed part of the heavily defended Eastern bloc frontier. To increase the festive mood, the German *Musikverein Waidhaus* played brass band music, and the cheering public waved with flags and shouted 'Bravo!' and 'Freedom, freedom!'. Responding to their enthusiasm, the ministers handed out pieces of 'Iron Curtain', an act reminiscent of the transformation of the Berlin Wall into chopped off pieces of history[4] (cf. Sporrer 1990). During the political ritual, different symbols were used to represent and engender emotion. The wire symbolised four decades of mutual enmity and fear, and by destroying it, the politicians symbolically transformed a symbol of fear into a symbol of hope. At the same time, the music and the act of cutting and distributing the 'actual borderline' stirred up feelings of trust in the post-Cold War political situation.

It took another six months before the compulsory visa requirements were abolished, and before the heavily defended Cold War border was transformed into a less forbidding borderline. Especially in the light of Czechoslovakia's intention to apply for NATO and EU-membership, the Czechoslovak and German governments now regarded the Bohemian-Bavarian border as 356 kilometres of potential contact. This shift in perception did not just take place on the level of governmental state policy. Many people who lived in communities close to the border welcomed the changes, and were curious about life on "the other side". Their optimistic feelings had social consequences. Quite a few people, especially those who lived in communities close to the state border, began to look for opportunities to establish cross-border contacts (cf. Svašek 1999).

One of the reasons why eastern Bohemian and western Bavarian border inhabitants were interested in 'the other side' was that for a period of over forty years, they had lived in the peripheries of two hostile ideological entities, the capitalist West and the communist East. The disadvantageous conditions that 'normally' characterise frontier zones, such as economic underdevelopment and political marginalisation (cf. Donnan and Wilson 1999) had been intensified in the Cold War context. The governments in Prague and Bonn simply regarded the regions as peripheral zones of defence, and did not invest much in their development. The Germans were of course much better off than the Czechs because of the advantageous economic conditions in former West Germany, and because of the policy of political decentralisation.[5] On the Czech side, the dramatic results of economic mismanagement, overcentralisation, and strict military control were clearly visible. People lived in run down houses, and to deter them from fleeing the country, a wide strip of land was only accessible with a special military pass. With the disappearance of the Iron Curtain, both Czech and German border inhabitants hoped that their situation would improve.

## Meeting at the Border

In the Spring of 1990, Czechs and Germans from the Bohemian village of Broumov and the small Bavarian town of Mähring, began meeting each other at the Broumov-Mähring border-crossing. The people who had been officially expected to see each other as ideological Others for a period of forty-one years, now talked and drank beer while hanging over the barrier. After several friendly exchanges, the idea was born to organise a communal party to celebrate the ending of the Cold War (cf. *Der Neue Tag* 1989; Zrenner 1990). The party would function as a social and emotional context in which the friendly relations could be further developed.

On the first of May 1990, two months before the official abolition of the compulsory visa requirement, the border crossing opened its barriers for one day. On the Czech side, a banner welcomed the Germans, saying: "Broumov vítá Mähring" (Broumov welcomes Mähring). A banner saying: "Herzlich Willkommen" (Welcome indeed!) on the German side expressed similar intentions. The transformation of the physical border into 'an open door', inviting people in and making them feel welcome instead of shutting them out, was obviously highly significant.

During the day, more than fifteen thousand Czechs took the opportunity to visit Mähring, and many Germans crossed the border to Broumov. The German newspapers described the event as a dramatic restoration of friendship. *Der Neue Tag* reported that Czech and German priests 'fell into each others arms and prayed', and quoted a German representative who had stated that this was "the beginning of reconciliation and friendship". The speeches by Czech and German representatives were highly optimistic about future co-operation. A Czech Mayor was reported to have declared: "We will build a new house without weapons, so that we can live in peace" (Sporrer 1990).[6] The local powerholders clearly used emotional rhetoric and performance to create an atmosphere of mutual trust, and to open up possibilities to co-operate on various levels.

If we should believe the local press, the optimistic mood in the Bohemian-Bavarian frontier zone was shared by all inhabitants. On the 1st July 1990, when the compulsory visa requirements were officially abolished, and six new border-crossings were ceremonially opened, the German local newspapers talked of "ein riesiges Volksfest", "ein Festival der Lebensfreude" (*Der Neue Tag* 1990).[7]

The opening of the border, however, did not only evoke positive, optimistic feelings of hope and trust in a better and peaceful future, as the press suggested. On the contrary, large groups of Czechs and Germans were reminded of the Second World War and of the Sudeten German expulsion, when they had been each other's fierce opponents. Their distrust and fear highlights an important area of research in the study of emotions: the impact of past experiences and social memories on people's emotional life. As Ilona Irwin-Zarecka noted, as people first articulate and share the sense they make of *their* past, it is their experience, in all its emotional complexity, that serves as a key reference point. If their interpretive strategies are indeed products of culture, the plausibility of resulting accounts depends on the fit with the individuals' emotional reality. Someone who suffered great physical pain is not likely to define what happened as a pleasant diversion' (Irwin-Zarecka 1994: 17, emphasis in original).

This article will focus on German and Czech expressions of old and new fears, as well as on attempts by local politicians and priests to create a mood of mutual trust through reconciliation. It will demonstrate that conflicting discourses and practices, expressing and reinforcing feelings of both hope and fear, influenced post-Cold War identification processes.

## Old Fears: Remembered and Re-experienced

When the Broumov-Mähring border crossing was officially opened, thousands of people participated in the celebrations.[8] Mathilde, one of the German visitors, told me about the event when I met her in 1997. Her account shows how the event evoked memories of a fearful past, as well as generated a feeling that things could be changed for the better.

It is necessary to make a theoretical distinction between *evoked* emotions, *remembered* emotions and *re-experienced* emotions. I define 'evoked' emotions as emotional reactions to specific events or incidents. By contrast, 'remembered emotions' are *memories* of past emotions that do not cause a (similar) emotional reaction in the person recalling them. 'Remember how angry I was?', somebody might say with a smile on his face, clearly being emotionally detached from the earlier experience of anger. By contrast, 're-experienced emotions' are past feelings that are remembered *and* re-experienced in the present, and that possibly empower a person to take certain actions, or, on the contrary, force him into a state of social paralysis. It is important to note that in this context, 're-experience' does not mean that the person experiences and interprets his or her feelings in exactly the same way as he or she did in the past. Instead, as Mathilde's case will show, their meanings and social consequences may be quite different.

The following case will show that Mathilde both remembered *and* experienced fear after she had crossed the Bohemian-Bavarian border. Since 1947, she had lived in Tirschenreuth, a small Bavarian town situated only 12 kilometres from Mähring. She had been born in 1940 in the Bohemian village of Brand (today mainly known by the Czech name of Milíře), less than 20 kilometres from her adopted Bavarian home. In 1946, at the age of six, she had been expelled from Czechoslovakia, together with over 3 million other Sudeten Germans.[9] To her, the opening of the border and a visit to Bohemia meant far more than to indigenous Bavarians: it not only evoked nostalgic memories of life in her old *Heimat*, but also confronted her with a dark side of her family history and personal past.

The Sudeten German expulsion had begun immediately after the liberation, two months before the signing of the Potsdam Agreements. Between May and October 1945, the Sudeten Germans had lost their citizenship rights, and the confiscation of their property had been given legal basis by a number of presidential decrees. During the first chaotic post war months, numerous Czechs had taken the opportunity to take revenge on the German population. From May till November 1945, during a period known as the "wild expulsion" (wilde Austreibung), many Sudeten Germans, in particular those who lived in ethnically mixed areas, had been terrorised, maltreated, and brutally killed.[10] In 1946, during the "organised expulsion" (geregelte Vertreibung), the Germans were generally treated in a more humane manner (cf. Hamperl 1996; Staněk 1991).

The village where Mathilde came from had been situated in the almost purely German district of Tachau[11], and the terror had been less severe than in other districts. Nevertheless, the experience of the sudden expulsion and the loss of *Heimat* had traumatised many, if not all expellees (cf. Hamperl 1996). Many of them had settled in Bavaria, often in areas not far from the Czech border, and it is not surprising that they experienced the opening of the borders with mixed feelings.

On the one hand, the expellees shared feelings of nostalgia and curiosity: how would their former homeland look after forty years? It was this mixture of feelings that made Mathilde decide to cycle past Broumov further into Bohemia, and that eventually drew her like a magnet to her old *Heimatdorf* (home village).[12] As she recalled:

"In 1990 the border crossing Mähring-Promenhof [Promenhof is the old German name for Broumov] was opened, and this had been officially announced to the inhabitants from Tirschenreuth (...). We read about it, my husband and I, and we said to each other: 'we should actually go, and have a look on the Czech side'. My husband said 'you know what we'll do? We'll take the bicycles with us'. So we put the roof rack on the car and we put the bicycles on top and we drove to Mähring, where we left the car and cycled to the border. There were so many people! Thousands! Thousands of people, and all walking, they must have thought 'the next village is Promenhof, that's not far (...)'. We recognised many people from Tirschenreuth, and they said: 'Aaah, you got your bicycles with you! My God, how far is it then still to Promenhof?' It was a lovely, warm day."

Cycling between the two border towns, surrounded by large crowds of Germans and Czechs, Mathilde felt light-hearted and experienced the event as a real celebration. When I asked her about the Czech visitors she answered: "Yes, there were Czechs as well. People ate sausages, it was a real celebration".

Judging from the tone of her voice, cycling the first few kilometres into Bohemia, she had still felt carefree and excited about the fact that she was back in her old Heimat.

"We had our bicycles and it was nice weather, so we, my husband and I, we cycled, and cycled, and cycled, further and further, the sun was shining brightly. We were already far inside the Czech Republic, and saw a sign that said 'direction Tachau' (the old German name for the city of Tachov). So we said to each other 'let's ride a bit further in the direction of Tachau'.

The tone in her voice changed, however, when she remarked:

"We no longer saw any Germans, because they did not go that far, they were all on foot". Unconsciously, she began to be haunted by memories and stories of the expulsion, and to perceive the Czechs as a potential danger. Nevertheless, her desire to get closer to home was strong enough to suppress her anxiety and to cycle on. She continued: "Well, and then we saw Tachau in the distance, [so we said]: 'we should go there'. We were curious. When we actually arrived in Tachau it was half past three in the afternoon... It could not be that far any more to Brand. We did not speak a word of Czech and nobody understood us, because, until 1990, nobody went to Czechoslovakia. In Tachau there were no Germans, and there was nothing. Today it is different, today they understand a bit of German. [But then] we asked everybody: 'Brand, Brand, Brand, where is Brand, how do we get to Brand? [Finally] a woman understood us, and directed us. So we cycled and cycled...' "

The experiences that people did not speak any German, and that they did not recognise the German name of Brand made Mathilde suddenly feel like a stranger. She was back home but she wasn't. She recognised the landscape, but things were different. It was like a nightmare.

"We saw the church [of Brand] all the time [on the hill], but there was a new road, leading around a reservoir that had not been there before so we had to go around the reservoir, it was much further than I thought. It was late, almost evening, and we were there alone in the Czech Republic, my husband and I. I cried and we were tired as well. My husband said 'it cannot be far any more, it cannot be far'. So finally we cycled up the Church Hill (Kirchenberg) ... "

Mathilde was physically and mentally exhausted. The sight of the familiar church, the shock when she noticed that a whole village had disappeared and made way for a reservoir, the frustration when she needed to find a new road, and the fact that it was getting later and later confused her. When I remarked that "it must have been hard, such a long trip", she repeated that they "had been all alone" (as Germans on Czech territory), and when I asked her whether she had been afraid (which was obvious from the tone of her voice), she almost screamed: "I was so afraid, my heart was pounding!"[13]

When they had finally reached the village, and Mathilde had entered the church, she had been overwhelmed by emotions. She recounted:

"Well, and then we stopped near the church to have a look. My husband said 'down here is a pub, I think they'll sell lemonade and beer. Sit down in the church, I'll get us something'. And I sat down in the church, and my husband gave the sexton twenty Deutschmarks. 'For the church, it's a donation', he said. The sexton lit a few candles, and he went up and rang the bells. I was alone in the church, I cried!"

When I suggested that she remembered things, she replied.

"Yes, I remembered, I remembered a lot. The church, and how I used to sit in the church, and the candles, and how they used to take photographs, and the annual festival that used to be held in the area in front of the church, on the *Festplatz*. It was rather moving."

In the church, Mathilde's memories of the pre-expulsion past (in Sudeten German texts often referred to as a timeless, mythical paradise), pushed away her anxiety caused by the trauma of the expulsion itself.[14] Once outside the safe church walls however, her fears returned. Yet being so close to the place where her old family house had stood (she knew from her father who had visited the place that it had been knocked down), she cycled on to see the spot. In her account she emphasised that she had been afraid: "By now it was already evening, and we were all alone in the Czech Republic! It was frightening! (*es war ganz schlimm*)".

Mathilde and her husband approached the house that used to be her neighbours', and saw American flags behind all the windows. She recalled: "'Look!', I said, 'thank God, everything [i.e. Western civilisation] is not so far away!' (*es ist doch nicht so weit weg, alles*). To me they were like a ray of hope."

As in a fairy tale, the story had a happy ending. The present Czech owner of the house came out and invited Mathilde and her husband in. Even though the memory of fear remained, her actual fear disappeared. The owner's wife spoke a few words of German, and offered them schnitzels with bread and a glass of beer. When the German couple decided to leave because it was getting late, and they still needed to cycle all the way back to Mähring, their Czech host protested and offered to take them and their bicycles by car and trailer.

Mathilde's account makes clear that the sudden disappearance of the Iron Curtain evoked contradictory feelings on the Bavarian side of the border. On the one hand, the inhabitants were happy that the Cold War had ended, and that Oberpfalz no longer formed the outer belt of a political, economic and military unit. They would be able to travel without restrictions to West Bohemia to go shopping and visit tourist attractions such as Karlovy Vary and Mariánské Lázně. The expelled Sudeten German inhabitants in particular, were interested in visiting their former homeland. On the other hand, however, the disappearance of the Iron Curtain also aroused feelings of distrust and fear, stirred up by memories of anti-Sudeten German aggression and for anxieties about the collapse of what some perceived as the outer boundaries of Europe. On the one hand, remembered emotions could easily transform into re-experienced emotions, and, as such, they could reinforce the perception of those on the other side of the border as 'dangerous others', and discourage cross-border co-operation. Re-experienced emotions could, however, also transform into emotionally detached memories, and loose their direct impact on social and political life.

## Distrust and Fear on the Czech Side

After I began visiting the Czech-German border area regularly from 1991 onwards, several people told me on different occasions that on the night before the official opening of the border, the inhabitants from the Czech village of Lesná had armed themselves with guns, sticks and pitchforks, in an attempt to defend the forest roads leading to the border in case the Sudeten Germans would attack. Lesná, also known by the German name of Schönwald, had been inhabited by Sudeten Germans until their expulsion in 1946, and was situated only a few kilometres from German territory. The current inhabitants, so the story went, had feared a Sudeten German invasion, and had prepared a 'military defence'.

The story, described by some of Lesná's inhabitant as sheer nonsense, was told to me on both sides of the border. Some narrators (Germans and Czech townspeople) presented it as an example of the 'simplistic, rural mentality' of Czech village people. Others hinted at the fact that Lesná's inhabitants were 'backward' Ruthenians, emigrants who had moved from northern Romania to Czechoslovakia in 1947 as part of Czechoslovakia's post-war immigration policy. One German argued that the story proved how brainwashed the Czechs were after forty years of Communism. *All* narrators, however, *also* argued that the story indicated just how deeply rooted were the Czech feelings of distrust and fear. Referring to (but not necessarily feeling) these emotions, they expressed their doubts in the optimistic image the media had presented of future Czech-German co-operation.

The dramatic political change, however, did allow Czechs to travel back and forth to Germany, and to replace the stereotypical view of Germans as 'dangerous invaders' with more realistic expectations. Many Czechs, especially those who lived close to the border, began to learn German, and a considerable number of them found jobs in the Oberpfalz district. Temporarily living in Bavaria, or commuting daily to their German jobs, they profited from the much higher wages.

## Cross-Border Politics: Other Fears and Concerns

Local politicians, mayors, and teachers began to look for ways to co-operate with their German counterparts. Many Czech and German cities and schools formalised their contacts through community-links and partnerships (cf. Giegold and Otto 1994), and in the Czech border city of Cheb, a number of active intellectuals began to search for possibilities to co-operate on a larger, regional scale. Gradually, more local Czech and German politicians became interested in the formation of a larger framework of euregional co-operation.[15] Especially the Czechs regarded it as a way to increase regional autonomy. An idea to join together four Czech and two German districts, and call it *Euregion Egrensis*, was proposed in 1992 (cf. Houžvička 1993, 1994; Svašek 1999).[16]

The propagation of cross-border, euregional co-operation rested heavily on standard discourses, common in other European frontier zones. Transnational problems such as environmental pollution and illegal cross-border movements of people, goods, and money were central issues. To find support for euregional policy, the adherents defined these problems as major causes of fear, and argued that they could not be tackled by individual state governments or local authorities alone.[17]

Many people I spoke with indeed identified ecological problems and illegal cross-border movements as worrying developments. They regarded refugees, smugglers, and prostitutes as unwelcome people who socially and morally polluting the area. Cross-border co-operation was presented as a way to 'purify' the frontier zone (cf. Douglas 1966).

Another cause of fear euregional policy makers promised to deal with was the problem of social, political and economic marginality. As noted before, border peoples often have a peripheral existence within their own countries, and receive less financial support for the development of their region than the state centres. Cross-border co-operation, implying the strengthening of cross-border loyalties and identities, was presented as a solution.

As citizens of two autonomous political states

that had been divided by the Iron Curtain for more than forty years, however, the Bohemian and Bavarian border inhabitants were used to seeing the frontier as a highly significant symbolic marker of cultural, political, and economic difference. Evidently, the politicians and regional representatives who supported euregional co-operation thought it necessary to change the border inhabitants' spatial and territorial perception. A colourful symbol was designed as a visual emblem for the new Euregion, and a new map was printed outlining the territory of Egrensis. In the new geographic scheme, the Iron Curtain was transformed into a much less important, intra-regional boundary. The tourist guide *Museums in Euregion Egrensis: A Journey through Time and History* even printed a map of Egrensis in which the Czech-German state border had totally disappeared. The map suggested that the heavily guarded outer border of the European Union (also known as "the electronic curtain") that split the new Euregion into two political and economic spheres, was non-existent. The spatial reclassification reflected the plans to include the Czech Republic in the European Union, and can be regarded as a sign of Brussels' policy of decentralisation, expressed by the slogan "Europe of the Regions" (cf. Cooke, Christiansen and Schienstock 1997; Preston 1997: 195–209).

## Memory, Mistrust, and Political Scepticism

Czechs who had experienced the Second World War, and who continued to distrust their former enemies, did not welcome the developments. "You can't trust Germans", I was told frequently by Czech border inhabitants. Communists and Republicans especially were sceptical of policies that created close cross-border co-operative ties, and found the high number of expelled Sudeten Germans who actively supported euregional co-operation disturbing. Continuously reminding people of Nazi terror, they attempted to stir up and strengthen anti-German and anti-Sudeten German feelings. Various articles appeared in the newspapers, warning readers that Germany was still a nation to be feared, and that the Sudeten Germans had serious aspirations to resettle in the Sudetenland. The journalist Karel Čtvrtek stated in the communist newspaper *Hálo noviny*: Transferred Germans do not hide their aim of taking back land, because without their own land, the Sudeten Germans are threatened with extinction as a national group, in as much as they are threatened by integration with the population among whom they live. They do not want to return to a Czech national state, they do not even want minority rights at a European level. They want land. It is of secondary importance to them whether that land will be 'Freistaat Sudetenland', or another federal land of Germany (Čtvrtek 1992).

*Hálo noviny* interpreted the creation of a new Czech-German geographical unit as an act of anti-Czech territoriality, an act that strongly reminded them of the assimilation of the Sudetenland by the Third Reich in 1938. Jiří Frajdl, who worked for the same newspaper, stated in 1994 that Euregion Egrensis was 'an old Nazi plan', a conspiracy between pro-German Czechs and anti-Czech Germans, meant to undermine the autonomy of the Czech Republic (Frajdl 1994).

The idea of a conspiracy was unintentionally reinforced by Cheb's Mayor, František Linda, when he attempted to prohibit a planned demonstration by the *Club of the Czech Border Area* (Klub českého pohraničí), an association established by Czechs who were afraid that the Germans would attempt to increase their power in the Bohemian border area. The official goal of the 1994 demonstration was 'to remind people of the Munich dictate and to commemorate its victims' (Tachovský deník 1994). According to Linda, an adherent of Czech-German euregional co-operation, the demonstrators' (mainly communists and republicans) true goal was to increase Czech-German tension, and to 'inflame national hatred'. The *Club* went to court, however, and appealed against Linda's decision to prohibit the commemoration. The High Court in Prague ruled in their favour, and the ban on the protest was repealed. On 24 September 1994 a few hundred people gathered on Cheb's main square, carrying banners with the slogan 'Never again Munich', 'Cheb must stay Czech', and 'People beware of the Sudeten Germans'.

The above demonstrates that the painful memories of German terror and oppression were easily evoked in the post-Cold War political arena. Politicians and interest groups reminded people of their past fears, and attempted to use emotional force to gain political power. The dynamics of politics and emotions hampered reconciliation and the construction of shared euregional and European identities. The following section will show how priests and local politicians attempted to turn the tide by creating emotional contexts in which Czechs and Germans would be willing to co-operate.

## Controlling Emotions through Divine Power

In the first few years after the border opened, Czech and German representatives of different churches[18] made particular efforts to establish cross-border contacts. Living and working in an area where large groups of people feared and distrusted each other, they regarded it as their Christian duty to convince the border inhabitants of the necessity of reconciliation.

'Reconciliation' is a common Christian theme, and both Czech and German clergy used the bible as a source of inspiration to connect notions of religious and political reconciliation. Father Götz, a young German priest who headed a Catholic parish in the border town of Bärnau, told me in 1996 that people needed to reconcile with God before they could reconcile with each other: "It is our task to retain peace. I mean, Christ says '(...) the peace given by Christ comes from the heart through the reconciliation with God [and] the forgiving of sins'".

In the same year, the Orthodox Father Hausar from the Czech village of Lesná noted: "Up to the present day, the hatred against the Germans, against the [German] nation, is deeply rooted in some people. I always take the Christian viewpoint, [and there is] a fundamental difference between the approach taken by such people and the Christian approach. I now talk from a Christian viewpoint: there is a proverb saying that 'Christians must hate sins but love sinners'. If a German commits an offence against somebody I will condemn his deed but [at the same time] I will love that person because through love and forgiveness, the relations can be restored."

Both priests conceptualised negative emotions such as jealousy and hatred as powerful forces that should be controlled by divine power and faith. In this view, feelings of hate and fear could be transformed into love and trust through personal reconciliation with God. Priests and ministers who worked in the border area used the ritual context of the sermon and their own religious authority to convince people of the necessity to reconcile. As David Kertzer noted:

"The dramatic quality of ritual does more than define roles (...), it also provokes emotional response. Just as emotions are manipulated in the theatre through the varied stimuli of light, colour, gesture, movement, voice, so too these elements and others give rituals a means of generating powerful feelings" (Kertzer 1988: 11).

To get their message across, some priests were quite inventive performers. 'Where is Hitler? ... Where is Stalin? ... and where is Jesus?!!', shouted a German Protestant minister in Milíře's Orthodox Church during the Easter ceremonies in 1998. He had been invited to this Czech village (Mathilde's place of birth) by the local priest, Father Hausar, who had asked him to deliver a short sermon on Easter Sunday to the Orthodox congregation.[19] The metaphorical construction in the sermon was based on three properties of symbols that are especially important in ritual symbolism: 'condensation', the embodiment and connection of diverse ideas; 'multivocality', the variety of different meanings attached to the same symbol, and 'ambiguity', the fact that symbols do not necessarily have single precise meanings (cf. Kertzer).

The reference to Hitler, Stalin, and Jesus undermined the image of Germans as 'the fearful arch-enemy'. First, by referring not simply to Hitler but also to Stalin, the minister emphasised that the Germans had not been the only enemy of the Czechs. Second, by classifying Hitler as an evil German *individual* he deconstructed the totalising image of The German Danger, and created a semantic space for more positive images of Germans.

The sermon sketched the image of Christianity as a transnational, pacifying force. By contrasting 'Hitler and Stalin' with 'Jesus', the minister stressed that although the former two had enjoyed political power and had terrified people during their lives, they had lacked the latter's divine, eternal authority. In other words, in comparison with God's almighty power, human force was limited, and only God could use His powers to restore damaged relationships, and to undermine national hatred. If the border inhabitants remained faithful, they would find the strength to continue living together in peace and harmony.

## Religious and Political Reconciliation

After the opening of the borders in 1990, an increasing number of local Catholic, Protestant and Orthodox priests established contacts with colleagues from the other side of the border, and actively propagated political reconciliation.[20] By May 1997 thirty-five of the forty-nine cross-border links between Bavaria and Bohemia were between religious communities.[21]

In the Bavarian town of Vohenstrauß, for example, the Protestant parish began to cooperate with the Bohemian Brethren in the Czech city of Cernošín in 1991. Their co-operation involved, amongst other things, occasional joint church services, mutual visits, and godparenthood relations between German godparents and Czech godchildren.[22] The Catholics from Vohenstrauß established connections with the Catholic community in the city of Stříbro. They organised joint pilgrimages, visited each others' churches, and the Germans helped the Czechs by offering financial support for the restoration of Stříbro's Catholic church. The priests hoped that people would be able to get to know each other through these mutual visits and shared experiences, and thereby, break down negative nationalist stereotypical images.

In many cases, religious connections were also stimulated by newly-established official citylinks. These cross-border links formalised contacts between mayors and town representatives, and stimulated activities in many different areas of life, such as education, sport, culture, and religion. Vohenstrauß, for example, established a citylink with Stříbro in 1992, and the Catholic and Protestant parishes from both cities were involved.

The religious connections were also advocated on a higher, euregional level. From 1993 onwards, Euregion Egrensis subsidised *Euregional Church Day*, an ecumenical annual event that combined political and religious discourses of reconciliation.[23] In 1996, the slogan was 'Under one heaven, we will find ways to each other'. A Czech-German booklet, published for the occasion, referred to the feelings of fear and mistrust people had in the region: 'Six years after the change, Czech-German relations show that the wounds of the past are far from healed' (Beyhl and Libal 1996). The introductory text also claimed that the ecumenical co-operation (between Catholics, Protestants and Orthodox) during the *Euregional Church Day* should be an example for political co-operation across national borders. However, the main inspiration was religious, and not political, as the booklet made clear: We invite you to find ways to one another. They should be ways of reconciliation, reconciliation through faith. The Bible recounts how prejudices and seemingly unbridgeable gaps can be overcome. This is what we will talk about during the Church days – about the Gospel – the Happy Message of God.

The organisers of the Euregional Church Day directly confronted the negative emotions that hampered reconciliation, arguing that they did not want to 'conceal our worries. When I know the thoughts, worries, fears, but also the hope of others, a common ground can be developed – under the heaven of God's promises'. The booklet also included a chapter entitled 'Reconciliation of Czechs and Germans: Excerpts from Church Reports', with fragments from an open letter written by Wilfried Beyhl, a member of the Church Assembly in Bayreuth, in which the author tried to dispel Czech fear about a German invasion: "As Germans we did not come with property claims, but as messengers of reconciliation, and we ask forgiveness for the crimes and damages that have been done in the name of the German nation. Let us live as reconciled sisters and brothers and as good neighbours." The chapter also included an announcement by the Synod of the Protestant

Bohemian Brethren which denounced the post-war Czechoslovak policy of collective expulsion, and stated that "we realize that the way to the future cannot be opened by never-ending accusations, but instead by sincere repentance, mutual efforts and understanding, and a longing for reconciliation".

It is hard to judge to what extend the discourses of reconciliation have generated an actual change in border peoples' feelings. I realized this when an expelled Sudeten German, who had attended a religious service in Bohemia, where the priest had emphasised the need for reconciliation, returned to Germany, and sat down in a *Biergarten*. After a few pints, he suddenly shouted: "The Czech nation is an evil nation!"

## Emotional Connections and Political Claims to the Old *Heimat*

The Sudeten German expellees in particular showed a keen interest in attending specially organised religious services on former Sudeten German territory.[24] Their main motivation was not reconciliation, even though numerous Sudeten Germans I spoke with emphasised that it was highly necessary to establish peaceful relations with the Czechs. Instead, most of them were motivated mainly by nostalgia, and simply wanted to visit their beloved homeland. They still felt an emotional attachment to their *Heimat*, and enjoyed spending some time in the villages or towns of their youth.

An expellee from the village of Labant who was twenty years old at the time of the expulsion, and who had settled in the Bavarian city of Bayreuth, explained:

"Of course we have a strong *emotional connection* with our homeland. Labant was a village in the Bohemian Forest, nicely situated, a *terrific environment*. The life of the farmers was tough, but somehow, *communal* life in the village was *harmonious*, and it still *lives inside us*, the *connection with our homeland*" (italics mine).

It is important to note that similar idealised accounts of 'life before the expulsion' and expressions of unconditional love for the homeland[25] have been reproduced endlessly in hundreds of Heimat books, Heimat exhibitions, and Heimat paintings. Evidently, the image of 'harmonious life in a beautiful world' is highly selective, and avoids accounts of Sudeten German involvement with the Nazi regime. As such, it offers a safe conceptual space in which expellees can engage with their pre-expulsion past without having to deal with the dark side of German history.

The end of the Cold War gave the Sudeten Germans the opportunity to visit their old homeland regularly. The generation that could still vividly remember the Sudetenland was slowly dying out, and the older people in particular were interested in trips to the country of their youth. During the first post-1990 years especially, individual Sudeten Germans crossed the border, and many attempted to make contact with the current inhabitants of their former homes. Some were heartily welcomed and were invited for a cup of coffee by the present owners of their houses, whereas others encountered suspicion. Whatever the reaction was, they were, unavoidably, at some point confronted with anti-German feelings.

Most Sudeten Germans were members of *Heimatvereine*, post-expulsion associations that connected people who had lived in the same Sudeten German villages, towns, cities or districts. Through various Sudeten German newsletters and newspapers they received news about post-Communist Czechoslovakia and exchanged experiences about recent trips to the old Heimat. The organisational networks were also used to organise communal trips, and to collect money for the restoration of their former churches, graveyards, and war memorials.

The expellees often felt a strong emotional attachment to the church they had attended before the expulsion. Commemorating the deceased in the actual churches and visiting the graves of close kin, they symbolically appropriated time and space, and strengthened the feeling that they were strongly rooted in former Sudeten German soil. The Sudeten Germans from Brand (Milíře), for example, held their first annual service in 1993. When I asked Mathilde how she and her relatives had experienced the ceremony, she replied:

"It was nice, yes, nice. I also have cousins; they are from Augsburg. They contact us every year, and stay with us [in Tirschenreuth] the night before. They always have *tears in their eyes*. They were older than me, they were fourteen and fifteen years old, and I was only six [at the time of the expulsion], so it was … I did not experience it like them … although … it is somehow … *where one is born, that is simply one's homeland"* (italics mine).

The discourse of nostalgia expressed strong feelings of belonging. It assumed a natural relation between identity and place, and, as such, had compelling political connotations (cf. Malkki 1992).[26]

The *Sudetendeutsche Landsmannschaft*, the biggest organisation of expelled Sudeten Germans with its seat in Munich[27], used the discourse of nostalgia in the representation and negotiation of political reality. Representatives of the organisation politicised the emotional claims to the old homeland by demanding the return of Sudeten property to its former owners. The annual *Sudetendeutsche Tag*, a three-day ritual event which included cultural, political, and religious ceremonies, and in which hundreds of thousands expellees participated, formed a focal point for the emotional and political discourse of *Heimatrecht*. The commemoration of the victims of the expulsion, and the political speeches by people such as Franz Neubauer, the leader of the *Sudetendeutsche Landsmannschaft*, and the Bavarian Prime Minister Edmund Stoiber, created powerful emotional contexts during which the participants remembered and re-experienced strong feelings of grief, loss, and anger. Even though not all participants agreed with the political aims of the *Sudetendeutsche Landsmannschaft*, the collective ritual experience reinforced their Sudeten German identity. As David I. Kertzer (1999: 5) noted, 'far from always creating solidarity by reinforcing shared values, one of the crucial functions of ritual is to produce solidarity in the absence of any commonality of beliefs'.

The speakers, powerful actors in the Christian-Democratic Party (CSU/CDU) used emotional discourse to increase their political strength by promising to continue their fight for *Heimatrecht*, and stressing that, to be able to do that, they needed support during the elections. The Sudeten German calls for justice were supported by influential Bavarian politicians, such as Stoiber and Finance Minister Theo Waigel. They put pressure on the German government to accept the Czech Republic as a European Union member state only *after* cancellation of the Beneš decrees (cf. Svašek 1999).[28] The German government, until 1998 led by Helmut Kohl, did not give in to the Sudeten German demands. Instead, it signed the Czech-German Declaration in 1996, in which both governments apologized for the harm done during and after the Second World War. The present German government, led by Gerhard Schröder, is even less likely to take the Sudeten German demands seriously. Like the former government, it stresses the importance of the creation of a shared, European identity.

Understandably, Czech border inhabitants have followed the news with mixed feelings. Numerous Czechs I spoke with felt uncomfortable with the increasing Sudeten German presence on Czech territory. In general, however, Czechs seem to accept the Sudeten German feelings of nostalgia, and believe that the property claims will never be granted.[29] In particular younger people assured me that they did not fear the Germans. In an essay assignment on the theme of ethnicity and nationalism, a fourteen year old female student from the Tachov *Gymnasium* stated:

"Germans. When I pronounce the word I associate it with the Second World War and the concentration camps. I guess that I am not the only Czech with such thoughts. I also think that fifty years have passed since the ending of the Second World War, and that the old generation will be replaced by a young generation which must distance itself from the crimes. They are not responsible, even though they may feel ashamed. We have to try to forget the past and create a new situation."

## Conclusion

Complex identification processes in border regions cannot be understood without a focus on emotions. People's emotional and social lives take shape in particular cultural, historical, and geo-political contexts. In border regions, these dimensions influence identification processes in particular ways.

The distinct geo-political situation in border areas may have a specific influence on border peoples' social and emotional life. On the one hand, border inhabitants live relatively close to people who are politically linked to potentially hostile neighbouring states. This implies that border inhabitants often feel more vulnerable than those who live in state centres. On the other hand, the proximity of the border may be an incentive for the establishment of close cross-border contacts, which may generate and strengthen mutual feelings of trust and friendship. Long histories of cross-border kinship increase people's cross-border loyalties, and weaken their emotional identification with the national state.

The Bohemian-Bavarian case demonstrated that geo-political aspects alone cannot explain why specific emotional discourses and practices may strengthen or weaken particular identification processes. It showed that it is necessary to take a historical perspective, and to examine how border people remember and re-experience the past, and how emotions influence their perception of 'those on the other side'. Remembered emotions must be analytically distinguished from re-experienced emotions to be able to understand how emotionally complex memories can become a political force. Re-experienced emotions in particular, evoked by memories of traumatic war and post-war experiences, influenced Czech, German, and Sudeten German perceptions, and hindered attempts to develop a sense of a shared interregional, European identity. At the same time, images of centuries of mutual co-operation were used by adherents of euregional co-operation to evoke feelings of trust, and to stimulate interregional identification.

Different interest groups and political actors used emotional display and discourses of emotion in distinct ways to generate social and political change. Numerous Sudeten Germans, as well as Czech republicans and communists tried to stir up past emotions during commemorations, annual meetings, and demonstrations. In these ritual contexts, they engaged people emotionally, and incited them to actively support specific political demands.

One of the ways in which both Czech and German priests attempted to create feelings of communal identity and solidarity, was by referring to the dangers caused by national hatred, while presenting ecumenic transnationalism as a way to control the situation and to encourage reconciliation. In the ritual context of the mass, well-known emotionally charged Christian signifiers such as 'Jesus' were connected to contemporary post-Cold War political arguments. Images of fearful political personalities and traumatic historical events, such as Hitler, Nazi oppression, and the expulsion, were transformed into emotionally compelling religious metaphors.

In contrast, euregional discourse focused on other major causes of fear, such as political and economic marginalisation, and environmental and social pollution. The adherents of Euregion Egrensis presented cross-border, euregional policy, and European identification as a political solution, and as a strong source of hope.

## Notes

1. The research referred to in this paper was funded by the University of Utrecht under the aegis of the Grotius grant. Additional funding was awarded by the Catharina van Tussenbroek Fonds. Different versions of this paper were presented in July 1998 at the EASA conference in Frankfurt, and in May 2000 at the Department of Social Anthropology, University of St. Andrews. I would particularly like to thank Hastings Donnan and Kay Milton for their critical remarks.
2. Even though emotional life in border areas has not been examined systematically, some anthropologists have been sensitive to the significance of emotions to border people's perceptions. For example, John Borneman (1998) has discussed Germans' changing expectations and their experiences of liberty and security after the collapse of the Berlin Wall. Stef Jansen (1998) has focused on the emotional confusion experienced by three female writers after the breaking-up of former Yugoslavia. Milena Veenis (1995) has looked at the ways in which desire and fantasy about West German consumer goods shaped East German perceptions of self and other.

3. He emphasized that it is necessary to abandon the common theoretical practice of reducing emotion to either meaning or feeling: 'emotions are *felt* in bodily experience, not just known or thought or appraised' (Leavitt 1996: 526).
4. A few days later, the German newspaper *Der Neue Tag* reported that nobody had guessed that "at the end of the dark tunnel, bright light would shine!" (Sporrer 1990). Ironically enough, this optimistic metaphor used to be very common in socialist rhetoric.
5. Munich, the capital of *Freistaat Bayern*, had more affinity with its own eastern border district of *Oberpfalz* than Bonn had.
6. Both Czech and German participants told me that they were relieved because, all of a sudden, they no longer felt as if they lived "at the end of the world". Politicians and journalists also used this image, arguing that what for a long time had seemed the end of the world, had now become the centre of Europe (cf. Zrenner 1990).
7. Local Czech papers did not yet exist at the time in the region. Several Czech participants, however, assured me that they enjoyed the day, and that a mood of optimism prevailed.
8. In particular, inhabitants from the Bavarian districts of Tirschenreuth and Weiden, and the Bohemian district of Tachov.
9. After the liberation of Czechoslovakia in 1945, the government, headed by President Edvard Beneš, declared *all* Germans 'collectively guilty' of German territoriality and the Nazi crimes, and decided that the Sudeten Germans would be expelled to Germany. The population transfer was legally backed up by the signing of the Potsdam Agreements in August 1945, which regarded the presence of ethnic Germans in states outside Germany as a danger to the political stability of Europe (cf. Svašek 1999).
10. Czech and German historians do not agree on the number of people who died during the expulsion. According to Sudeten German sources, around 250,000 people lost their lives. Czechs have argued that the number is much lower, between 20,000 and 40,000.
11. Until the expulsion, Brand had been inhabited exclusively by Roman Catholic Sudeten Germans, but after the expulsion, the village was renamed "Milíře" and re-populated by Orthodox Ruthenians from Romania, and by Czechs and Slovaks from the Czechoslovak interior. Tachau was renamed Tachov.
12. Sudeten Germans often felt a certain nostalgia for their old *Heimat*. Numerous poems that have appeared in Sudeten German newspapers, newsletters, journals, and *Heimatbücher* reveal this.
13. I agree with John Leavitt (1996: 523) that bodily feelings (like a pounding heart) are as much part of emotions as interpretations of these changes.
14. She was not bothered by the fact that the Roman Catholic church had been transformed into an Orthodox church. The village had initially been re-populated by Unionist Ruthenians from Romania, who, after the 1948 Communist coup, were forced to become Orthodox.
15. Euregional policy was introduced in the 1970s by the European Union member states to encourage European integration, and to stimulate economic development in border areas. In 1992, Euregion Egrensis was established in the Czech-German border region, integrating parts of Western Bohemia, Eastern Bavaria, Thuringia, and Saxony (cf. Svašek 1999). Co-operation and integration with the Czechs was supported by the German government as part of European Union politics. Tensions and conflicts in the post-Communist countries caused concern among the European Union member states. In particular, Germany pressed for measures to secure stability in the East. A special subsidiary programme called Phare was established to support the reform process in most post-Communist countries, and plans were made to enlarge further the European Union to the East (cf. Preston 1997: 197).
16. The imagined geographical unit included parts of former West Germany (East Bavaria), former East Germany (Saxony and Thuringia), and the Czech Republic (the West Bohemian districts of Karlovy Vary, Sokolov, Cheb, and Tachov).
17. The inhabitants of border regions, as such, have been confronted with the powerlessness of the nation state to deal with the effects of specific aspects of globalisation.
18. Roman Catholic, Protestant, and Orthodox.
19. The latter were mainly Ruthenians from Romania who had moved to the village in 1950. The German minister was a Sudeten German from Silesia, who had been expelled with his family to Germany after the Second World War.
20. Some priests took up important positions in growing cross-border networks. The Protestant Dean Father Lubomír Libal, who lived and worked in the Bohemian border city of Cheb, had connections in Bayreuth, Selb, Schönwald, Regnitzlosau, Wunsiedel, Marktredwitz, and Lautertal-Neukirchen. People like him were very active propagators of Czech-German reconciliation.
21. This information was taken from an unpublished report written by the *Arbeitsgruppe EKD / EKBB* (a German Protestant organisation), which mapped the newly established religious and intercommunal connections in Bavaria, Saxony, and Bohemia. The 35 community links between Saxony and Bohemia included 31 contacts between different parishes.
22. In 1997, the German priest noted that due to 'really existing atheism of post-Communist and neo-capitalist forces', missionary work was highly necessary on both sides.
23. Euregionaler Kirchentag/Euregionalní setkání krest'anů.

24. In the past eight years many have travelled to their *Heimat* to celebrate mass in the churches they used to attend as children or young adults, and in a number of cases they have crossed the border to restore old graves and war memorials. Their activities can be regarded as symbolic acts of re-territorialisation, and as temporary re-appropriations of religious space (cf. Svašek 1999).
25. Benedict Anderson argued that 'nations inspire love, and often profoundly self-sacrificing love. The cultural products of nationalism – poetry, prose fiction, music, plastic arts – show this love very clearly in thousands of different forms and styles' (Anderson 1983:141).
26. Cf. Smith (1998: 83) on the emotional sources of national sentiment.
27. In 1999, the *Sudetendeutsche Landsmannschaft* had approximately 100,000 members, but its leaders claimed to represent the whole *Volksgruppe*. In 1990, representatives travelled to meet with representatives of the Czechoslovak government and called for the cancellation of the Beneš decrees.
28. The *Sudetendeutsche Landsmannschaft* has been trying to negotiate with the German and the Czech governments on the basis of global human-rights discourses. Their discourse of *Heimatrecht* was based on the image of Europe as a just legal community, protected by the outer boundaries of the European Union.
29. The most serious 'confrontation' took place in 1994, when a combined Czech-German pilgrimage to the Loreta Church in the Bohemian city of Bor had to be delayed because of a bomb scare for which no one took responsibility.

## References


Beyhl, Wilfried & Libal, Lubomir 1996: *Unter einem Himmel, Wege zu einander zu finden*. Cheb and Bayreuth: Euregion Egrensis.

Borneman, John 1998: Grenzregime (Border Regime). The Wall and Its Aftermath. In: *Border Identities. Nation and State at International Frontiers.* Wilson, Thomas and Donnan, Hastings (eds.), Cambridge: Cambridge University Press, Pp. 162–190.

Cheater, A.P. 1998: Transcending the State? Gender and Borderline Constructions of Citizenship in Zimbabwe. In: *Border Identities. Nation and State at International Frontiers.* Wilson, Thomas and Donnan, Hastings (eds.), Cambridge: Cambridge University Press, Pp. 191–214.

Cooke, Phil, Christiansen, Thomas & Schienstock, Gerd 1997: "Regional Economic Policy and a Europe of the Regions". *Developments in West European Politics*. Rhodes, Martin et al. (eds.). Hampshire and London: Macmillan. Pp. 190–206.

Čtvrtek, Karel 1992: Stanou se z Československa Euroregiony? *Hálo noviny*, 23 May 1992.

Der Neue Tag 1989: "Eine Karawane in die Freiheit", *Der Neue Tag*, 27 December 1989.

Der Neue Tag 1990: "Europa blickt nach Böhmen und Ostbayern", *Der Neue Tag*, 30 June/1 July 1990.

Douglas, Mary 1966: *Purity and Danger. An Analysis of the Concept of Pollution and Taboo.* London: Routledge.

Donnan, Hastings & Wilson, Thomas M. 1999: *Borders: Frontiers of Identity, Nation, and State*. Oxford: Berg.

Douglass, William A. 1998: A Western Perspective on an Eastern Interpretation of Where North Meets South. Pyrenean Borderland Cultures. In: *Border Identities. Nation and State at International Frontiers*. Wilson, Thomas and Donnan, Hastings (eds.). Cambridge: Cambridge University Press, Pp. 62–95.

Driessen, Henk 1992: *On the Spanish-Moroccan Frontier. A Study in Ritual, Power and Ethnicity.* Oxford: Berg.

Driessen, Henk, 1998: "The 'New Immigration' and the Transformation of the European-African Frontier". In: *Border Identities. Nation and State at International Frontiers*. Wilson, Thomas and Donnan, Hastings (eds.), Cambridge: Cambridge University Press. Pp. 96–116.

Green, Sarah, 1997: Post-Communist Neighbours. Relocating Gender in a Greek-Albanian Border Community. In: *Surviving Post-Socialism*. Bridger, Sue and Pine, Frances (eds.), Pp. 80–105.

Hamperl, Wolf-Dieter 1996: *Vertreibung und Flucht aus dem Kreis Tachau im Egerland, 1945–1948. Schicksale in Berichten, Dokumenten und Bildern* (I and II). Trostberg: Private publication.

Houžvička, Václav 1993: *Česko-Německé Vztahy Všedního Dne. Sociologická Sonda Obyvatelstva Euroregionu Egrensis*. Usti nad Labem: Sociologicky Ustav. Research Report.

Houžvička, Václav 1994: *Euroregions as Factors of Increasing Cooperation within the Czech-German Relations*. Usti nad Labem: Sociologicky Ustav. Unpublished paper.

Irwin-Zarecka, Iwona 1994: *Frames of Remembrance. The Dynamics of Collective Memory*. New Brunswick and London: Transaction Publishers.

Jansen, Stef 1998: Homeless at Home. Narrations of Post-Yugoslav Identities. In: *Migrants Identity.* Rapport, N. and Dawson, A. (eds.). Oxford: Berg. Pp. 85–111.

Kearney, Michael 1998: 'Transnationalism in California and Mexico at the End of Empire'. In: *Border Identities. Nation and State at International Frontiers* (Wilson, Thomas and Donnan, Hastings (eds.). Cambridge: Cambridge University Press. Pp. 117–141.

Kertzer, David I. 1988: *Ritual, Politics, and Power*. New Haven and London: Yale University Press.

Leavitt, John 1996: Meaning and Feeling in the Anthropology of Emotions. *American Ethnologist* 23(3): 514–539.

Lutz, Catherine & White, Geoffrey M. 1986: The Anthropology of Emotions. *Annual Review of Anthropology* 15: 405–436.

Lyon, Margot L. 1995: Missing Emotion: The Limitations of Cultural Constructionism in the Study of Emotion. *Cultural Anthropology* 10(2): 244–263.
Malkki, Liisa 1992: National Geographic: The Rooting of Peoples and the Territorialisation of National Identity among Scholars and Refugees. *Cultural Anthropology* 7 (1): 24–44.
Preston, Christopher 1997: *Enlargement and Integration in the European Union*. London and New York: Routledge.
Reddy, William M.1999: Emotional Liberty. Politics and History in the Anthropology of Emotions. *Cultural Anthropology* 14 (2): 256–288.
Smith, Anthony 1998: *Nationalism and Modernism*. London and New York: Routledge.
Sporrer, Thomas 1990: Schlagbaum hebt sich für einen Tag, *Der Neue Tag*, 2 Mai.
Staněk, Tomáš 1991: *Odsun Němců z Československa*. Prague: Academia naše vojensko.
Storch, Ralph (ed.) 1992: *Standpunkt. Magazin der CSU in der Oberpfalz*, Special Issue on "Brückenschlag. Die Öffnung der ČSFR-Grenze". Regensburg: CSU Bezirksverband Oberpfalz.
Svašek, Maruška 1995: The Soviets Remembered. Liberators or Aggressors? Czech History, Memory, and Memorial Sites *Focaal. Journal of Anthropology* (25). Theme Issue on 'War and Peace'. Pp. 103–124.
Svašek, Maruška 1999: History, Identity, and Territoriality. Redefining Czech-German Relations in the Post-Cold War Era. *Focaal. Journal of Anthropology* (32). Theme Issue on Ten Years After: Hidden Histories and New Mythologies in Post-Communist East-Central Europe'. Pp. 37–58.
Svašek, Maruška 1998: The Ritual Paradox. The Construction of Cultural Unity and Diversity in a Combined Orthodox (Ruthenian) Czech / Roman Catholic (Sudeten) German Religious Ceremony. Unpublished paper presented at the session 'Multiculturalism', ISA World Congress of Sociology, Montreal, 1998.
Veenis, Milena 1995: "Only Because of the Bananas..." Western Consumer Goods in East Germany. *Focaal. Journal of Anthropology* (24): 55–69.
Wikan, Unni 1990: *Managing Turbulant Hearts. A Balinese Formula for Living*. Chicago: University of Chicago Press.
Wilson, Thomas & Donnan, Hastings (eds.) 1998: *Border Identities. Nation and State at International Frontiers*. Cambridge: Cambridge University Press.
Zrenner, Paul 1990: Die Adressen sind schon getauscht. *Standpunkt*. Special Issue Brückenschlag. Regensburg: CSU Bezirksverband Oberpfalz.

# Contents

## Vol. 30: 1 – 2000



## Vol. 30: 2 – 2000

# Ethnologia Balkanica

Journal for Southeast European Anthropology
Zeitschrift für die Anthropologie Südosteuropas
Journal d'anthropologie du sud-est européen

***Ethnologia Balkanica*** is the journal of the *International Association for Southeast European Anthropology*. Combining the traditions of ethnology, European Ethnology, cultural and social anthropology, and folkloristics, the journal publishes studies related to Southeast European folk cultures in order to contribute to a better understanding of the region. Languages of publication are English, French and German.



**Topics of vol. 1 (1997)**
*The Danube – a Bridge of Cultural Interchange; Ethnology of Modernisation and Transformation; Ethnicity, Identity, and Interethnic Relations.*

**Topics of vol. 2 (1998)**
*Ideology in Balkan Anthropology; The State of the Discipline.*

**Topics and authors of vol. 3 (1999)**
*Identity and Interethnic Relations*: Christian Giordano, Ulf Brunnbauer, Asen Balikci, Cvetana Georgieva, Veselin Tepavičarov, Jasna Čapo-Žmegač, Zdenek Uherek, Thede Kahl, Albert Doja, Radost Ivanova, Nicolae Constantinescu.

**Topics and authors of vol. 4 (2000)**
*Family and Kinship*: Michael Mitterauer, Karl Kaser, Zafer İlbars. *Everyday Culture*: Doroteja Dobreva, Gabriele Wolf, Dorothea Schell. *Folk Religion, Mythology and Politics*: Petăr Petrov, Jordanka Telbizova-Sack, Mirjana Prošić-Dvornić, Stelu Şerban.

**Subscription** (one volume per year):
Institutions: 20 Euro, individuals: 16 Euro, students: 10 Euro.
Individuals and institutions in Southeast Europe: 5 Euro.
**Subscription address:**
Waxmann-Verlag, Steinfurterstr. 555, D-48159 Münster, Fax +49251-216075,
e-mail: order@waxmann.com